Lizzie Siddal

Lizzie Siddal

The Tragedy of a Pre-Raphaelite Supermodel

Lucinda Hawksley

ANDRE
DEUTSCH

First published in 2004 by André Deutsch
An imprint of the Carlton Publishing Group
20 Mortimer Street
London
W1T 3JW

Reprinted in 2008

10 9 8 7 6 5 4 3 2 1

A CIP catalogue record for this book is available from the British Library.

ISBN 978 0 233 00258 3

Typeset in Liverpool by E-Type
Printed and bound in the UK by CPI Mackays, Chatham, ME5 8TD

Contents

Dedication

For Dominique, Laura and Vanessa, with love and thanks for the encouragement, inspiration and wonderful conversations.

In memory of Hugh De Fonblanque, a wonderful godfather and a wonderful man.

Picture Credits

The publishers would like to thank the following sources for their kind permission to reproduce the pictures in this book:

Section One

Page 1   **'Walter Howell Deverell'** – William Holman Hunt/Birmingham Museums and Art Gallery/The Bridgeman Art Library

'Twelfth Night' – Walter Howell Deverell/Private Collection/The Bridgeman Art Library

Page 2   **'Dante Gabriel Rossetti'** – Self Portrait/The National Portrait Gallery London/Topham Picturepoint

Page 3   **'Ophelia'** – John Everett Millais/Tate Gallery/The Art Archive

'Study for Ophelia' – John Everett Millias/Birmingham Museums and Art Gallery/The Bridgeman Art Library

Page 4   **'William Holman Hunt'** – Self Portrait/Birmingham Museum and Art Gallery/The Bridgeman Art Library

'A Converted British Family Sheltering a Christian Priest' – William Holman Hunt/Ashmolean Museum University of Oxford/The Bridgeman Art Library

Page 5   **'How They Met Themselves'** – Dante Gabriel Rossetti/Fitzwilliam Museum University of Cambridge/Topham Picturepoint

'Paolo and Francesca da Rimini' – Dante Gabriel Rossetti/Cecil Higgins Art Gallery/The Bridgeman Art Library

Page 6   **'Rossetti Sitting to Elizabeth Siddal'** – Elizabeth Siddal/Birmingham Museums and Art Gallery

'Writing in the sand' – Dante Gabriel Rossetti/The British Musuem London/The Bridgeman Art Library

Page 7   **'Portrait of Mother & Daughter'** – Dante Gabriel Rossetti/National Portrait Gallery London

Photograph of Dante, Christina, Mother and William Rossetti – Charles Lutwidge Dodgson/Private Collection/The Bridgeman Art Library

vii

Acknowledgements

With many thanks to my agent, Christopher Sinclair Stevenson, and Miranda West at André Deutsch, both of whom were superbly supportive.

With extra special thanks to Sandra Sljivic-Georgiadis.

Many thanks to Peter and Julie Peel; Dominique and Pam Kenway; and Louise, Paul, Natalie and Dani Ruse for being such lovely hosts while I was researching. Also to Joanna Baldwin, Clare Double, Helen Povall and Becky Sherrington-Cross for timely help with the research.

I am indebted to the staff and facilities at various local studies libraries, in particular Southwark, Holborn, St James's, Hastings and Sheffield; also to Denise Chantry and the Bath Library. Thank you to the staff at the British Library, the Wellcome Library and the Sheffield Archives; to Ann Price at the Hope Historical Society; to Helen Elletson at the William Morris Society in Hammersmith; the curators of Red House, in Kent; and all those scholars and biographers who knew, or have researched the life of, Lizzie Siddal.

CHAPTER ONE

The Red-Haired Model

I n mid-nineteenth-century London, if you wanted to buy a hat, you would have made your way to the area around Leicester Square. The narrow thoroughfares that were Cranbourne Street, Cranbourne Alley and Cranbourne Passage were *the* places to go, crammed with milliners, mantle-makers and dressmakers. The streets were so narrow, the shops so numerous and the roads so crowded that it was difficult to pass along them unimpeded. Any lady naïve enough to find herself in this district while wearing an unfashionable bonnet or cloak would be swamped by over-whelming offers of assistance and numerous entreaties to buy a new one, often accompanied by tussles over the potential customer by rival shops' assistants. There were incidences of women having their clothes ripped or even being temporarily "kidnapped" by over-eager salesgirls, who would seize the witless wanderer and hurry her into their shop before any rival snapped her up. In the late 1840s, 3 Cranbourne Street was a hat shop, owned by a Mrs Mary Tozer. To help her in the business, Mrs Tozer employed several attractive girls and women, who not only made the hats and worked as shop assistants but could also model the headgear to its best advantage. One of these was a young woman named Elizabeth, or "Lizzie" Siddall (later changed to Siddal).

In 1849, Lizzie was twenty years old and had lived an unremark-able life. She was tall and slender with large eyes and long hair the colour of pale copper. Striking, rather than beautiful, especially with those huge, heavy-lidded eyes in such a small face, Lizzie did not conform to the contemporary ideal of beauty. Her greatest considered attributes at this date were that she had perfect deportment, fine facial bone structure and was unusual looking. A woman one would look at and remember. By fashionable dictates, however, she was too tall, not womanly because she was not curvaceous and her hair was red – most definitely *not* considered an attribute. Superstition still deemed that red hair was unlucky and associated it with witches, black magic and a biblical reference to Judas Iscariot having red hair. Although the educated classes would have scoffed at such a notion of a hair colour being unlucky, there was a far larger number of uneducated people in Britain, who continued to believe red hair was something to be shunned and to be afraid of. The poet Algernon Swinburne (1837–1909), who was to become one of Lizzie's most devoted friends, had hair of an almost identical colour to hers. He related stories of how, when he was a child, the people in his local village had regular forays to throw stones at red squirrels, as their coppery fur was believed to be the cause of bad luck. Common folklore dictated it was unlucky if the first person you saw in the morning was a redhead, particularly a woman with red hair. Maritime superstition decreed that redheads brought bad luck to a ship (so, apparently, did flat-footed people); if a sailor could not avoid making a voyage with a redhead, he was warned he must speak to the red-haired person before that unpropitious being uttered even a syllable to him, in order to reverse the bad luck.

These superstitions sound ridiculous today, but they were long lived and deep seated. The belief that red hair is unlucky dates back to the Egyptians, who burned redheaded women alive in an attempt to wipe them all out. Queen Elizabeth I finally made red hair popular in England, and stopped the English persecution of redheads for being witches or warlocks, but even three hundred years after Elizabeth's reign other prejudices against red hair remained among the ignorant. Throughout her childhood and adolescence, Lizzie often suffered teasing for the hair that was destined to become her greatest feature.[1]

Mrs Tozer's employees worked long hours and in tiring conditions. Although the shop itself had a large display window so potential customers could see the hats, the working area where these were created was badly lit, with just one small window that looked out to the back of the building on a scrubby patch of mud and grass. The girls would start work early in the morning and usually continue until 8 p.m. During especially busy times, such as the London Season, their hours would be extended and they could sometimes work all night. Lizzie, who lived in Southwark, often walked home from work with a colleague named Jeanette, who also lived south of the river. The girls were not particularly close friends, but it was not safe to be on one's own in the dark, so the company of someone else was necessary as well as welcome on such a long walk.

Little is known of Jeanette except that she had a host of admirers, including the Irish poet William Allingham (1824–89).[2] At the end of 1849 Allingham was working as a customs officer, but had finished his first volume of poetry, had had it accepted and was waiting for it to be published. He did not live in London but made frequent visits there, both on business and to see friends. These friends included the recently formed Pre-Raphaelite Brotherhood and their circle – in particular, the promising young artist Walter Howell Deverell (1827–54). When Allingham made his visit to London in the winter

---

[1] Mary Howitt, a Victorian writer who contributed articles to magazines aimed at young women, made the sarcastic comment that the Pre-Raphaelites had ushered in an age in which "plain women" could be considered beautiful. She added that the painters had made "certain types of face and figure once literally hated, actually the fashion. Red hair – once to say a woman had red hair was social assassination – is the rage".

[2] Allingham is best known today for his poem, "The Fairies", which begins: "Up the airy mountain / Down the rushy glen, / We daren't go a-hunting, / For fear of little men ...".

of 1849–50, he found his friend struggling with a painting he wanted to exhibit at the Royal Academy. It was of a scene from Shakespeare's *Twelfth Night* and Deverell was desperately seeking a model for Viola. In the end, it was Allingham who found the solution to his friend's problem, and that was quite by chance. Being in London, he decided to visit Jeanette and offer to walk her home from work. They were accompanied by a tall, silent workmate, Lizzie Siddall.

Allingham was not initially overly impressed by the redheaded girl, finding her "stuck up" and dull; although he was presumably somewhat prejudiced against her for her unintentional intrusion on his intended romantic walk. Despite this unpropitious start, Lizzie and Allingham went on to become good friends. After her death, Allingham wrote that "She was sweet, gentle and kindly, and sympathetic to art and poetry ... Her pale face, abundant red hair and long, thin limbs were strange and affecting, never beautiful in my eyes." At this first meeting, however, he did know she would be perfect as Deverell's model, not least because she was so slim. Deverell wanted to paint Viola in boy's clothing and was despairing of finding a woman without prominent curves; he had also hoped to find a red-haired model.[3] He was painting the episode when Viola disguises herself as Cesario, Duke Orsino's page-boy, and he needed a woman who would look plausible in a pair of breeches.

After being told about Lizzie, Deverell made a visit to Cranbourne Street – one hopes he had the foresight to wear a fashionable hat – to observe Lizzie through the display window. He was thrilled by her and agreed wholeheartedly that Allingham had discovered a genuine "Stunner" (the Rossettian word for any beautiful woman and a term quickly adopted by all the Pre-Raphaelites). It was out of the question for Deverell to approach an unknown

---

[3] In wanting a red-haired model, Deverell was following Dante Gabriel Rossetti's example. The previous year, Rossetti had sought in vain for a red-haired girl to be painted as the Virgin Mary, but had ended up using his sister, Christina, and painting her brown hair as auburn.

young woman himself, so he asked his indulgent mother to talk to Lizzie on his behalf.

Mrs Deverell visited Mrs Tozer's shop, accompanied by her son, and promptly introduced herself and Walter to Lizzie, voicing his request in the most tactful manner possible. It was a shock to this previously unfêted young woman to be singled out and offered quite bluntly such a very unusual proposition. Although deeply flattered, Lizzie was wary of the offer and uncertain of exactly what it entailed – in the 1840s modelling for an artist was perceived as being synonymous with prostitution and Lizzie's upbringing had been strictly religious. Modelling was not something any respectable woman thought of doing, unless either related to the artist or sitting for one's elegant portrait, yet Walter's mother carried her audience beyond this very understandable prejudice and into an entirely favourable frame of mind; she seemed, indeed, unaware that there could be even the vaguest of reasons to demur, so, in the end, they did not. Mrs Deverell's very obvious respectability and her reassurances of propriety at all times allowed her to convince both Lizzie and the more worldly-wise Mrs Tozer to agree to the proposition. Walter's indomitable mother then set out for an entirely different part of London from the one she inhabited – to visit Lizzie's equally formidable mother in the Old Kent Road.

CHAPTER TWO

A Pre-Raphaelite Muse

Elizabeth Eleanor Evans, although of Welsh extraction, was brought up in Hornsey, Middlesex. It was here that she married Charles Siddall, a cutler from Sheffield, on December 13, 1824. They lived for a while in London after their marriage, before returning to Sheffield for an unspecified period. By 1828 they had moved back to London, where they remained for the rest of their lives. Charles was not a rich man, but he had a rich heritage, of which he was extremely proud. In a tale reminiscent of Thomas Hardy's *Tess of the D'Urbervilles* he spent the greater part of his life – and any profits from his business – attempting to prove he was the rightful owner of the Crossdaggers, a family business, in the Derbyshire village of Hope.[1] The Crossdaggers, which was still referred to by locals by its former name of Hope Hall, was a coaching inn set within its own seventy acres of farmland. It would have provided Charles with a good, steady income and was considerably grander than anything he could hope to aspire to while working as a cutler. From 1720 until 1756, the property was owned and run by a James Siddall, who passed it on to Thomas Siddall (presumably his son). Thomas ran it from 1757 until 1807,

---

[1] In the 1600s, the Crossdaggers was called Hope Hall and was a small ancestral home owned by the Balguy family. It became a coaching inn around the start of the eighteenth century and the building remains a pub/hotel to this day. In 1876 its name was changed to the Hall Hotel; it is now called Old Hall.

when the direct family line died out and it was taken over by George Bentley.[2]

The Siddall family was, by a convoluted route, descended from a wealthy and influential Derbyshire family, the Eyres.[3] Hope Hall was, at one time, the property of the Eyre family and, although there were a great many branches of both families, Charles Siddall did have a legal right to claim ownership of the property. He was, however, to be frustrated at every turn and died without securing the home and recognition he wanted so desperately for his children and grandchildren. The legal battle placed an enormous strain on the family and drained them financially. Charles's children dreaded every new development in the lawsuit, knowing it would lead to yet more legal bills and place even more stress on their father's health. Eventually, Lizzie's sister, Clara, decided to spare her father – and the rest of the family – any more worry and expense from the distressing legal case and threw all the relevant documents and papers on the fire. Charles's reaction to this has not been recorded.[4]

The Siddalls' two eldest children, Annie and Charles, were born before their parents decided to make a permanent home for their family in London. In the early years of their marriage, Eleanor and

---

[2] After 1807, no Siddalls appear in the records of the inn's ownership.

[3] The Eyres' heritage can be traced back to the time of the Norman Conquest and several branches of the family remain in the Derbyshire region today. Charlotte Brontë, who had very fond memories of the Peak District, paid homage to the area's great landowning family by naming Jane Eyre after them. Today, the surnames Eyre and Siddall are commonly found throughout Derbyshire and Yorkshire. Lizzie's great-grandfather, Christopher Siddall, grew up in Hope, but moved with his family to Sheffield, presumably to find work. Since then, Lizzie's ancestors had lived in Sheffield, but dreamed of returning to Hope Hall.

[4] The incident of Clara throwing the papers on the fire was revealed in an interview given in March 1930 by one of the daughters of Lizzie's sister, Lydia; the daughter was named Elizabeth Eleanor in memory of the aunt who had died around the time of her birth. The interview also records the dramatic assertion, "I have always understood … that Hope Hall should have been inherited by my grandfather. There is a local tradition that until a member of the Siddal family lives again at Hope Hall, ill-luck will always pursue the people who live there."

Charles deliberated between London and Sheffield, trying to decide which was the better location to start up a business and raise their children.[5] By the time Lizzie was born, they had made the decision to leave Sheffield for good and were living in the London borough of Holborn. Named Elizabeth Eleanor Siddall, after her mother, Lizzie came into the world on July 25, 1829 at the family's home at 7 Charles Street, Hatton Garden.

It is popular in biographies of Dante Gabriel Rossetti (1828–82) (who later became Lizzie's husband) for Lizzie to be described as growing up in a "slum" and for their class differences to be greatly magnified. In reality, however, the social gulf between them was not so enormous. Rossetti's parents had come to London as political refugees from Italy; they later married and raised a family, never returning to their native country. His father, Gabriele, attained a position as a university lecturer, which afforded him social status, but not a particularly large salary. The family struggled to keep up with the strict requirements of the society into which they had moved, such as the need to have servants and to maintain a rigidly particular way of life. When Gabriele's health began to deteriorate, Dante Rossetti's sisters and mother felt the need to work – albeit at more genteel pursuits than millinery – and it was his younger brother, William, who kept the family finances afloat by securing a good salary while still a teenager and taking over from his father as the breadwinner.

Lizzie Siddall's parents arrived in London as reluctant refugees from the middle class to the lower, but with great aspirations of one day owning their own home and employing a servant. It was this dream that led to a relentlessly downward spiral in their finances,

---

[5] The 1841 census states that Charles and Elizabeth's second child, Charles, born in 1828, was born in Yorkshire. Annie, born in 1825, was baptized in London, so it is likely she was born in London as well. She is not mentioned in the census, presumably being away from home on the night it was taken. Neither is she mentioned in the 1851 census, having by that time married a printer named David MacCarter and moved to his native Scotland.

caused by the extravagant burden of legal fees and Charles Siddall's refusal to accept defeat in the lawsuit. If he had been able to give up the dream of Hope Hall and had invested his profits more wisely, Charles's family might have ended up in quite different financial circumstances. They would never have been wealthy, but they could have been more comfortable, financially.

At the time of Lizzie's birth, her parents were not poverty stricken, as popular belief would have it. Her father had his own cutlery-making business, run from home in Charles Street. He also had an interest in another cutlery business at 13 Cecil Street, the Strand, run by a Mr J. F. Taylor.[6] Over the years, Charles Siddall is described variably in official directories as being a "cutler", an "optician" and an "ironmonger". At one time, he is described as owning a "Sheffield Warehouse", though as this was run from his home premises, it was obviously the same business and not a larger concern. Despite this inconsistency, the main business was the making and selling of cutlery, sharpening knives and scissors and, in later years, running a general ironmongery shop.

When the Siddalls lived in Hatton Garden, it was most definitely not a slum. It was not yet renowned for the jewellery and diamond shops which make it famous today – they didn't start arriving until after the Australian gold rush in the early 1850s – but it was certainly not one of London's worst areas. The area has a rich history and was a fascinating place to live. In the twenty-first century, Hatton Garden is mainly an area of retailers, but in the 1820s and 1830s it was a varied mixture of teeming commercial premises and family homes with people of several social classes and brackets of income intermingling. Charles Street (now called Cross Street) ran perpendicular to Hatton Garden itself. Part way along it was Bleeding Heart Yard, immortalized by Charles Dickens in *Little Dorrit*.

---

[6] Taylor may have been Charles Siddall's employer when the latter first arrived in London, or they may have been business partners; the relationship is unclear.

Dickens was very fond of setting his plots around this historic area of London: just up the road from the Siddalls' home is the police station to which Oliver Twist was taken after being caught stealing Mr Brownlow's handkerchief; the area is also mentioned in *Barnaby Rudge, Martin Chuzzlewit* and *Bleak House*.

There were, however, some definite slum areas around Holborn and several very undesirable streets within easy reach of Lizzie's home. Not far away was an area known as Coldbath Fields, named for the presence of a "healing" spring which had been discovered in the 1700s, although by the 1830s the spring had been all but forgotten. By this time, the fields housed a prison and the toddler Lizzie and her older siblings would have regularly seen prisoners being marched (or dragged) along nearby roads to incarceration. At the other end of the scale, Hatton Garden was also home to some eminent and prosperous inhabitants, including one of the Siddalls' near neighbours, Sir Moses Montefiore, business partner of the great financier Baron M. N. Rothschild.

Although Coldbath Fields no longer housed a public bath, there was no need for residents to go unwashed. At 32 Hatton Garden, a canny homeowner had built new public baths in his garden, a facility the Siddall family would certainly have made use of. A few years after the Siddalls left the area, a young lodger moved into the house at number 32. He was Samuel Plimsoll, the man who invented the Plimsoll mark on ships and to whom so many sailors have owed their lives. Ironically, a few decades later, Hatton Garden was to become the home of someone indirectly responsible for more deaths than almost any other inventor: Hiram Maxim, the man who gave the world the machine-gun. It was developed just metres away from the place of Lizzie Siddall's birth.

Around 1831, the Siddall family moved to the borough of Southwark, in south London, a less salubrious area than Hatton Garden. The move may have been prompted by the fact that Charles had been going through the business's profits in his fruitless attempts to claim back his family's heritage. Or it could have been simply a matter of the family growing in size and needing more space, which they could not afford to rent in Holborn. By 1833, Charles was working on his own and had only one business, run from his home at 8 Kent Place, just off the Old Kent Road.[7] This new home was rented from a greengrocer, Mr James Greenacre, who lived at number 2 Kent Place. Their homes were opposite an imposingly large Georgian building, the Asylum for Deaf and Dumb Children, and near several popular coaching inns. It was in Southwark that the rest of Lizzie's siblings were born: Lydia, to whom Lizzie was particularly close, Mary, Clara, James and Henry. The Siddalls' youngest child, who was born in 1843, suffered from unspecified learning difficulties, though these were apparently not serious enough to prevent him entering into the family business.[8] For a couple of years, the Siddall family rented two properties in Southwark, the one in Kent Place and another in Upper Ground, very close to Blackfriars Bridge. They lived briefly at Upper Ground, before returning permanently to Kent Place when Henry was about a year old.

In 1831, the population of Southwark reached 85,000; over-crowding was a serious problem and many Southwark residents had no access to clean running water. The Thames was desperately unhygienic, still used by many Londoners as a bottomless rubbish tip and choked by having untreated sewage poured into it. In 1832, the borough – in common with much of London – suffered a cholera outbreak. As the cause of cholera was still unknown, thousands of needless deaths were caused by people continuing to drink contaminated water from the river.

There were, however, many positive aspects about the family's new home. Southwark was far less built up than Hatton Garden,

---

[7] Kent Place no longer exists.
[8] The census of 1861 lists an 18-year-old Henry as a "cutler".

with wide open spaces and green fields for the children to play in; there was even a nearby zoo, which opened in 1831 and became a popular tourist attraction. The local economy was relatively stable, with high employment in the area and new labour continually needed to help build the London and Greenwich Railway and, when that was complete, to work on the Thames Tunnel, an underwater passageway that was the project of Marc Brunel (father of Isambard Kingdom Brunel).

Charles Siddall was not alone in running his business from home. Almost all their neighbours did the same, including their landlord. Lizzie was later to recall how Mr Greenacre, a "giant" of a man, was kind to her and occasionally carried her across the street when the paving stones were covered with sewage or effluent from less savoury businesses than greengrocery or cutlery. When Lizzie was seven years old, however, the "giant" Mr Greenacre disappeared most sensationally from Kent Place, never to return. It was not long before the Siddalls – in company with the rest of the newspaper-reading public – discovered their neighbour and landlord had committed one of the most notorious murders London had yet seen. His case caught the popular imagination, filled the newspapers with sensational "scoops" and even inspired a book. As an adult, Lizzie dwelt quite regularly and with ghoulish melancholy over the fact she had known a murderer and that his unfortunate victim had been killed very close to her childhood home.

A widower with children, Greenacre had been due to marry a childless widow, Mrs Hannah Brown, a laundress who had a small amount of savings. On Christmas Eve, just days before their intended wedding, she disappeared and he told his friends that they had had an argument, the wedding was off and she had left him. That winter was extremely cold, with several inches of snow on the ground. When it started to thaw, a couple of days after Christmas, a scruffy bag, which had been discarded on the Edgware Road and ignored, suddenly attracted attention, because of the red colour that seeped out of it into the surrounding snow. When the bag was opened, it was found to contain severed limbs. A woman's torso and, a few days later, the head of James Greenacre's fiancée were discovered in two other locations in London, but she had been dismembered and killed (in that order) in a building very close to Kent Place. James Greenacre was hanged in 1837.

Murderous landlords and impoverished circumstances aside, Elizabeth and Charles Siddall were determined their children would aspire to return to the social class from which they believed they had been wrested. Although there is no record of her having attended school, Lizzie was able to read and write, presumably having been taught by her parents. She developed a love of poetry at a young age, after discovering a poem by Tennyson on a scrap of newspaper that had been used to wrap a pat of butter. This discovery was one of Lizzie's inspirations to start writing her own poetry.

The Siddall children's lives were animated with tales told by their father of his family's former greatness and a belief that they should be living in a minor ancestral hall. Mindful of his origins, Charles and Elizabeth strove to see that their family, though very poor, had the manners of children from a more genteel home. They were taught general lessons about how to behave in public – to eat correctly, to have gracious manners, to converse intelligently, to sit, stand and walk elegantly and how to dress themselves (making their own clothes, of course) with style. This early education was to stand Lizzie in good stead later in life, allowing her to charm several of Rossetti's more highly connected friends.

Unfortunately, being brought up to consider themselves as equals to their social superiors did not prevent the Siddall children from having to find work as soon as they were old enough. Charles was apprenticed to another cutler in Southwark, James and Henry worked with their father and the girls, except Annie, drudged in the poorer-paid end of the fashion industry. Annie married very young, at the age of fifteen, moved to Scotland and had six children, but

Lydia had two jobs, working in her aunt's candle shop and as a dressmaker. Mary was also a dressmaker and Clara worked as a mantle-maker.

Their wages were not considerable. Mrs Tozer paid Lizzie £24 a year – the modern-day equivalent of just under £1,500 – and her sisters' salaries would have been similar.[9] As Lizzie was to discover, by sitting for an artist she could more than double the money she earned from millinery. The going rate for an artist's model in 1849 was "a shilling an hour, five shillings for a morning or seven and sixpence a day"[10] – and the work was far less backbreaking than making bonnets in a poorly ventilated and meagrely lit little workshop.

When Mrs Deverell paid her visit to Southwark, she was aided in her quest by Mrs Siddall's galling knowledge of her daughters' hard lives. Their careers were physically challenging and modelling would be far less harmful to Lizzie's always delicate constitution than millinery. There was also the element of surprise: the appearance of an elegant woman, arriving by coach, at the front door of 8 Kent Place was an occasion to be remarked upon. Mrs Siddall, unused to receiving such fine visitors and by now mournfully accepting of the fact that she would never be mistress of Hope Hall, was in awe of this friendly but grand lady who appeared so unexpectedly and spoke to her as an equal, from one mother to another. Mrs Deverell later related that Lizzie's mother was haughty and painfully refined. She had the same very correct manner of walking and sitting, keeping her spine perfectly erect, as her daughter, and possessed beautifully kept, very long hair of a paler, but equally arresting, colour than Lizzie's. The house was faultlessly clean, and emanated

[9] Statistic obtained from http://eh.net/hmit/ppowerbp/

[10] The rate affirmed by Mrs Frith, wife of the popular artist William Powell Frith, when asked by either Mrs Deverell or Mrs Rossetti (the legend is unclear) to find out how much her son should pay Lizzie, his first professional model. Until then both Walter Deverell and Dante Gabriel Rossetti had painted their mothers and sisters when they needed a female sitter.

the impression that its owners had "come down in the world" and were now waiting to be elevated once more. The pleasure of receiving such a guest was tempered by the knowledge that this woman came from a far superior home, which was perhaps the reason for Mrs Siddall's haughty demeanour. She was an intelligent woman, however, with a large number of daughters to consider. This rich woman's son was obviously captivated by Lizzie's looks and a modelling career might lead to something more – it could be Lizzie's chance to break out of the social mould into which she had been reluctantly cast and to marry her way into a higher echelon of society. Such a marriage would benefit the whole family. Mrs Deverell assured Mrs Siddall that she and her daughters would be on hand to ensure Lizzie was not placed in any awkward or compromising situations. Walter's mother made the offer sound appealing and lucrative and, if Mrs Tozer had no objection, indeed was being more than generous in her terms, so why should Mrs Siddall object? It was fortunate for the history of art that Lizzie's father was not at home, as he most certainly did object to his daughter's new role – when he found out about it. In his absence, however, Lizzie's mother stiffly gave her permission and Mrs Deverell returned home across the river to tell her son the good news.

At the start of her modelling career, Lizzie was in the enviable position of being allowed to remain working at Mrs Tozer's part time, thereby ensuring herself a regular salary even if the modelling did not work out. This was an unusual opportunity for a woman of her time, and suggests that the milliner was reluctant to lose such a capable assistant. As later reports of Lizzie (written by friends or admirers of Rossetti) suggest she was a languid, dull and lacklustre person, this more favourable opinion of her and her capabilities makes a welcome change. As was to be demonstrated many times throughout Lizzie's life, she could charm anyone she believed worth charming and snub without compunction anyone she was not in the mood to entertain.

Lizzie was smuggled into and out of the Deverells' house, in Kew, in order to reach Walter's slightly damp, makeshift studio in the garden without being seen by his father. Mr Deverell, despite being the head of the Government School of Design, vociferously disapproved of his son's decision to be an artist. He was not being snobbish, but was worried about his family's financial situation and needed his son to start earning a decent salary in a reliable job. Mr Deverell was not even aware that Walter had his own studio, let alone one in his own garden. Later reports, by biased commentators such as William Rossetti, claim Lizzie was angry about the indignities of this subterfuge and complained bitterly about the secrecy. In fact, the reverse was true, Lizzie was always touchingly fond of Deverell and all such reports about her being complaining and bitter were written in hindsight, with knowledge of what Lizzie was like later in life, when disappointment and laudanum had so altered her personality. At the time she began working with Deverell, Lizzie was young, naïve and had grown up in a world that led her to expect social and sexual inequality. She had absorbed the works of Tennyson and longed for a more poetic existence than the drudgery of the workroom in Cranbourne Street could ever provide. Modelling was an exciting, entirely new experience, from which she was earning double her usual rates of pay for a great deal less work, and being idolized into the bargain. A little embarrassed secrecy cannot have been too galling under those circumstances. Walter's nervousness *was* unsettling and her pride was, of course, dented by the knowledge that his father would disapprove of her, but none of this was any more remarkable than the treatment she received every day from customers at the bonnet shop, all of whom were on a social par with Walter's father, if not more exalted.

Lizzie's introduction to modelling was an extremely pleasant entrance into what could be a sleazy world. Mrs Deverell and her daughters took great pains to make Walter's charming new model feel at ease and were often in the studio with her, so she did not have to be alone with a man she barely knew. They were happy to take her food and cups of tea to sustain her as she worked and, by all accounts, were equally as fascinated by her as he was. Lizzie and Deverell became friends and she was encouraged to show him her own sketches and to share with him her desire to be an artist.

Walter Deverell was charming, kind and generally perceived as the best looking of all the Pre-Raphaelites. William Holman Hunt (1827–1910), a fellow Pre-Raphaelite and student at the Royal Academy with Deverell, describes him as having been a lively, witty companion, usually in infectious high spirits. Deverell was actually suffering from a kidney disease (Bright's disease) that would kill him at the age of 26, but he refused to admit he was ill and always looked so healthy that it was difficult for his friends to believe the doctor's diagnosis. It was fortunate for Lizzie that he did not attempt to take advantage of her, as his reputation amongst his friends was one of a practised – and successful – flirt. Perhaps mindful that he needed to fit all life's experiences into a drastically shortened time frame, he was more adventurous than his friends – most of whom longed to live a wild bachelor experience, but were far too middle-class to do so. Deverell joked that, in his case, the letters "PRB" would not translate to "Pre-Raphaelite Brotherhood", but would stand for "Penis Rather Better".

Deverell was two years older than Lizzie. He had been born in America, in Charlottesville, Virginia, in 1827, returning to England with his parents while still a baby. At the age of 17, he had enrolled at Sass's art school, where he had met and befriended Rossetti. Deverell exhibited at the Royal Academy for the first time in 1847 and, thus far, his reception had been favourable. *Twelfth Night* was, he felt, his most ambitious picture and he was anxious to finish it in time to be shown at the Academy in spring 1850.

The painting focuses on three central figures: Viola, on the left, Orsino, in the centre, and Feste, the jester, on the right. It is Act 2, Scene 4 of the play and Orsino is pining over his unrequited love for

Olivia. Lizzie was painted sitting sideways on, gazing up at Orsino, a self-portrait of Deverell. Feste was modelled by Rossetti – but the figure of the jester was already finished before Deverell started painting Lizzie so the future lovers did not pose together. The one aspect of the painting Deverell found difficult to paint to his satisfaction was Viola's hair, so Rossetti, in a prophetic gesture, finished it for him. In addition to the oil painting of *Twelfth Night* that was exhibited at the Royal Academy, Deverell painted another version of the play, using a different scene. Lizzie was employed once again as the model for Viola and the painting was printed in the Pre-Raphaelites' short-lived journal, *The Germ*.[11]

Twelfth Night, now considered Deverell's best surviving work, was released at an unfortunate time and received mixed reactions from the critics. It was not given a fair trial, being exhibited at the excruciating moment when the artistic world had just discovered what the letters "PRB" daubed onto certain paintings meant. Although he was not one of the original seven members of the Pre-Raphaelite Brotherhood, Walter was known to be one of their circle, and thereby guilty by association. Indeed, when James Collinson resigned in May 1850, Walter Deverell was the name suggested by Rossetti as his replacement. In the end, no formal decision was made and Deverell was never actually elected, but he was thought of by the rest of the Brotherhood as an honorary member of the PRB.

---

[11] This journal was initially titled *Monthly Thoughts in Literature, Poetry and Art*, but later changed to *The Germ*. Rossetti was much inspired by the current publication the *Art Journal*, which he wanted to emulate, but using the PRB's own unique interpretation of things artistic. The first edition of *The Germ* was published on New Year's Eve 1849. As well as the PRB, contributors to *The Germ* included William Allingham, Coventry Patmore, Walter Deverell, William Bell Scott and Christina Rossetti. The journal was to prove a particularly good career move for William Rossetti, making his name in the journalistic world and leading to other commissions. *The Germ*'s aim was to enforce and encourage an entire adherence to the simplicity of nature. It's pages were scathing of any critic who had spoken against the Pre-Raphaelites and unreservedly laudatory in their reviews of the latest works by Robert Browning and Alfred, Lord Tennyson.

The Pre-Raphaelite Brotherhood was a society set up by seven very idealistic young men who were passionate about art, depressed by the current, very conventional state of the art world and idealistically desirous of bringing about dramatic changes. The group held its first meeting in the autumn of 1848. Its members were: John Everett Millais (1829–96); William Holman Hunt; Dante Gabriel Rossetti and his brother William Rossetti (1829–1919); Thomas Woolner (1825–92); Frederic George Stephens (1828–1907); and James Collinson (1825–81). All, except William Rossetti, were artists who had studied at London's best schools – Sass's and the Royal Academy – and were disillusioned by the instruction they had received. William Rossetti, although not a serious artist, was a great lover of art and a "man of letters"; his journalistic talents were to prove of great benefit to the group. When they met, the "brothers" talked earnestly about their love of art and literature and how the conventions of these artistic schools were stifling the progress of painting. As they saw it, art was being taught in too stylized a manner, with no room for individual expression or original ideas. There was no scope for using any subject matter other than that deemed suitable by the powers that be – and those "suitable" subject matters were highly limited. The Pre-Raphaelite Brotherhood also objected strongly to the use of boring, sombre colour palettes. They wanted to paint vibrantly coloured works that would *mean* something to the viewer, subjects that would provoke the imagination and cause discussion. They wanted to experiment with new techniques and to create robust new paint colours. They wanted to turn the course of British painting around, harking back to a time when bold colour and imagination were not disdained as being beneath the notice of so important a personage as a Royal Academician.

These seven idealists – all aged between 19 and 23 – came up with a list of "Immortals": people and legends that could inspire wonderful paintings. They placed Jesus Christ at the top and went on to list revered poets and authors, from Chaucer to Tennyson. All the members of the PRB were inspired by medievalism, in particular the legends of King Arthur, as well as by the Bible, the works of Shakespeare and more modern poets, including Byron, Keats and their hero-worshipped contemporary, Robert Browning. They harked back to the paintings of Botticelli and other early Italian artists and they admired the style of medieval frescos, so rich in colour and depicting animated subject matter. Eventually, the group pinpointed the time at which they believed art had "gone wrong": it had been with the advent of Raphael (1483–1520). Although not denigrating Raphael's abilities, they believed that it was his style that dictated the rigid codes now adhered to by the British artistic establishment. The new society swore to return to the artistic ideals displayed before Raphael, and so the name "Pre-Raphaelite" was born.

The group's ideals were a secret intended to be known solely by the seven members, although very honoured friends, such as Ford Madox Brown (1821–93), Walter Deverell and Charles Allston Collins (1828–73), were often present at, and involved in, their discussions. The group was sworn to secrecy and marked their allegiance only by the presence of three little letters, "PRB", painted on to their canvases. There was mild speculation about what this could mean, but no one had made any great attempt to find out. In 1850, however, just as *Twelfth Night* and several other Pre-Raphaelite paintings were to be exhibited, the secret was betrayed. The sculptor Alexander Munro (1825–71) was a close friend of the group. During an animated discussion, Dante Rossetti revealed to him, in strictest confidence, the significance of the letters "PRB". Munro, perhaps in ignorance of the identity of the man to whom he was speaking and filled with excitement at this revolutionary society created by his friends, told a journalist what Rossetti had divulged to him. The story hit the papers and a scandal of breathtaking fury ensued.

The idea that a group of such very young men, most of them barely out of their teens, was arrogant enough to suggest it knew more about art than such luminaries as Sir Joshua Reynolds (whom the Pre-Raphaelites had dubbed "Sir Sloshua"), Thomas Gainsborough or Raphael himself, appalled the critics, and journalists were suddenly extremely harsh. Brotherhood members, including John Millais and William Holman Hunt, who had been so lauded for their works the previous year, were now destroyed in print. Deverell, known to be an intimate of the group, could not escape unscathed. It was an extremely difficult time and responsible for the failing of more than one artistic career – if their works were not bought, the majority of artists could not afford to keep on painting and, for a while, any painting that seemed to have even a hint of the Pre-Raphaelite about it was reviled, regardless of whether or not the artist had any connection with the group. Not every critic was so harsh, however, and Deverell's picture did receive an occasional favourable review. An article in the magazine *Critic*, published in July 1850, described *Twelfth Night* in the following words:

> The head of *Viola* is beautifully intended, but not physically beautiful
> enough, owing, as we fancy, to inadequate execution; and her position
> is in perfect accordance and subordination to the pervading idea ... Mr
> Deverell has here, for the first time in a form at all conspicuous, entered
> on art boldly and with credit to himself; his faults are those of youth,
> and his beauties will doubtless mature into the resources of a true artist.

By the time Deverell's painting was ready to exhibit, his friends had all heard his many raptures over Viola, the new "Stunner", with whom it was apparent he was more than a little infatuated. Holman Hunt later wrote an account of the first time he heard about Lizzie Siddall:

> Rossetti at that date had the habit of coming to me with a drawing
> folio, and sitting with it designing while I was painting at a further
> part of the room ... Deverell broke in upon our peaceful labours. He
> had not been seated many minutes, talking in a somewhat absent

manner, when he bounded up, marching, or rather dancing to and fro about the room, and, stopping emphatically, he whispered, "You fellows can't tell what a stupendously beautiful creature I have found. By Jove! She's like a queen, magnificently tall, with a lovely figure, a stately neck, and a face of the most delicate and finished modelling; the flow of surface from the temples over the cheek is exactly like the carving of a Phidean goddess ... I got my mother to persuade the miraculous creature to sit for me for my Viola in 'Twelfth Night', and to-day I have been trying to paint her; but I have made a mess of my beginning. To-morrow she's coming again; you two should come down and see her; she's really a wonder; for while her friends, of course, are quite humble, she behaves like a real lady, by clear commonsense, and without any affectation, knowing perfectly, too, how to keep people respectful at a distance."

Eager to see this paragon, most of the Pre-Raphaelites hurried to Deverell's studio to glimpse her as she was being painted, and several were eager for her to sit for them, too. Rossetti, never one to be concerned about encroaching on a friend's territory, asked her to sit for him on her second day at Deverell's studio and Holman Hunt wrote to her almost immediately afterward, asking that she model for him also. He had not even seen her, but was convinced that she was the right model for him, based on Deverell's and Rossetti's ecstatic accounts of her. It was a mesmerizing time for Lizzie. A hitherto unrealized world was opening up in front of her, offering a life that need not follow the much-trodden rut she had previously assumed it would. She had a new, unusual and quite lucrative career that was taking off with a passion; her life would never be the same again.

CHAPTER THREE
Dante and Beatrice

L izzie met Dante Gabriel Rossetti for the first time in the winter of 1849–50. At the time Lizzie and Deverell were attracted to one another, but Deverell knew he could not have a relationship with a woman his family would never approve of him marrying and he was too kind to attempt to seduce Lizzie and not marry her. She was not a streetwalker or the usual coarse model; she was fervently respectable, desperate to be acceptable and, most important, she trusted him. Rossetti, believing himself unbound by social rigidity, was ready for an unconventional and life-changing passion. By 1851, Deverell was out of the frame, whether he liked it or not, and Rossetti and Lizzie were recognized by their friends as a couple. Lizzie quickly became Rossetti's main – at times, only – source of inspiration. Their courtship was to continue, sometimes passionate and wonderful, at other times limping sickeningly, until their belated marriage in 1860, by which time Lizzie was so ill, it was uncertain whether she would live long enough to make it to the church.

Rossetti, a year older than Lizzie, was born on May 12, 1828; the second of four children, two boys and two girls, born to Gabriele and Frances (née Polidori) Rossetti. He was christened Charles Gabriel Dante Rossetti, but due to his adoration of the medieval Florentine poet Dante Alighieri (1265–1321) he changed the order of his names in his late teens and recreated himself as Dante Gabriel Rossetti (losing the more prosaic

Charles entirely).[1] The Pre-Raphaelites always called him Gabriel, but he preferred the name Dante. Fluent in Italian, he translated Alighieri's poetry into English and spent his life re-creating scenes from Alighieri's work in paintings.

Rossetti came to identify strongly with his hero, in particular with the poet's early and enduring passion for a girl named Beatrice, about whom much of his poetry revolved. Enchanted by this story of impossible love, the agony it caused and the creativity it inspired, Rossetti became obsessed by an ideal that the only true love was one that caused pain – but such an exquisite pain that it could be channelled into the world's greatest artistic works.

Dante Alighieri and Beatrice Portinari were just children when they met, but he decided at once that he loved her. He remained adoring throughout adolescence, although he was so shy and hid his feelings so well she had no idea of the emotions she had engendered. So worried was Dante that someone would discover his secret that he went to elaborate lengths to hide his feelings by pretending to be in love with a woman of Beatrice's acquaintance and, when she left town, then pretending to have fallen for someone else. Beatrice believed him to be a flirt and to be insincere; she had no suspicion that she was the true object of his adoration. When she was 15, Beatrice's parents arranged her marriage to a suitable nobleman, Simone de Bardi. Although Dante himself had been betrothed at the age of 12, to Gemma Donati (whom he married in 1285, four or five years after Beatrice's wedding), he had not yet given up hope of being with Beatrice – until her wedding foretold the end of his dreams. Dante was so desperately unhappy that, when he saw Beatrice on her wedding day, he had to turn his head away from her

---

[1] Rossetti changed his name after the untimely death of his English godfather, Charles Lyell, whom it had been hoped would be a prominent patron of his works. After Lyell died, Rossetti saw no need to keep "Charles" in his own name and reversed the order of his remaining Christian names to become Dante Gabriel Rossetti.

so she could not see his tears. Having no idea how he felt, Beatrice believed he was insulting her and refused to acknowledge him again.

Unable to express his love of another man's wife, Dante turned his emotions inward, dreaming of Beatrice and willingly allowing her to haunt every waking and sleeping moment. One night he had a dream of a winged figure, named Amor: the dream showed Amor taking Dante's heart and giving it to Beatrice, the rightful owner, telling Dante to use his love for Beatrice to write poetry. Dante also had a prophetic vision about Beatrice: when he was ill and feverish, he had a dream about her dying at a young age and becoming an angel. Beatrice did die, very suddenly, in 1290. She was 24 or 25 years old at her death. Despite being married to Gemma, Dante was distraught by the death of the woman he truly loved. His love had been unconsummated and unrequited, but instead of diminishing with the years had grown stronger.

After her death, Dante turned Beatrice into a saintly figure. She became the inspiration for some of Italy's most famous poetry, *Vita Nuova* and *The Divine Comedy (Divina Commedia)*. *Vita Nuova*, which means "new life" and refers to a life renewed by love, is the story of his passion for Beatrice, beginning with their first meeting, when she was just eight or nine years old. Beatrice also appears in *The Divine Comedy,* an epic in which Dante travels through heaven and hell and in which she is his guiding angel. Although Gemma bore Dante several sons and remained married to him for many years, his name has become inextricably connected with Beatrice, the wife of another man. Gemma Alighieri is barely ever remembered.

Dante Gabriel Rossetti was a deeply romantic figure to whom many aspects of Alighieri's story appealed. Although born and raised in London, he clung proudly to his parents' Italian roots and identified his father's exile from Italy, for his political views, with Alighieri's fourteenth-century exile from the city state of Florence, also because of political allegiances. Rossetti became obsessed with the idea of Dante and Beatrice and, from the time he met Lizzie, identified her strongly with Beatrice. After Lizzie's death, she was no longer his troublesome, flawed wife. Instead she became a beatified beauty, who would never grow old, like Beatrice. A disproportionately large number of Rossetti's paintings were born out of the poetry of Dante Alighieri; in later life it was not always Lizzie who was painted as Beatrice, although she is without doubt the strongest presence in his Alighieri-inspired works.

Rossetti, in his youth, was deeply attractive, with flowing black curls and intense, seductive eyes. Georgiana Burne-Jones, wife of Edward Burne-Jones, later recalled, "no one could reproduce the peculiar charm of his voice with its sonorous roll and beautiful cadences". In later years he became portly and grotesque and the eyes which had held such depth now appeared to hold a look of insanity. Towards the end of his life he fought a constant battle with depression, chloral addiction and severe mental illness, but in his youth, when he first met Lizzie Siddall, he breathed passion, raw vitality and excitement into every gathering. At this period, he did not drink alcohol, neither did he smoke – he appears to have had enough natural adrenalin to negate the need for any artificial stimulants.[2] There was something mesmerizing about him, a quality that attracted men and women to love, admire or want to emulate him. The painter Valentine Prinsep (1838–1904) was a minor Pre-Raphaelite, an admirer of their works and a member of the younger circle who longed to be a part of the group. He described his mentor in the following way: "Rossetti was the planet round which we revolved ... we copied his very way of speaking. All beautiful women were 'stunners' with us. Wombats were the most delightful of God's creatures. Mediaevalism was our *beau idéal* and we sank our own individuality in the strong personality of our adored Gabriel."[3]

---

[2] Ford Madox Brown wrote that Rossetti abstained from "tobacco, tea, coffee, stimulants" and described how, after a party or at the end of an evening, he would always pour himself a glassful of cold water.

[3] Rossetti was fascinated by wombats; see page [163 n3.]

Bessie Rayner Parkes (1829–1925),[4] a close friend of both Rossetti and Lizzie, wrote the following description of him in 1854, "He is slim Italian; English born and bred, but a son of Italy on both sides of the house – short, dark hair, lighter eyes, a little moustache and beard; very gentlemanly, even tender in manner; with a sweet mellow voice." The Victorian poet Coventry Patmore (1823–96), most famous for his poem "The Angel in the House", also knew the Pre-Raphaelites when they were young. He was an admirer of their art and a contributor to *The Germ*. In his memoirs he wrote: "Rossetti was in manners, mind, and appearance completely Italian. He had very little knowledge of or sympathy with English Literature; and always gave me the impression of tensity rather than intensity."

Not only was Lizzie as equally "tense", or nervously inclined, as Dante Rossetti, but both were headstrong and wilful; they were also both depressive; prone to wild mood swings, ranging from the elevated to the depressed; had a tendency to addiction and shared a destructively jealous need to be the most important figure in their – or, indeed, any – relationship. When they were in love and happy, they were deliriously so, not needing anyone else and perfectly content to stay cocooned together in Rossetti's rooms for days at a time. When one – or both – of them was unhappy, ill, depressed or jealous, they made one another's lives hellish. Throughout the nine long years of their strange courtship, they tested each other's patience and trust to the limits. Self-destructive and self-loathing at

---

[4] Bessie Rayner Parkes was a poet, essayist and champion of women's rights. Today, she is mostly remembered as the mother of two more famous writers, Hilaire Belloc and Marie Lowndes Belloc, but she was an equally important figure in her own right. She met Barbara Leigh Smith, who introduced her to Rossetti and Lizzie, in 1846 and they remained lifelong friends. Together they founded *The Englishwoman's Review* in 1858, and in 1866 co-founded the first Women's Suffrage Committee. In 1867, Bessie was on holiday in France where she met and fell in love with Louis Belloc, an invalid several years her senior. Both families and Barbara were against the marriage (the two women's friendship suffered a temporary coldness as a result), but the Bellocs enjoyed five very happy years of marriage before Louis's early death. After his demise, Bessie returned to England with her children.

times, as well as being arrogant about their abilities, both must have been extremely difficult to live with.

The first indication we have of the quite cloying nature of their affection for one another is in 1851, when Holman Hunt proposed making a painting trip to Syria. Rossetti expressed a wish to go with him and Lizzie was desperate at the idea that he might leave her.

Holman Hunt was a fervent believer in the powers of natural light: he would paint outside in all temperatures, weather and seasons in order to re-create the most realistic light conditions for his paintings. When he painted his famous *The Light of the World* (1853, now in St Paul's Cathedral), he slept by day and painted in his garden at night in order to be able to capture the true essence of moonlight and lantern-light.[5] His desire for painting in the open air led him all over the world in a quest to seek out different light forms, subtleties and strengths. He grew especially fond of the Middle East, through which he travelled extensively.

Holman Hunt's passion to experience other lands, cultures and art was seductive and Millais and Rossetti were among several artists who pledged to travel with him, although when Holman Hunt finally set out on a big trip to the Middle East – in 1854 – neither of them accompanied him.

In 1851, when the possibility of such a voyage was first mentioned, Christina Rossetti wrote a sulky letter, commenting that her brother would never go to Syria because he was too "ensnared" by Lizzie. Christina had not yet met her future sister-in-law – they were not introduced until 1854 – but she was already convinced this unknown woman was unworthy of her brother. To Christina's mind,

---

[5] This behaviour engendered several local rumours of eccentricity. One night, after an evening out, Holman Hunt was taking a cab home and his driver asked if he knew "the madman" who had a house on this street but chose to live in his own garden, rather than sleep in his bed. Holman Hunt listened, amused, to the cabbie – before apparently asking him to stop the cab a few doors away from his home, so the cabbie would not know that it was his passenger who was "the madman".

no doubt encouraged by William's unfavourable opinion, Lizzie was merely a common model from the Old Kent Road, no matter how grand her pretensions. Annoyingly, however, this common model was also proving a challenging, and often unbeatable, rival for Christina's brother's affections.

This petulant impression was largely the fault of Rossetti himself who, despite telling everyone how wonderful "Miss Sid" was, did not introduce her to his mother until 1855. Neither did he introduce her to his friends outside the immediate Pre-Raphaelite circle. Despite his anti-establishment stance where art was concerned, in other areas of his life Rossetti was more conventional than he would have liked to believe. He was embarrassed by the financial differences between his and Lizzie's families and the gulf between their social circles, yet he could not help himself falling in love with her. Perhaps he also kept her separate from the other areas of his life in an attempt not to lose his ideals: in his mind Lizzie had become the adored one, the Beatrice to his Dante, a woman with no flaws; by introducing her to his family and friends she would have left thirteenth-century Florence and been rooted very firmly in nineteenth-century London.

Lizzie was unlike the women he had met before, far removed from his often suffocatingly conventional sisters, Christina and Maria, and a world away from the whores with whom he joked on the streets and wished he had the courage to approach properly. Lizzie was of a lower social class, yet with an image of herself as his social superior – she did not introduce him to her family because her parents would never approve of an artist, or an Italian (the first time Lizzie took Rosetti home was in 1855). She also dressed very differently from other women, wearing floating, unstructured dresses without a corset, the style that has come to be known as Pre-Raphaelite. Although it is usually assumed that the PRB invented the medieval-influenced style that later became fashionable wear for women, Lizzie was renowned for her own very individual and elegant style. Her sartorial sense was as much of an influence on Rossetti as his eye for colour and fabric was on her. Georgiana Burne-Jones described Lizzie's style c. 1860: "[her] slender, elegant figure – tall for those days ... – comes back to me in a graceful and simple dress, the incarnate opposite of the 'tailor-made' young lady ..."

When he fell in love with her, Rossetti wanted to "improve" Lizzie, to make her more worthy of being his companion. One of the first things he did was to persuade her to change the way she spelt her surname. He convinced her that "Siddal" looked more genteel than "Siddall", so Lizzie changed it permanently. This belief was one she passed on to her family. Her father, in yet another effort to establish his eligibility for his ancestral home, followed suit for a while: in the census of 1851, the family at 8 Kent Place is listed as "Siddal". However, he changed the spelling back again quite rapidly.

In spite of persuading her to make changes to her name and her career – by teaching her and helping her to be recognized as an artist – the contrary side to Dante Rossetti did not allow him to introduce Lizzie to his family because he *wanted* this love to be complicated and painful. He wanted it to inspire him as the painful desire for Beatrice Portinari had inspired his namesake.

Although she was not allowed to become a part of his family, Lizzie was ever present in Rossetti's life – once he had started to draw and paint her, he could not stop. Despite her jealousy and dislike of Lizzie, Christina was also fascinated by the woman who had gained such a hold over her brother. At Christmas 1856, after visiting Rossetti at his home in Blackfriars, where the walls were covered in sketches and paintings of Lizzie, Christina wrote a poem about his obsession:

In An Artist's Studio

One face looks out from all his canvases,
One selfsame figure sits or walks or leans:
We found her hidden just behind those screens,
That mirror gave back all her loveliness.
A queen in opal or in ruby dress,
A nameless girl in freshest summer-greens,
A saint an angel – every canvas means
The same one meaning, neither more nor less.

He feeds upon her face by day and night,
And she with true kind eyes looks back on him,
Fair as the moon and joyful as the light:
Not wan with waiting, not with sorrow dim;
Not as she is, but was when hope shone bright;
Not as she is, but as she fills his dream.

Her image may have adorned almost every inch of Dante's walls, keeping her within his gaze even in her absence, yet in the words of his sister, four years before Rossetti eventually married her, Lizzie had already grown "wan with waiting". Even Christina felt pity for Lizzie's very female nineteenth-century predicament of being wasted by not being married. The real Lizzie was not a favourite with Christina, but her painted image nonetheless inspired the poet. The words "Not as she is, but as she fills his dream" emphasize Rossetti's Alighieri-like desire to keep his Beatrice a vision of something she is not. Christina believed she could see the "true" Lizzie, a side of her of which Rossetti continued – by choice – to be in ignorance.

Painting the Dream

T he year 1850 was an important one in the Pre-Raphaelites' calendar: the Poet Laureate, William Wordsworth, died and his successor was named as Alfred, Lord Tennyson, one of the PRB's "immortals". It was also the year in which Dante Rossetti painted Lizzie Siddal for the first time. The result was a small water-colour entitled *Rossovestita*. The picture was exhibited at the Old Water Colour Society in November 1852 and later given as a gift to Ford Madox Brown. There is some dispute that Lizzie was the model for *Rossovestita*, as it is not a great likeness of her, but Pre-Raphaelite legend is insistent it was Rossetti's first painting of her. William Holman Hunt also painted Lizzie in 1850, using her as one of several central figures for his striking composition, *A Converted British Family Sheltering a Christian Priest from the Persecution of the Druids*.[1] Lizzie is not the most central figure in this painting, although she is prominent. The central figure is the gentle-looking, Christ-like priest; Lizzie stands at his left side, holding a bowl and

---

[1] Holman Hunt later admitted that this picture of Lizzie does not look like her. In his memoirs of 1905, he magnanimously wrote about the woman who had disliked him so much by the end of her short life: "With my desire to give a rude character to the figure, and my haste to finish, certainly the head bore no resemblance to her in grace and refinement." Another problem with his depiction of Lizzie in this painting is that her left arm and hand appear to have been painted from someone else who possesses much larger bone and muscle structure. Although her right hand, in which she holds the cloth, is dainty and feminine, the left hand, which supports the bowl, looks unfeasibly larger and out of proportion in comparison. The muscles of the exposed left arm also seem extremely over-developed for someone as slight as Lizzie.

cloth with which to clean his wounds. The painting was one of the first to demonstrate the Pre-Raphaelites' new-found technique of painting on a "wet-white ground". The artist would prepare his canvas by covering it with a specially mixed white paint before beginning the picture. This white background added luminosity to the colours and allowed the artists to create such glowing tones as those seen in the face of Holman Hunt's priest. The picture is now considered a masterpiece, but at the time it was criticized as ferociously as Deverell's *Twelfth Night,* and for the same inartistic reasons. At the 1850 Royal Academy exhibition, it was blighted not only by its "PRB" connection, but also for complaints of there being too much nudity in the picture.[2]

Despite this setback, Holman Hunt painted Lizzie again, and more famously, in 1850–1, as Sylvia for his *Valentine Rescuing Sylvia from Proteus,* a subject taken from Shakespeare's *Two Gentlemen of Verona.* Although there are four figures in the painting, Lizzie's face is almost directly in the centre and it is she who draws the eye. Wearing an elaborate silk dress, with her hair drawn back and fully revealing her face, she is the most striking element in the picture; even though she is kneeling down, her face is still in the centre of the composition, suggesting that Holman Hunt composed the painting's other elements around her features. The additional three figures are dressed in darker, autumnal colours, in keeping with the woodland background, but Sylvia's silver-and-white embroidered dress stands out dramatically. It is apparent from this painting and its careful composition that Holman Hunt felt as drawn to Lizzie's face as Deverell and Rossetti were.

In 1904, when Georgiana Burne-Jones wrote the memoirs of her husband Edward Burne-Jones's life, she recalled meeting up with an

---

[2] Although the lack of a buyer cast Holman Hunt into despair at the time, it was eventually bought by Thomas Combe, who was to become one of the Pre-Raphaelites' most important patrons and is largely responsible for the wealth of Pre-Raphaelite art that has remained in the UK. Combe paid £160 for *A Converted British Family* ...

unnamed woman[3] who had once been one of the Pre-Raphaelites'
favoured models:

> Her regard for [the Pre-Raphaelites] … was still fresh and she loved
> to dwell on their memory. "I never saw such men," she said; "it was
> being in a new world to be with them. I sat to them and was there with
> them, and they were different to everyone else I ever saw. And I was
> a holy thing to them – I was a holy thing to them."

How intoxicating to be made to feel this way, to be praised as a
muse without whom there would be no painting. There is no question that when Lizzie first worked for them these remarkable young
men made her feel equally idolized, or that her early days of modelling were some of the happiest times of her life. The
Pre-Raphaelites, so different from most of the men of her acquaintance, did not look upon her as a lowly shop girl but deified her as
a possessor of rare beauty, "a holy thing". Once she had entered this
world, how very difficult it would be ever to go back to the life she
had known before.

Lizzie was not, however, to remain Holman Hunt's favourite
model for long, because 1850 was the year in which he picked up a
young stunner of his own, named Annie Miller. It was at this time
that Lizzie's world started to darken – after just a few months of such
unexpected and unalloyed happiness. Annie was most definitely a
working-class girl, with no illusions of being otherwise. She was
gorgeous, sexy, entirely at ease with her sexuality and willing to use
it to get whatever she wanted. Like Professor Higgins, Holman Hunt
misinterpreted his lust as a genuine desire to do good and set about
the long process of educating and grooming Annie until she was
"suitable" for him to marry. After four years of slow courtship and

---

[3] The woman may well have been Fanny Cornforth, though she could have been
one of several other former models.

delay, he then set off for the Middle East for two years, expecting her to stay patiently at home and learn her lessons, waiting chastely for his return. He was to be sorely disappointed.

Between Lizzie and Annie there was antipathy at first sight. Lizzie, grown accustomed to being adored and petted by the group as a whole, suddenly had to make way for a woman with whom she would never have dreamt of associating previously. Had her parents known she was consorting with a woman such as Annie Miller, they would have been furious. Annie was not a wide-eyed innocent like Lizzie. She was earthy, mature beyond her years and malicious, taking obvious delight in Lizzie's misery (though it is a fair presumption that both women were equally unpleasant to one another). Whether it was genuine foresight or simply unintelligent jealousy, Lizzie was wise to distrust Rossetti to be around Annie Miller.

Lizzie was also working up another reason to dislike Holman Hunt, of whom she had at first been in awe. This dislike of him was largely irrational, blown up out of all proportion and related not just to Annie Miller but also to his closeness to Rossetti. In the early days, Rossetti looked up to Holman Hunt as a mentor. The latter had been his teacher for a while and he was a superbly original painter, very much worthy of Rossetti's admiration. The way he could so easily command Rossetti's loyalty represented another severe threat to Lizzie's potential happiness, especially with Hunt's desire to go travelling to remote parts of the globe.

Lizzie's additional reason for disliking Holman Hunt began in September 1850 when Holman Hunt, Fred Stephens and Lizzie paid a visit to a friend of the Pre-Raphaelites, Jack Tupper, and his aged father, who was known affectionately as "The Baron". Jack was the brother of George Tupper, an artist and early contributor to and important financial backer of *The Germ*. For whatever reason, it was decided to play a joke upon the Tuppers by having Holman Hunt pretend Lizzie was his wife. The reason for this joke and its result have been lost in history – all that remains is an angry letter written by Dante Rossetti to his brother William in which he describes it as a "disgraceful hoax" and relates how he made Holman Hunt write a letter of apology to the Tuppers.[4] Rossetti's anger had more to do with jealousy because Holman Hunt had publicly claimed Lizzie as his own, rather than with his professed fury at Holman Hunt and Stephens being rude to a friend. (Rossetti's own manners were not usually notable for being overtly correct.) Lizzie was quick to make use of this potential rift and swiftly decided that she was also furious with Holman Hunt. Her early fondness for him began to fade – leaving the latter reeling as he had no idea why – and, with a strange rapidity, became replaced by passionate dislike. Although some biographers dispute that Rossetti and Lizzie had become romantically involved as early as 1850, Holman Hunt's letter of apology to the Tuppers makes it explicit. Included with the letter was a sketch. It shows a chastened-looking bearded man – Holman Hunt himself – who is holding a handkerchief to his eyes. Fred Stephens is depicted rubbing his eyes with the back of his hand, as though wiping away tears. Below them is a sketch of a starry-eyed couple, identifiable as Rossetti and Lizzie, drifting languidly in a boat beneath a romantic crescent moon.

Later biographers of Lizzie claim it was the incident at the Tuppers' home that soured the relationship between her and Holman Hunt, though precisely why it upset her so much is not related. She was, it seems, content to go along with the joke at the start, but there is always the possibility that he sprang it on her, that she had not had any idea of what he intended to do and was therefore dismayed and embarrassed when he introduced her as his wife, and was uncertain of how to get out of the deception. Perhaps she worried that the Tuppers – and Rossetti – might think she was cheap for having been willing to pretend to be married to a man she barely

---

[4] In this apologetic letter, Holman Hunt describes Lizzie as "a modest, agreeable girl … not a common model".

knew. Or maybe she felt the joke had been aimed at her and that Holman Hunt was being particularly cruel in intention – Lizzie could be highly over-sensitive and Holman Hunt could be thoughtless and brusque. Rossetti's reaction to the joke made matters worse because it was obvious that one of the reasons he was cross was because he was worried the Tuppers would be offended when they learned that Holman Hunt's supposed wife was actually a mere model and shop girl. His reaction, although defensive of her, also led her to the humiliating realization that she had not been accepted as one of the group, but would always be seen as an outsider, a parvenue from a lower class who could never quite be accepted as an equal.

Unable to sever all contact with Holman Hunt and Annie Miller, as she would have liked, Lizzie was forced to suppress any overt displays of dislike, reserving her anger for the occasional outburst. She was beginning, instead, to show a cold, haughty side the group had not previously experienced. In October 1850, while Holman Hunt was using both Annie and Lizzie as models, he and several other Pre-Raphaelites decided to spend a weekend in the country to allow them to paint in the natural light and for Holman Hunt to be able to work his background for *Valentine Rescuing Sylvia from Proteus* from nature. The venue was decided on and the plans laid: they would visit Knole Country Park, near Sevenoaks in Kent, where Rossetti and Holman Hunt had already spent time painting. It would be a weekend of "picnics and painting real girls under real trees", the artists and their models would all go – and there came the sticking point. When Lizzie discovered Annie was to be included in the party, she absolutely refused to attend. No amount of persuasion was effective and she stayed behind in London while a furious Gabriel, an irritated Holman Hunt and a triumphant Annie Miller joined the rest of the group.[5]

---

[5] During this sojourn at Knole, Rossetti began painting the background for his *Beatrice, Meeting Dante at a Marriage Feast, Denies him her Salutation*.

Playing the waiting game alone in London was agonizing: Rossetti had not capitulated and stayed with her, as Lizzie had expected, and she was terrified Annie's very obvious charms would work on him as effectively as they had on the smitten Holman Hunt. In the end, however, she had the satisfaction of welcoming back a thoroughly dejected party. The weather had been appalling, it had rained and been utterly cold and miserable; painting had been impossible, Annie had been soaked and had looked distinctly unappealing to the painterly eye; the light had been all wrong and the intended hearty picnics in the sunshine had been impossible.

The smugness Lizzie felt over this ill-fated jaunt was to be emulated by Annie in a few months' time. Although *Valentine Rescuing Sylvia* was to prove very popular at the Liverpool Autumn Exhibition of 1851, where it sold for £200, its first exhibition at the Royal Academy was far less successful. Here it was caught up in the aftermath of the anti-Pre-Raphaelite storm that had so blighted Deverell's picture and Holman Hunt's own *Druids* painting the year before. The fact that this furious storm was still raging was instrumental in earning the Pre-Raphaelites one very valuable supporter: the overweening criticism of such genuinely talented painters brought the celebrated writer John Ruskin into the fray, to speak up on their behalf. A respected critic, Ruskin had been growing increasingly interested in the Pre-Raphaelites, both personally and professionally, and was moved to defend them against the barrage of journalistic vituperation. The artists had even been criticized by Charles Dickens – a dangerous opponent in a world full of people who seemed willing to believe that his word was almost the stuff of gospel.[6]

---

[6] Charles Dickens ridiculed Millais's *Christ in the House of his Parents* (1850) to such an extent it seems remarkable that, just a few years later, Millais was a close enough friend of the Dickens family for the author to allow his younger daughter, Katey, to model for the artist.

To counteract Dickens's influence, the Pre-Raphaelites were in desperate need of an equally influential supporter. Fortuitously, Ruskin could no longer tolerate this one-sided argument and in 1851 began publicly declaring his support for the Pre-Raphaelites. Part of that support involved him writing two famous letters to *The Times* in which he extolled the virtues of the group and put forward an alternative, favourable opinion of their works. He had not met Lizzie at this point and it was unfortunate that his only criticism of *Valentine Rescuing Sylvia* was about Sylvia herself: he lamented "the commonness of feature" and "unfortunate type chosen for the face of Sylvia", a criticism which seems unfair. The painting shows Sylvia as a pretty, pensive girl with delicate and finely formed features; it is certainly the most flattering view of Lizzie of all the non-Rossetti oil paintings she modelled for. By now, with three of the paintings she had posed for so publicly humiliated and even her own looks criticized in *The Times,* Lizzie felt that her dreams of artistic fame were coming to nothing and queried her wisdom in ever choosing to enter this cut-throat world. Annie Miller was delighted.

The unfortunate incidents of 1850 and 1851 were, however, to be forgotten as Lizzie prepared to sit for what has become considered one of the most important of all Pre-Raphaelite works. It was to be another Shakespearian scene, this time taken from *Hamlet.* In John Everett Millais's *Ophelia* (1852), the artist chose to depict the scene in which Ophelia, driven mad by Hamlet's rejection, gathers flowers for her own bridal/funeral wreath and drowns herself in the river, having strewn the flowers all around her. In 1899, John Guille Millais, son of the artist, recorded the following:

Miss Siddal had a trying experience whilst acting as a model for *Ophelia*. In order that the artist might get the proper set of the garments in water and the right atmosphere and aqueous effects, she had to lie in a large bath filled with water, which was kept at an even temperature by lamps placed beneath. One day, just as the picture was nearly finished, the lamps went out unnoticed by the artist who was so intensely absorbed in his work that he thought of nothing else, and the poor lady was kept floating in the cold water till she was quite benumbed. She herself never complained of this, but the result was that she contracted a severe cold, and her father wrote to Millais, threatening him with an action for £50 for his carelessness. Eventually the matter was satisfactorily compromised. Millais paid the doctor's bill; and Miss Siddal, quickly recovering, was none the worse for her cold bath.

It is said that Millais's mother had devised the heating system for the bath; an ingenious invention, if it had been properly attended to. The perfect model, Lizzie did not risk speaking or moving to draw Millais's attention to the fact that the lamps had gone out; she just lay there and suffered for his art. No wonder she was so much in demand – she placed the Pre-Raphaelites' work far above her own needs. She was a willing martyr to the cause in which they all believed so passionately. It is noteworthy that it was shortly after this incident that Lizzie's poor health came to the fore in Rossetti's correspondence and, from this time onward, it remained a permanent theme.

In order to set the historic scene, Millais had found an antique wedding dress for Lizzie to wear, which billowed out around her in the bathwater, adding dramatic shape and tension. In the finished painting – which William Rossetti described as being more like Lizzie than any other picture – Ophelia appears to have expired very recently. Her skin is starting to lose its bloom and her eyes seem only just to have relinquished their vision. It is a powerfully haunting painting which, even today, regularly attracts large crowds of observers at London's Tate Britain. It is the best known image of Lizzie – and one that is remarkably apt for a woman whose life ended so sadly and not so very differently from that of Shakespeare's doomed heroine.

At around this time Lizzie was in mourning, following the unexpected death of her eldest brother, Charles. Her wages were suddenly even more important than before as Charles had been one of the Siddall family's major wage earners and his death placed the family in a difficult financial position. In anticipation of the modelling fee, she suppressed her dislike of Holman Hunt and sat for him again. Both she and Christina Rossetti were tried out as models for the face of Jesus in *The Light of the World*. Hunt used many models – male and female – trying to find exactly the right expression for Jesus. In the end it was Lizzie's hair – the supposedly unlucky red hair – that was chosen to frame Christ's face. Her church-going parents must have been proud – and no doubt even her father was a little mollified after his horror at her choice of career.

CHAPTER FIVE

Falling in Love with Ophelia

Not long after Lizzie had posed as Ophelia, Rossetti decided that he could no longer abide the thought of sharing her. He asked her not to sit for anyone else and requested that his friends no longer ask her to model for them. This was not as difficult for the group as it would have been two years earlier – inspired by Deverell's success with Lizzie, and because each artist now wanted to discover his own, even more beautiful stunner, the men had been busy approaching suitable-looking women and by now had quite a variety of models at their disposal. Rossetti was no exception, always scanning the streets, theatres and pleasure gardens for stunners.[1]

What Lizzie felt about the loss of this extra income is unrecorded. She also gave up working for Mrs Tozer, so by agreeing to model solely for Rossetti – a man not renowned for wisdom where money was concerned – she was placing herself in a very vulnerable position. However, it was around this time that Lizzie's health, which

---

[1] The Cremorne and Vauxhall "pleasure gardens" were large parks that had been intended to provide respectable entertainment, but became notorious for prostitution, debauchery and generally un-Victorian activities. Hugely popular from Regency times onward (when there was also a third garden, at Ranelagh), pleasure gardens were the site of dancing, theatre, concerts, travelling shows, firework displays and even – on several memorable occasions – ballooning. By the mid-Victorian years, however, the pleasure gardens had acquired a dubious reputation, particularly in the evenings. Any unchaperoned young women Rossetti and his friends were likely to encounter in the gardens were most probably prostitutes. Vauxhall Pleasure Garden was closed in 1859, but Cremorne was still in existence in the 1870s.

had never been robust, began to become a recurrent theme in Rossetti's letters, so it became of sudden import that she should not continue with millinery or any similarly exhausting career. Rossetti did not make Lizzie regular payments for modelling incessantly for him, but one must assume that he supported her (not least because, in 1854, Lizzie moved out of the family home and rented rooms in a house in central London).

In 1852, Charles Allston Collins – the younger brother of Wilkie Collins and, at one time, an unsuccessful suitor for the hand of Maria Rossetti – wrote to Lizzie asking her to model for him, hoping that she would make an exception to her rule of sitting solely for Rossetti. He was prompted to try because of his long association with Rossetti, having been his friend in the pre-Brotherhood days and been present at the start of the PRB itself.[2] A letter written by Millais relates that she "answered in the most freezing manner, stating that she had other occupations". Collins, a romantic and quite neurotic young man, was deeply dejected by her refusal, feeling it especially painfully as he seemed unable to find another model whom he believed would fulfil the role as Lizzie would have done. According to Millais, that particular picture was never painted.

At the start of 1852, Rossetti was living at The Hermitage in Highgate, the house of a friend, the designer Edward Latrobe Bateman. As Bateman was often away, Rossetti was allowed the run of his home and the freedom to invite over whomever he chose. In 1860 (at the time of Rossetti's and Lizzie's marriage), William Bell Scott wrote to William Rossetti reminiscing about the occasion in early 1852 when he had first encountered Lizzie. Arriving unannounced at The Hermitage, at a time "when the place seemed to be in the sole occupancy of Gabriel and Miss Siddall"[3] he had let himself into the house. On walking up the stairs, he came upon the

---

[2] Collins later went on to marry the artist Katey Dickens, daughter of the novelist.
[3] It is interesting to note that Bell Scott still used the old spelling of Lizzie's surname, even in 1860.

couple looking very cosy in a dark nook lit by candlelight, with Rossetti lovingly reading poetry out loud to Lizzie. In the words of Bell Scott: "I came upon them like Adam and Eve in Paradise, only they *wasn't* naked, and he was reading Tennyson."

Much has been made of this meeting in books about Rossetti, as he did not introduce Lizzie to his friend and she left almost as soon as Bell Scott arrived, apparently slighting him. Bell Scott told friends at the time that he supposed Rossetti to be ashamed of her. In this letter of 1860, however, Bell Scott admits he was tactless, coming upon them unexpectedly and grinning at their discomfiture, where-upon an embarrassed and annoyed Lizzie glowered at him and left without a word. An unsurprising action, considering she found herself in a particularly compromising position, being discovered alone in a house with a man. Bell Scott obviously assumed she was Rossetti's mistress and she took exception to his leering.

In November 1852, Dante decided it was time to rent a place of his own and persuaded William Rossetti to take on the lease of a flat at 14 Chatham Place, in Blackfriars, London.[4] William was still living at home, so renting a place in Blackfriars made sense, as it was within convenient walking distance of his office in Somerset House on the Strand. In Dante's eyes, the flat was located satisfyingly close to Lizzie's home in Southwark, from which Bateman's home in Highgate was a considerable distance. As well as a small bedroom, the flat had a large sitting room, walls covered in bookshelves and – most impor-tantly – a large studio. There were no cooking facilities, which was quite usual at the time. A bachelor with no cook was expected to eat out or to order food from a local tavern or his landlady.

Chatham Place was on the river, which was occasionally a beau-tiful sight worthy of an artist's eyes. The apartment had a convenient sunny balcony on which the light conditions for painting were perfect – and the balcony was large enough to house the painter,

[4] Chatham Place no longer exists.

his easel and a model. More often, however, the river proved a stinking, unhealthy encumbrance that forced Rossetti's guests to leave his parties early, or to decline future invitations, in order to escape the foul odour he claimed he could not smell. At times the stench was strong enough even to force Rossetti out, on which occasions he would overstay his welcome at friends' houses or spend some time at home, being pampered by his doting sisters and mother. The rent of 14 Chatham Place was £60 a year, a sum William considered too expensive. It was almost triple the yearly amount Lizzie had been earning when she had been discovered by Allingham, just three years previously.

The year he moved to Chatham Place was also the year in which Rossetti decided to become Lizzie's art teacher. From an early age she had shown an aptitude for painting and drawing, as well as for poetry. Rossetti knew that she had shown her works to Deverell and, discovering that she had received no formal education, Rossetti offered to tutor her. This arrangement was a welcome development for him as their relationship was unsettled and he was obviously reluctant to commit himself. Despite the fact that by 1853 Lizzie was regularly staying alone or with Rossetti at the one-bedroomed flat in Blackfriars, he often described her to friends as his "pupil". The offer to teach her was intended kindly and genuinely – Rossetti always believed Lizzie had a prodigious undiscovered talent – but it had also the extra attraction for him of providing an ideal excuse for not needing to place their relationship on a more permanent, or official, footing. In September 1853, Rossetti sketched an image of the two of them in the studio at Chatham Place. In it, he reclines on a couple of chairs – sitting on one with his feet resting on the other – while an eager Lizzie bends over her canvas to sketch him. The scene is dimly lit by a tall lamp, her canvas rests on the backrest of his second chair and she peers intently at him. Meanwhile, Rossetti sits in a relaxed fashion, his hands in his pockets, observing her as keenly as she is observing him. The brown-ink sketch, swiftly executed, captures a wonderfully intimate moment in their relationship.

There has been much speculation about precisely when Rossetti did propose. After both Lizzie and Dante were dead, William Rossetti made a vague claim that they had become engaged in 1851, but there is no proof for this and it seems that William was attempting to salvage his brother's reputation – which was badly sullied by Lizzie's death and the resulting scandal – by claiming he behaved in a more gentleman-like manner than he had. Violet Hunt, who wrote a florid biography of Lizzie in the 1930s, claims they became engaged in 1854, during a passionate moment in the Sussex countryside, but this is also unsubstantiated. Despite having attempted to meet one another's families in 1855, it seems no formal engagement did take place until Rossetti was called to what everybody thought was Lizzie's deathbed in 1860, and swore to marry her if she would only live long enough.

Rossetti was an odd and intriguing mixture of selfishness and self-lessness. Although he could be quite astonishingly heedless of other people's feelings and needs, he could also be extremely kind and hospitable. He was generous enough to offer to share his studio space at Chatham Place with painters struggling even more than himself, such as Arthur Hughes (1832–1915).[5] In later years, when he was famous and wealthy, he would suggest to impecunious artists that they live with him at Cheyne Walk when they could not afford to pay rent.[6] Rossetti was also well known by his friends for giving money to beggars and even for handing out his own clothes to the homeless when he could scarcely afford to buy himself food. He frustrated his great friend and one-time tutor, Ford Madox Brown, by continually borrowing money he did not repay, yet then parading expensive new clothes in front of him, or by jaunting off to Paris when he should

---

[5] One of Hughes's most famous paintings is *April Love* (1855), now in the Tate Britain, London.

[6] Rossetti most famously gave living space at Cheyne Walk to the artist Frederick Sandys (1829–1904), with whom he fell out spectacularly, having irrationally accused Sandys of plagiarism.

have been finishing a paid commission. The Madox Browns were not in particularly solid financial circumstances, especially when their children were very young – there was no free health service in the nineteenth century – but Rossetti's charm was such and his friend-ship so very genuine and, in his unique way, loyal, that both Ford and his wife Emma regularly forgave him. William Rossetti treated his brother with equal indulgence, selflessly giving up his own dreams of studying to become a doctor so he could start work at the age of 15 to pay for his older brother's erratic lifestyle and support Dante's refusal to even think about getting a regular job and income.

Although William's name was on the lease, and he paid the rent and bills with far greater frequency than his brother, it seems William never actually lived at Chatham Place, just staying over occasionally. Lizzie, on the other hand, was there almost incessantly. On November 25, just days after moving in, Dante wrote to his brother:

> My dear William,
>
>   I have written to Hunt, as I told you I should, to decline attending the meeting tomorrow. In case I should not see you before then, I beg that you will avoid asking him (should it enter your head) to come down here on Saturday, as I have Lizzy[7] coming, and do not of course wish for anyone else. I have written to him that I am engaged that evening …

Yet just a couple of months later, Rossetti was writing to Ford Madox Brown, describing Lizzie as his "pupil".

Madox Brown, affectionately called "Bruno" by Rossetti, was a few years older than the members of the Pre-Raphaelite Brotherhood. He was a groundbreaking artist, who has since become famous for works such as *Take Your Son, Sir* (1851), *The Last of England* (1855–66) and *Work* (1863), but he was already disillusioned by the time the band of seven brothers set out on their quest to change the world.

---

[7] Rossetti spelled her name as both "Lizzy" and "Lizzie", but she preferred the latter spelling and the very few letters written by her that remain are signed "Lizzie".

Rossetti and Madox Brown had met for the first time in March 1848. Rossetti, having seen some of Madox Brown's work and been profoundly moved by it, determined to be taken on as a pupil by this great master. He wrote a richly complimentary letter to the older artist, begging him to become his art tutor. Unhappy with the direction his life had taken and distrustful of people in general, Madox Brown was convinced this young swaggerer's letter was intended to mock him, so he turned up at the Rossettis' home in Charlotte Street, complete with a sturdy stick, where he threatened to beat Dante Rossetti for his impudence. The mistake was eventually cleared up, Dante's adulation for Madox Brown's work discovered to be genuine and an astonished Madox Brown agreed to take on the promising new pupil. "Bruno" later swallowed his pride when Rossetti left his tutelage, after just five months, for that of Holman Hunt and he remained one of Rossetti's closest – and certainly his most altruistic – friend until death. Madox Brown was also among the few people of Rossetti's acquaintance who genuinely liked Lizzie.

Madox Brown had been widowed early and left with a young daughter, Lucy (who lived with her grandparents).[8] Around the time that Rossetti met Lizzie, Madox Brown had also fallen in love again, with another young model called Emma Hill, "a very young girl, with little education or domestic training". For a few years, Madox Brown and Emma were lovers without being married. On November 11, 1850, while Rossetti and Lizzie were fast falling in love, Emma gave birth to Madox Brown's baby, Cathy (also known as "Catty").[9] The

---

[8] Lucy Madox Brown was later to marry Dante Rossetti's brother, William.

[9] Cathy also became an artist, mainly of watercolours, exhibiting for the first time in 1869. In 1872 she married the musicologist Dr Franz Hueffer, who had been born in Germany but moved to England where he became the music critic for *The Times*. Their son was Ford Madox Hueffer, later renamed Ford Madox Ford (because of anti-German feeling), author of the classic novel *The Good Soldier* (1915) and the Editor of *The English Review* which published such unknown writers as Ezra Pound, James Joyce and Ernest Hemingway.

couple eventually married in April 1853. Coincidentally, Emma's family were acquaintances of the Siddalls, a shared history that led to a close friendship developing between her and Lizzie. Because of this intertwined relationship, Madox Brown's diary contains valuable information about Dante's and Lizzie's relationship (as well as his own). It reveals a relationship that was intense, often troubled but always exceedingly close. It also tells of Rossetti's jealousy of the closeness between Lizzie and Emma.

Another key source to discovering Rossetti's true feelings for Lizzie are his own letters. In August 1852, a few months before moving to Blackfriars, Rossetti wrote a revealing missive to Christina. Maria had told him that Christina was trying her hand at portraiture and he asked to see an example. Though he added, with a tactless air of teasing, "You must take care however not to rival the Sid, but keep within respectful limits." Not a comment calculated to endear the un-met girlfriend to a sister's heart. In smitten tones he added, "I have had sent me, among my things from Highgate, a lock of hair shorn from the beloved head of my dear, and radiant as the tresses of Aurora, a sight of which may perhaps dazzle you on your return." He also told her that Lizzie had recently made herself two dresses, one in grey and one in black silk. The grey "bringing out her characteristics as a 'meek unconscious dove'" and the black one making her as graceful as a swan. Rossetti used the word "dove" as one of his nicknames for Lizzie; in correspondence, he would often draw a picture of a dove instead of writing her name (doves were also one of his favourite artistic devices, featuring regularly in his paintings).

Giving a man a lock of one's hair was a sure symbol of love and fidelity. It was not an action a woman was supposed to undertake unless she was engaged to the recipient, which suggests that Rossetti had led Lizzie to believe at this early date that he intended to marry her. In this letter, Rossetti seems to be suggesting this unspoken intention to Christina.

August 1852 is also the first time that mention is made of Lizzie's poor health. In that month, she went to Hastings to take a rest cure and Rossetti followed her, unwilling to stay in London without her, even forsaking his precious studio. Lizzie was by now experimenting excitedly with her art, enthused by Rossetti's own passion for painting. By the following January, Rossetti was writing to Madox Brown to come to Blackfriars and see Lizzie's drawings. She had been illustrating poems from Wordsworth and he particularly wanted "Bruno" to see a finished piece inspired by Wordsworth's poem, "We Are Seven". It was a typically melancholy subject to be chosen by Lizzie: the story of a child who insists that she has six siblings, even though two of them are buried in the local churchyard. The poem, which starts with the lines, "A simple Child, / That lightly draws its breath, / And feels its life in every limb, / What should it know of death?" is in a similar vein to Lizzie's own poems, all of which centre on gloomy subjects, usually death or betrayal in love. The death of a child – a tragically common occurrence in Victorian England – was a subject sentimental enough to be guaranteed commercial success.

On June 20, 1853, Dante sent a letter to William Rossetti which he marked PRIVATE. He sent it from Newcastle, where he was staying with a friend, William Bell Scott, and attempting to recover from an illness. In the letter, he confided to William that while he was out of London Lizzie was staying at Blackfriars, but he did not want anyone else to know. As he was expected back in London sooner than he was now able to return, he anticipated friends attempting to call on him at Chatham Place in his absence, and he did not want any of them to discover Lizzie in residence in his rooms. Being discovered in a man's rooms, even while he was not in residence, was strictly taboo, according to the conventions of the time. Lizzie's reputation would have been ruined and Rossetti would never have been able to marry her if her behaviour became discussed. Dante requested that his brother discourage anyone from going to the studio and explained that he had told Lizzie to keep the doors locked while he was away and not to answer to anyone who called round. However, as there was no kitchen, she must have left and returned to the studio quite regularly. Despite Rossetti's attempts at this stage to keep the relationship – and Lizzie's presence in his rooms – a secret, the other residents of the building already believed that she was his mistress.

It was not until March 28, 1854 that Dante Rossetti finally decided to introduce this adored "dove" to his sister, asking Christina to visit him at his studios, where she was to have the pleasure of seeing Lizzie's artwork. Rossetti had been talking to Allingham about the possibility of getting Christina's poems published and was keen for Lizzie to be their illustrator (Christina's poems were not published until 1862, the year of Lizzie's death, and Lizzie was not invited to help with the project). Rossetti attempted to forge a friendship between the two women, hoping their shared love of writing poetry would create a bond, but it was something that would never be. Christina, a little shrewish at times and eventually disappointed by life, was unimpressed by this rather common, but uncommonly attractive, woman who had usurped her in "Gabriel's" life. However, there was also a measure of fascination for the woman whose friendship she shunned (after her sister-in-law's death, a genuinely remorseful Christina encouraged her brother to publish Lizzie's poems).[10]

Six months after this first meeting, Christina composed a poem entitled "Listening", which demonstrates how much of an impression Lizzie's adoration for Dante had made upon his sister:

---

[10] After Lizzie's death, Rossetti wanted Christina to publish Lizzie's poetry in a volume of her own works. Christina was eager to do so until she received the poems, whereupon she decided they were "too hopelessly sad" to be published.

Listening

She listened like a cushat dove
That listens to its mate alone;
She listened like a cushat dove
That loves but only one.

Not fair as men would reckon fair
Nor noble as they count the line:
Only as graceful as a bough,
And tendrils of the vine:
Only as noble as sweet Eve
Your ancestress and mine.

And downcast were her dovelike eyes
And downcast was her tender cheek
Her pulses fluttered like a dove
To hear him speak.

Lizzie and Rossetti had been recognized by their friends as a couple for two years, but there was no sign of an engagement ring, neither was there any indication that his mother or Maria were aware of the true nature of their relationship. Lizzie hoped that her meeting with Dante's sister would be the start of the formalities of a betrothal, but it was not to be. Despite Rossetti's obvious adoration of her, he was not willing to make any formal declaration to the world. It was humiliating and also frightening – what would she do if he decided he preferred someone else and abandoned her? She had given up her career and her reputation for him. Whether intentionally or not, he had encouraged her to become entirely dependent on him without offering any genuine security in return. She had placed herself in a frighteningly precarious position.

The following is believed to be one of Lizzie's earliest poems, written c.1854; its alternative title is "Sleepless":

Fragment of a Ballad

Many a mile over land and sea
Unsummoned my love returned to me;
I remember not the words he said
But only the trees moaning overhead.

And he came ready to take and bear
The cross I had carried for many a year,
But words came slowly one by one
From frozen lips shut still and dumb.

How sounded my words so still and slow
To the great strong heart that loved me so,
Who came to save me from pain and wrong
And to comfort me with his love so strong?

I felt the wind strike chill and cold
And vapours rise from the red-brown mould;
I felt the spell that held my breath
Bending me down to a living death.

The ballad emphasizes Lizzie's impossible situation: her belief that Rossetti loves her, but also the wounding knowledge that although he wants to "comfort" her, he is unable to do the one thing that will make her security – and therefore her happiness – complete. By this time Lizzie was no longer the adored, unique supermodel – she was rapidly becoming merely a mistress, a status reluctantly forced upon her and one that felt like "a living death".

CHAPTER SIX

"Why does he not marry her?"

On March 10, 1855, an entry in Ford Madox Brown's diary reads, "She is a stunner and no mistake. Rossetti once told me that, when he first saw her, he felt his destiny was defined. Why does he not marry her?" It is a question that Lizzie must have asked herself hundreds of times and one that continues to be posed by countless biographers and scholars. Dante Rossetti's and Lizzie Siddal's relationship has inspired conversational debate ever since 1850 and still excites discussion today. Despite William Rossetti's claim in his memoirs that they had become engaged around 1851, there was no formal announcement and, indeed, at that date the Rossetti family were almost all in ignorance of Lizzie's existence. The latter was with good reason – Gabriele would never have approved of his son marrying an artist's model, or a lower-class girl whose parents lived in an insalubrious area of Southwark. Neither was William Rossetti ever a fan of "The Sid", though whether he disliked her for a specific reason or was simply jealous of the way she usurped his brother's affection is uncertain. William idolized his older, often ungrateful brother and Lizzie's sudden hold over him was galling – not least because she ended up holding court in Chatham Place, a home provided by William for himself and Dante. Most contemporary accounts of Lizzie were either written by, or at least edited by, William, so it is almost impossible to receive an objective view. After her death, William described Lizzie in the following terms: "Her character was somewhat singular – not quite easy to understand, and not at all on the surface … I hardly think I ever heard her say a single thing indicative of her own character, or of her serious underlying thought. All her talk was of a 'chaffy' kind – its tone sarcastic, its substance lightsome. It was like the speech of a person who wanted to turn off the conversation …"

Rossetti would not have been the first of his acquaintance to make a match of which society would not approve. Emma Madox Brown had been one of her husband's models, and had far less education and social ability than Lizzie, and Holman Hunt was getting ready to marry one of his models – a woman of far lower social standing than Lizzie. Even the wealthy and deeply respectable John Everett Millais had not managed to make a suitable match without causing a scandal. Rossetti cannot have been so worried about his reputation that his fears of marrying someone of a lower social class would have put him off spending his life with the woman with whom he was in love. After all, he believed he was above needing to worry about the bourgeois conventions of reputation and was perfectly happy in later life to have his friends and acquaintances meet the irrepressible Fanny Cornforth – a good-natured but coarse and very obviously working-class woman, without the benefit of Lizzie's graces.

If Rossetti was so concerned with his reputation, why did he flaunt his affair with Annie Miller? Especially as the affair was conducted largely during Holman Hunt's sojourn abroad, thereby earning Rossetti a scandalous reputation both because of Annie's dubious sexual history and because he was betraying a friend. Reputation, therefore, cannot have been the overriding factor in his hesitation.

There has been much speculation about whether Lizzie and Rossetti consummated their relationship before marriage – surprisingly, the general consensus appears to be that they did not. Many biographers and academics claim that Lizzie refused Rossetti – some even describe her as frigid (surely an extremely odd term to use in reference to a Victorian woman who declined to have sex with a man she was not even engaged to). Some claim that it was Rossetti himself who refused to move their relationship onto a sexual level, citing a conversation he had with friends in which he denounced the concept of free love. However, it must be remembered that this conversation was itself in stark contrast to an earlier comment Rossetti had made when he shocked a young Holman Hunt by complacently commenting that women were "so much nicer when they have lost their virtue". (It seems, though, that Rossetti was most probably still a virgin himself at the time he made this provocative comment, aged about 20.) If Rossetti was so against sex outside marriage, why did he sleep with Annie Miller and Fanny Cornforth? His fervent admiration for Giovanni Boccaccio's *Decameron*, a medieval exponent of the wonders of sex before marriage, is another factor in believing he was perfectly at ease with his sexual needs and willing to satisfy them without worrying about the conventions of society.

It has been claimed that it was Lizzie's refusal to have sex with Rossetti that pushed him into the arms of Annie Miller, Fanny Cornforth and the other women he had affairs with during his relationship with Lizzie, but these affairs began while Lizzie was abroad, when they were fighting or when they had become estranged from one another. I dispute that Lizzie continued to refuse him and believe they did have a sexual relationship before marriage. My main reason for this is that I cannot see any other reason for him not marrying her. If she had refused to have sex with him without being married, he would, at the height of his feelings for her, have married her in order to sleep with her, as so many Victorian men did. He was in awe of his father, with whom he occasionally argued about his unconventional behaviour and his inability to earn a proper income, but after the death of Gabriele, in 1854, Dante was the head of the family, able to do as he pleased – and around the time of Gabriele's death Dante's and Lizzie's relationship was at its height, with his feelings for her apparent to all who saw them together. By the time Rossetti's year of mourning for his father was at an end, Lizzie was receiving a generous annuity from Ruskin and, as

Jan Marsh suggests, if Rossetti had married her then, she would have been expected to give up Ruskin's allowance because a married woman could not accept payments from a man who was not her husband. Rossetti's precarious finances meant he could not afford to allow Lizzie to give up such a generous amount of money, which may add another dimension to his reluctance to marry her at that time.

Another strong indication that their relationship was sexual is the fact that they stayed together in Rossetti's rooms on many occasions. In an age when it was considered intimate for a man to talk to an unmarried woman without the presence of a chaperone, spending the night alone in the same apartment was unheard of and absolutely taboo, even if they slept in separate rooms. There was no sense in Lizzie taking such an enormous risk – with her family's home a comparatively short distance away – if she did not have an overwhelming reason for wanting to be alone with Rossetti.

Lizzie's poems provide another hint at a sexual side to their relationship. The final line of "Sleepless" talks about a relationship bringing the heroine to "a living death". This pays reference to Lizzie's own sense of loss caused by Rossetti's lack of a proposal, though it may have a double meaning. The term "little death" is a poetic device for referring to an orgasm. Lizzie's poem could, therefore, also refer to her sexual relationship with Rossetti. Many of the poem's lines are sexually suggestive: "the trees moaning overhead"; "he came ready to take and bear / The cross I had carried for many a year" and the "great strong heart" of her lover relieving her "frozen lips" and offering "comfort". This is not the poetry of a repressed virgin who continually kept her lover at arm's length while teasingly staying the night in his one-bedroomed apartment. It is also worth remembering that Lizzie's closest friend was Emma Madox Brown, who had an overtly sexual relationship with Ford Madox Brown for several years before marriage, a circumstance that could not be ignored after the birth of their daughter two and a half years before their wedding day.

Lizzie was brought up by very religious parents who attended a

Congregational church and were well known in the Christian community both in Southwark and in Sheffield. There have been suggestions, however, that she was not particularly devout herself – until she met the Pusey family in Oxford in 1855. If this was the case, and Lizzie suddenly decided in 1855 that she was doing wrong by sleeping with Rossetti and wanted to stop, it could well explain his sudden rush of infidelities at around this time and the many arguments that began to colour their relationship from the mid-1850s onwards.

Lizzie poem "The Lust of the Eyes" contains more than a subtle suggestion that their relationship was sexual. The date on which it was written is unknown but the bitterness of the subject matter makes it unlikely to have been composed after their wedding:

The Lust of the Eyes

I care not for my Lady's soul
Though I worship before her smile;
I care not where be my Lady's goal
When her beauty shall lose its wile.

Low sit I down at my Lady's feet
Gazing through her wild eyes
Smiling to think how my love will fleet
When their starlike beauty dies.

I care not if my Lady pray
To our Father which is in Heaven
But for joy my heart's quick pulses play
For to me her love is given.

Then who shall close my Lady's eyes
And who shall fold her hands?
Will any hearken if she cries
Up to the unknown lands?

This poem illustrates Lizzie's own realization that she has been duped; that the lover she trusted so entirely and fully expected to marry was in fact content to keep her solely as his mistress. Lizzie's religious background makes it unlikely that she would have taken a succession of lovers, like Annie Miller, but she was in love with Rossetti and believed from the beginning of their relationship that they would be married – as soon as he had earned enough money to support her. Lizzie's sister Lydia, to whom she was very close, became pregnant before her wedding. It seems likely that the sisters would have shared similar views on sex before marriage – believing that it was acceptable as long as there was the proviso that there would soon be a wedding. This attitude would also explain Lizzie's martyr-like devotion to Rossetti and her refusal to leave, even when he treated her badly. She knew she could not leave him because she would no longer be acceptable to other men.

The fact that Lizzie did not become pregnant before marriage is not proof that no sexual relationship was in existence. Lizzie's addiction may well have prevented conception. There is also the possibility that, as a result of becoming painfully thin at regular intervals, her periods may have ceased for long stretches of time, as can happen to anorexics. There was also fairly effective contraception available in the mid-nineteenth century. Condoms, or "sheaths", were easily available for men to buy, although they must have been extremely unpleasant to use, made as they were of animal intestines, usually sheep gut.[1] Women could use a specially treated sponge, a pessary or a "rubber pad" (which was similar to the modern contraceptive cap). They were also advised to douche or syringe themselves immediately after sex, using an astringent solution made with a substance such as vinegar or lemon juice, in an

---

[1] Hector France, an aptly named Frenchman living in London in the mid-1800s, wrote a letter home revealing that he had seen condoms on sale in Petticoat Lane market, which were decorated with a portrait of the Prime Minister or the Queen!

attempt to prevent conception. None of these methods was fool-proof, but they were more effective than leaving it to chance.

That Lizzie had a sexual relationship with Rossetti which she later regretted is implicit in her poem "Worn Out", written around 1856:

Worn Out

Thy strong arms are around me, love
My head is on thy breast;
Low words of comfort come from thee
Yet my soul has no rest.

For I am but a startled thing
Nor can I ever be
Aught save a bird whose broken wing
Must fly away from thee.

I cannot give to thee the love
I gave so long ago,
The love that turned and struck me down
Amid the blinding snow.

I can but give a failing heart
And weary eyes of pain,
A faded mouth that cannot smile
And may not laugh again.

Yet keep thine arms around me, love,
Until I fall to sleep;
Then leave me, saying no goodbye
Lest I might wake, and weep.

Diana Holman Hunt, granddaughter of William Holman Hunt and revealer of the family secrets, claimed that Lizzie became pregnant by Rossetti, resulting in either a miscarriage or an illegal abortion. She claimed Lizzie then went off sex and attributed Rossetti's affairs to her new reluctance to sleep with him. This rumour was gossip passed down through the family which may have been true or may have been malicious. It is unlikely Lizzie had an abortion – abortion in the 1850s was crude and usually resulted in infertility, and Lizzie went on to conceive more than one child. In a tragically high percentage of Victorian cases abortion proved fatal to the mother, through haemorrhaging after the operation or via infection sustained during the crudely executed procedure. A miscarriage is, however, possible as Lizzie was addicted to laudanum early in their relationship, which would have made the chances of a pregnancy going to full term highly unlikely. There were also various "remedies" suggested to unwilling mothers-to-be, which included sudden and rigorous exercise, such as horse-riding, running or vigorous walking. This could explain the long, exerting walks Lizzie and Rossetti took when he visited her in Sussex.

It has been common for biographers to question whether Rossetti ever genuinely loved Lizzie, offering instead the suggestion that, having made vague promises to her, he was reluctant and too guilty to shake her off entirely, perhaps fearful of a breach-of-promise lawsuit (after all, her father was famous for lawsuits, what with Hope Hall and his threat to take Millais to court after *Ophelia*). Yet when one reads through Rossetti's correspondence, as well as through letters and diaries written by others in his circle, there is no doubt that Rossetti was very much in love with Lizzie. In the years 1853 to 1855 they were almost inseparable – they rowed passionately and occasionally spent time apart, but the bond between them remained intensely strong. Their relationship survived Lizzie's bad health and Rossetti's hurtful infidelities and they were still able to remain adoring of one another. They did separate for around 18 months in the late 1850s, but it was not a permanent separation and neither began a serious relationship with anyone else while they were apart. Rossetti became convinced that what he and Lizzie had was an almost celestial relationship, building on his initial comment to Madox Brown that he had glimpsed his destiny the first time he saw Lizzie. In 1854 he wrote his poem "Sudden Light" which contains the lines:

> *You have been mine before –*
> *How long ago I may not know.*

Perpetuating the Dante and Beatrice legend, Rossetti cast himself and Lizzie in the roles of reincarnated lovers, evinced in his doppel-gänger painting *How They Met Themselves* – a painting he worked on for the entire length of their courtship.

Even the sceptical William Rossetti recorded that his brother was "deeply and profusely in love" with Lizzie and that he presumed she was "sincerely in love with him". Like all couples, they had their problems, but at no time did Rossetti end the relationship perma-nently. He was unfaithful and for the duration of these affairs may well have believed he was no longer in love with Lizzie – in 1856, Ford Madox Brown records in his diary: "Emma called on Miss Sid. yesterday who is ill and complaining much of Gabriel. He seems to have transformed his affections to Annie Miller and does nothing but talk of her to Miss Sid. He is mad past cure." But whenever these affairs reached their conclusion, Rossetti always returned to Lizzie, apologetic, cajoling and apparently as deeply in love with her as before.

On October 6, 1854, Ford Madox Brown recorded in his diary a loving scene he had witnessed at Rossetti's studio. In writing about it he used the pet name Lizzie and Rossetti used for one another, "Guggum", sometimes abbreviated to "Gug":

Called on Dante Rossetti. Saw Miss Siddal, looking thinner and more deathlike and more beautiful and more ragged than ever; a real artist, a woman without parallel for many a long year. Gabriel as usual diffuse and inconsequent in his work. Drawing wonderful and lovely Guggums one after another, each one a fresh charm, each one stamped with immortality, and his picture never advancing.

Almost a year later, in August 1855, Rossetti's obsession had not been muted and Madox Brown wrote, "To see Rossetti … He showed me a drawer full of 'Guggums'; God knows how many, but not bad work, I should say, for the six years he has known her; it is like a monomania with him. Many of them are matchless in beauty, however, and one day will be worth large sums." Another visitor to Rossetti's studio, while Lizzie was absent, wrote that all the while he painted, Rossetti kept repeating the word "Guggum" ceaselessly to himself.[2]

Rossetti's all-consuming passion for Lizzie was, however, worrying Madox Brown. Rossetti was not yet a rich man and he was reliant entirely on the goodwill of relations – one of his aunts was very adoring and William was always generous – and friends, namely Madox Brown himself, who seemed to be constantly lending Rossetti money. Yet even though he had commissions to complete in 1855 and he was in real need of the money these would bring, Rossetti could not stop drawing and painting Lizzie. She was more than a muse. Through no fault of her own she had become an obsession – and one that was endangering his career. At the end of 1855, when Lizzie travelled to France for her health, Madox Brown noted with relief that at last Rossetti would be able to get on with some work. In fact, several of his associates commented on how much better Rossetti worked when Lizzie was not around.

Yet, though he may have worked better, Rossetti could not bear the separation and continued to ignore the unfinished commissions.

---

[2] Rossetti was convinced that no one else could do justice to Lizzie's ethereal beauty. After her death, Georgie Burne-Jones asked for a photograph of her as a remembrance, Rossetti told her that no photographs of Lizzie had been kept as none of them was a flattering enough likeness. Though, as Jan Marsh notes, at least two very small photos did survive at that time.

He chose instead to work day and night to complete a new painting as fast as possible,[3] so he could sell it and use the money to go and join Lizzie for ten days. Alexander Munro, who joined Rossetti in his trip to Paris so they could visit the French Great Exhibition, wrote home: "We enjoyed Paris immensely, in different ways of course, for Rossetti was every day with his sweetheart of whom he is more foolishly fond than ever I saw lover."

That he genuinely loved her cannot be in dispute but, to echo Ford Madox Brown, why did he not marry her? It seems the answer lies not with Lizzie, but with Dante Rossetti himself and his aversion to being married. It is notable that, despite having passionate relationships after Lizzie's death, he did not ever marry again and, in spite of spending many years obsessed with Lizzie, he found himself unable to make the ultimate commitment until he was so torn apart by the belief she was about to die that he did the only thing within his power to make her happy – he married her almost on her deathbed. William's daughter, Helen, later described Dante by saying he "was not a man with any particular propensity for the married state". Why Dante had this distaste for marriage is unknown, but of the four Rossetti children, only William actively embraced the concept (and this was only after he had already suffered one broken engagement).[4] Both Christina and Maria turned down eligible suitors; Christina was engaged once and proposed to twice, but neither culminated in marriage.[5]

---

[3] He completed the painting in one week, a speed that astonished Madox Brown.

[4] William became engaged in 1856 to Henrietta Rintoul, the daughter of one of his colleagues. The engagement was dissolved in 1860 when she told him that she wanted a celibate marriage. In 1874, he married Lucy Madox Brown, whom he had known since she was a small child.

[5] Her first suitor, James Collinson, was a Catholic, a faith which he attempted to renounce for her sake, but was unable to do. His return to Catholicism in 1850 caused the end of their engagement, leaving Christina broken-hearted. In the 1860s, she had a romance with the linguist and translator Charles Cayley, with whom her brother William believed she was in love. Unfortunately, Cayley was an agnostic, which could also not be reconciled to a life allied to Christina. He proposed in 1866, after several years of acquaintance, but she refused him.

In 1856, after Rossetti and Lizzie had fought furiously about his infidelity with Annie Miller (a misdemeanour that had also been discovered by an angry Holman Hunt), their relationship took an unexpected upward turn. Rossetti was apologetic and loving; he bought Lizzie a sumptuous evening cloak to wear and rashly announced that there would finally be a wedding. In November he arrived at Madox Brown's studio, interrupting a private meeting between Ford and William Rossetti, and joyously proclaimed that he and Lizzie would be married as soon as possible and that he intended they should honeymoon in Algeria, at the time a popular spot for invalids and a place he had decided Lizzie would benefit from visiting. Barbara Leigh Smith had recently taken her consumptive sister, Isabella, to Algeria. No doubt Rossetti was also inspired to travel abroad having viewed the magnificent works Holman Hunt had been producing since his time overseas. A honeymoon in Algeria would be the perfect excuse for him to paint its landscapes and people. He told Lizzie he would fix the wedding date as soon as he received an expected payment from one of his patrons.

The payment arrived within a couple of weeks but, to Lizzie's humiliation, Rossetti suddenly stopped talking about wedding plans and Algeria, and spent the money elsewhere. As far as Lizzie was concerned, their relationship was now at an end. Mortified and miserable, she fled to Bath with her sister Clara, but Rossetti followed her and persuaded her to come back to him. Like the addict she was, she did so, returning to London and living, as before, entirely on Rossetti's terms, while her health deteriorated even more rapidly.

CHAPTER SEVEN

Lizzie's Mysterious Illness

To examine the state of Lizzie's health and the way it affected her relationship with Rossetti, we need to return to 1852 and the first time it was mentioned in Rossetti's letters. It was August and Rossetti wrote to Christina, mentioning that he was about to make a trip to Hastings. He was going there to visit Lizzie, who was convalescing by the sea – this was shortly after her experience of modelling for *Ophelia* and is suggestive that the extended cold bath had more seriously endangered Lizzie's health than John Millais's son was prepared to admit. From this time onward, Lizzie's poor health was to become a recurrent theme in Rossetti's correspondence. Her mysterious illness has long baffled medics and scholars. In her lifetime she was erroneously diagnosed as having consumption (tuberculosis) and curvature of the spine, but since then it has been suggested she suffered from an eating disorder, such as anorexia or bulimia, or that she was simply "neurotic" – a vague description that can encompass myriad symptoms and mental illnesses.

The long-accepted belief that Lizzie was consumptive does not tally with the many sudden recoveries she made, or with the fact that she lived for so long after the diagnosis was made. If she had been a victim of tuberculosis, her symptoms would have continually worsened and eventually proved fatal – this did not happen. Instead, she would languish and appear to be hovering on the brink between life and death and then quite suddenly – usually with the arrival of Rossetti at her side, or with the ending of one of his affairs – she would rally. Within days – sometimes within hours – she would have risen from what was believed to be her deathbed and be striding across the Downs or visiting an art exhibition with him. In the end it was not her poor physical health that killed her: she died from a self-administered overdose.

Lizzie did suffer from an undiagnosed digestive disorder. This could have been something as commonplace as severe indigestion or irritable bowel syndrome, or it could have been indicative of an eating disorder. The pain, however, may have been unconnected with her digestive system – "stomach pain" was a useful phrase to cover the embarrassments of gynaecological problems, such as period pains. Whatever the original ailment was, Lizzie began alleviating it with one of the nineteenth century's most common drugs, laudanum. It was that which was to prove her downfall.

Many of her symptoms – which included nausea, lack of appetite, a continually nagging nervous cough, sudden bouts of vomiting, breathlessness, a general feeling of weakness and dizzy spells – can be attributed to the effects of laudanum addiction. The suggestions that Lizzie had some kind of eating disorder seem to be borne out by the fact that Rossetti makes several references in letters to Lizzie having refused to eat – at one point she tells him she has not eaten for two weeks. These periods of starvation coincide with a time when Rossetti has been unfaithful or neglectful, indicative that her illness was emotional rather than physical. As their relationship deteriorated, it became common for her to emotionally blackmail him by refusing to eat. She remained unhealthily thin and suffered from a multitude of emotional miseries and feelings of self-loathing, which attacked her at around the same time as her apparent inability to eat, or an inability to digest what she did eat without vomiting. All these symptoms, including her lack of appetite, can also be attributed to laudanum addiction.

Laudanum, otherwise known as "tincture of opium", was a mixture of opium and alcohol. It was available widely and without need of anything as regulatory as a prescription. Laudanum was perceived as a cure-all painkiller, much as aspirin or paracetamol are viewed today. During Lizzie's lifetime, thousands of kilograms of opium were imported into the UK from China and until 1868 opium was not even classified as a poison.[1] The profession of pharmacist was recognized in Britain only in the 1840s, so in Lizzie's lifetime there were relatively few professional pharmacies. As a result, laudanum was sold over the counter in an eclectic variety of outlets. One could buy the drug from the greengrocer, the barber, the ironmonger or at market stalls. In 1865, a local government survey conducted in Preston discovered that the large number of people selling drugs at that time hailed from such disparate trades as a basketmaker, a baker, a tailor and a rent collector.

Laudanum was sold regularly to mothers to soothe their babies. The practice of spiking a baby's bottle with laudanum, to be sure of a good night's sleep, was common and several preparations created specifically for children were on the market, including the famous Godfrey's Cordial (which continued to be sold during the first decades of the twentieth century). The cordial was especially coveted by working mothers. In working-class areas, almost all able-bodied people were out working themselves, so the lot of child care usually fell to anyone who was not eligible for paid work – older children, the elderly and the infirm. Laudanum was therefore a vital part of ensuring that the children they were looking after did not become unmanageable. As a result, many children grew to adulthood already addicted to the opium-derived drug.

To understand why laudanum was so widely taken, one needs to look at the vast list of disparate symptoms it was claimed to alleviate.

---

[1] In 1830, more than 22,000 lb (10,000 kg) of opium was imported into the UK from China. By 1860 Britain was buying more than four times that amount each year.

These included symptoms of alcoholism (even though alcohol was the main ingredient of the "medicine"), bedwetting, bronchitis, chilblains, cholera, coughs and colds, depression, diarrhoea, dysentery, earache, flatulence, gout, gynaecological problems, headaches, hysteria, insanity, menopause, morning sickness, muscle fatigue, nausea, nervous tension, period pains, rheumatism, stomachache, teething in babies and toothache in adults. Lotion made with laudanum was said to heal a variety of complaints, including bruises, chilblains, piles, sprains and ulcers.

One can see how easy, and how acceptable, it was for Lizzie to become addicted to laudanum. In fact, laudanum addiction was so common that it was rarely referred to, treated much as drinking alcohol is accepted in society today. Lizzie was not alone in her addiction. Walter Scott and Coleridge were well known for their dependence on it, and Wilkie Collins and Elizabeth Barrett Browning (also an habitual invalid), were both regular imbibers of the alcohol-based drug.[2] Charles Dickens also took laudanum from time to time.

Lizzie's overwhelming problem, in addition to her addiction, was that she suffered from severe depression. Whether this was caused by the laudanum or whether she originally took laudanum to combat the depression is impossible to determine. Much of Lizzie's ill health originated in her mind, stemming from her desire to receive attention and love. Dr Acland, a friend of Ruskin's who made a close study of Lizzie over a fortnight, and Mrs Kincaid, with whom she spent several months abroad for her health, both became aware that much of Lizzie's illness was imaginary, or self-inflicted. On rare occasions, and increasingly toward the end of her life, she was genuinely very ill, but at other times her poor health seldom prevented her from undertaking anything she really wanted to do, although it was extraordinarily effective in stopping her from carrying out other people's wishes.

---

[2] Elizabeth Barrett Browning died just a few months before Lizzie, in 1861.

Very few letters between Lizzie and Rossetti survive, so the information we have comes from letters he wrote to his friends and family. One very revealing aspect of these letters – although unrecognized by Rossetti – is the extent to which Lizzie manipulated him through the medium of her ill health. Time and again when they were apart, Rossetti would leave whatever he was doing and rush to wherever Lizzie was as he had been told she was dangerously ill. More often than not, his next letter would enthuse that Lizzie had made a remarkable recovery thanks to his arrival and within a day or two they would be off walking for miles and carving their initials in the bark of unfortunate trees. It was also very common for him to write that he would be returning home in a couple of days, only for this letter to be followed rapidly by another saying he had been forced to change his plans as Lizzie had had a sudden relapse and needed him to stay with her.

It is interesting to see how often Lizzie's ill health coincided with Rossetti's affections being taken up by another woman. By his refusal to marry her, Rossetti had forced her to blackmail him emotionally and she used every opportunity to do so. At the start of their relationship it seems the balance of power was very much in his favour as she struggled to prevent him tiring of her, but by the end of her life she had become overtly manipulative and controlling, to the point that his friends claimed he shrank when she spoke to him, always expecting a rebuke or for her to sink dangerously into illness, blaming him wordlessly for its onslaught.

On August 25, 1853, Rossetti mentioned in a letter to Ford Madox Brown that Lizzie had been "very ill lately". Six months later she was in extremely poor health again, following Walter Deverell's death, on February 2, 1854.[3] Lizzie had remained very fond of

---

[3] After Deverell's death, Rossetti finished off his deceased friend's last painting so it could be sold and his family receive the money. Deverell must have been painting the picture for a long time as Lizzie had been one of the original models. Rossetti did not like the way Deverell had painted her hair, so he repainted it, sadly reminiscent of how he had repainted her hair in *Twelfth Night*.

Deverell, in later years telling friends that she had loved him before Rossetti. She was always grateful for his life-changing discovery of her and the kindness he showed her; his death caused her great sadness, as well as being a shocking reminder of her own mortality. Despite knowing that Deverell's doctors had warned him of the extent of his illness, his friends were unable to believe, until the very end, that this vivacious star of Pre-Raphaelitism, and of their social group in general, would ever let the disease get the better of him.

In 1857, when she and Rossetti were temporarily separated, Lizzie told an acquaintance in Sheffield that she and Deverell would have been married if he had lived. Although there is no apparent truth in the statement, Lizzie and Deverell had been very fond of one another. After Deverell's death, both she and Rossetti were dogged by depression, neither able to help the other as each was so wrapped up in their own misery.

A month after Deverell's death, when Lizzie's health was still exhibiting no improvement, Rossetti's friends, the Howitts, suggested that Lizzie be seen by a friend of theirs, the Swedenborgian physician Dr Garth Wilkinson. Anna Mary Howitt (1824–86) was engaged to Edward Bateman, whose home Rossetti had shared in Highgate, and it was through Anna Mary that he and Lizzie were introduced to Barbara Leigh Smith (1827–91) and her great friend, Bessie Rayner Parkes. The three women were to prove invaluable friends to the couple, especially to Lizzie.[4] Anna Mary was an artist, a serious female artist who had been trained at the

---

[4] Barbara Leigh Smith Bodichon was a great social reformer, particularly concerned with women's rights, and a philanthropist; she was also a prominent member of the religious movement known as the Dissenters and a cousin of Florence Nightingale (1820–1910). In addition, she was an amateur artist and the author of several works about social reform. Her father was a controversial MP who actively used his wealth to benefit the poor. In the enviable position of being independently wealthy, Barbara Leigh Smith was very generous with her homes in London and Sussex, always entertaining friends and concerned with their welfare. She took a considerable interest in Lizzie and often nursed her through times of illness. This interest may well have stemmed from the fact that her parents were

Royal Academy "pre" school, Sass's – although her gender precluded her from going on to the Royal Academy itself. Bessie and Barbara were amateur artists. Rossetti was hugely impressed by the three women and took their advice about Lizzie seriously. He related the resultant medical consultation to Ford Madox Brown:

> The Howitts insisted on Lizzy seeing a Dr Wilkinson, a friend of theirs, and I believe an eminent man. He finds that the poor dear has contracted a curvature of the spine, and says she ought not to paint at present; but this, of course, she must. He says her case is a very anxious but by no means a hopeless one ...

Curvature of the spine was an extremely odd diagnosis to make about a woman whose main symptoms were fainting, serious digestive disorders, loss of appetite and severe and sudden weight loss. It also seems a singularly strange report to give of a woman whom all contemporary reports claim had such perfect deportment and who never even wore a corset to keep her back straight. Lizzie was famed for being tall and elegant of bearing, and it was remarked that she walked with a superbly erect spine. It is interesting, however, that one of the symptoms of laudanum addiction, as noted by nineteenth-century observers, was a stooped posture. It seems likely that when Lizzie saw Dr Wilkinson, at the height of her depression, she had been dosing herself liberally with laudanum to try and numb the misery. It is also safe to assume that she suffered back pains as a

---

unmarried and her mother, who came from a much poorer family than her father, had been a milliner. It seems likely that Barbara's parents never married because the laws of the time – against which Benjamin Smith was totally opposed – meant that marriage was not at all an equal partnership, effectively making a woman the property of her husband. Barbara was a lifelong and active supporter of reform for married women's rights and of women's suffrage; she was also a fervent supporter of the poor and followed her father's example of using her wealth to help the needy. In 1857 she married the eccentric French physician Eugene Bodichon, whom she had met in Algeria where Bodichon was working. They had no children, but supported one another's many causes until his death in 1885.

result of her many hours of modelling for Rossetti, as well as from sitting huddled over her own easel. Curvature of the spine was not, however, the reason she was such an invalid and Wilkinson's diagnosis was to be dismissed by the several doctors who attended her in the coming years.

This letter of Rossetti's is interesting for his instant dismissal not of the diagnosis but of the recommended treatment: that she should give up art. To Rossetti the idea that one could give up art was as preposterous as suggesting that one should give up breathing. He would never entertain the idea, either for himself or Lizzie. He was also not going to deprive himself of his favourite and always available model, even if modelling was the cause of her constant illness. He loved her, but he loved his art even more.

By mid-April, Lizzie was still no better. Rossetti was concerned enough to arrange for her – on the advice of Barbara Leigh Smith – to return to Hastings and convalesce. On first meeting Lizzie, Barbara had written to Bessie expressing great interest in this needy woman's welfare:

I have a strong interest in a young girl formerly model to Millais and Dante Rossetti, now Rossetti's love and pupil ... She is a genius and will, if she lives, be a great artist. Alas! Her life has been hard and full of trials, her home unhappy and her whole fate hard. Dante Rossetti has been an honourable friend to her and I do not doubt if circumstances were favourable, would marry her. She is of course under a ban, having been a model (tho' only to two PRBs) ergo do not mention it to anyone ...

Barbara added, as the greatest of compliments, "although she is not a lady her mind is poetic". Lizzie's and Rossetti's reinvention of her life had been broad. Her modelling for Millais could not be ignored as *Ophelia* had become so well known, but neither Holman Hunt's nor Deverell's paintings were widely recognized, so the lovers were able to cut away at the truth, revealing it only piece by piece. Lizzie was, for some reason, keen to develop a fiction about a terribly hard, unhappy childhood – related here with undertones of abuse. Rossetti had also been told this version of her early years.

Barbara's interest was genuine and when Rossetti required assistance in solving the problem of Lizzie's poor health, Barbara was quick to offer hers. At last she had an opportunity of helping this interesting and tragic girl with whom she had become quite enthralled. Barbara found Lizzie suitable accommodation in Hastings town centre and explained that she would be at her own property, Scalands Farm, in the countryside outside the town, so she, Bessie and the visiting Anna Mary would be on hand to nurse Lizzie if necessary and to keep her company when she needed friendship.

Hastings' popularity as a health resort was due largely to its clean, clear sea water. At that date, it was not the concept of *swimming* in the sea that was seen as especially beneficial, but *drinking* the sea water.[5] The town was also famed for its plentiful supply of fresh fish, perceived as ideal food for invalids, and the presence of nearby natural springs, whose water could be drunk as a cure. Hastings was equally favoured by doctors because of its mild climate, which meant not only that the weather was usually clement enough for even the most delicate of invalids to journey outside but also negated the need for constant indoor fires – the smoke from coal fires being the main contributory factor to London's choking smog. Because of this, Hastings was often recommended for anyone suffering from respiratory problems, such as consumption or asthma.

For the non-invalid, there was not a great deal to do in this newly

---

[5] Health treatments for some invalids, however, did include sea bathing and "total immersion", the latter would be performed by a large-muscled bathing attendant who carried the invalid out into the sea and dropped them unceremoniously into it before carrying them back to the shore.

popular town. The local government was strictly moral so there was no theatre or concert hall (one was finally built in 1876), although there was a bandstand. The biggest attraction, and the one that drew in day-trippers from London and elsewhere, was the beach. In 1857, an article in the *Illustrated Times* commented:

> [there are] visitors here of all sorts from the noble Lord to the poor London warehouseman and occasionally the great Premier comes down for a day or two to see his step-daughter, Lady Jocelyn. On Sunday, shoals of Londoners swarm upon the beach ... The gentlemen do little all day long but bathe, and promenade, and lounge, and look through telescopes ... You can scarcely meet a lady who is not reading a shilling volume ... The most elegant and healthful recreation is riding on horseback.[6]

April 1854 was a severely trying time for Rossetti. Lizzie was desperately ill and wanted him to be with her in Hastings. Barbara, Bessie and Anna Mary all wrote several times from Sussex, urging him to hurry there and see her as they were so worried about the consequences if he did not. Meanwhile, in London, Gabriele Rossetti was dying. Dante was having to come to terms not only with his father's imminent death but also with his own new position as head of the family, ultimately making him responsible for his mother and sisters. Gabriele's health had been very poor for the last decade. His eyesight had started to fade first, after which his general health had deteriorated humiliatingly. In 1843 he had been forced to give up work, leading to his daughters and wife needing to find employment. Maria quickly found full-time employment as a governess, but Mrs Rossetti and Christina seemed doomed not to be successful in their chosen sphere. They wanted to run a school and, over the next few

---

[6] In the mid-nineteenth century, riding was also one of the most common ways for a woman to bring an end to an unwanted pregnancy, which may add another dimension to Hastings' popularity as a health resort for ladies.

years, set up two schools, the first in London and the second in Somerset, but neither were any good at making money and they ended up relying, as Dante did, on the sensible, solid salary earned by William.

When the children had been growing up, the Rossetti family had lived at the fashionable address of 50 Charlotte Street in central London, but in 1850, seven years of Gabriele's poor health and financial insecurity had taken their toll and the family relocated to the less salubrious and less central 38 Arlington Road, in Mornington Crescent. The following year, Gabriele, Frances and Christina left London for the Somerset countryside, partly so that Gabriele could convalesce and partly so that the two women could follow their favourite minister, who had recently moved to the Frome area and promised to help them set up their new school. They had remained in Somerset, failing miserably at making their fortune, for a year, until William was able to pay for them to move back to London in March 1852. Maria had stayed behind in London to keep house for William. She had also earned a small wage from teaching Italian to private students. Gabriele, a proud and erudite man, must have found his failing eyesight and his forced reliance on his younger son galling in equal parts. Added to this was the dilettante lifestyle of his eldest son and namesake, the one who should have been providing for the family but was instead not earning enough from his painting, refusing to work at anything else and flirting with models. Gabriele was inordinately proud of his eldest son's painting, but he knew that it would not make enough money to support the family after his own death. His knowledge that his son was right to pursue the career he was so obviously destined for fought against Gabriele's desire for Dante to be as reliable as William in providing for his family.

Gabriele died on April 26, 1854, after a demeaningly lingering illness. There is scant mention of his death in Rossetti's remaining letters and he seemed reluctant to grieve, preferring instead to concentrate on his plans to visit Lizzie as soon as the funeral was over. In later years, Rossetti's grief over the death of his father would resurface and contribute to his very poor mental health at the end of his life. In 1854, however, he was determined to cope and to do the right thing both for his family and for the woman with whom he was in love.

On May 1, Barbara Leigh Smith sent him an urgent letter, requesting he come and see Lizzie as she was so dangerously ill and enclosing a similar missive from Bessie Parkes, which made him "very uneasy". For once Lizzie was moved to let him know that she was not as ill as their friends feared, but he was too distracted to know what to believe. He replied to Barbara on May 2, letting her know he would set off as soon as possible:

My dear Miss Smith,

I shall try and come to Hastings tomorrow evening or the next day to see Miss Siddal. Thanks most sincerely for your letter, the kindest you could have written. If possible, I shall take the liberty of calling on you at the address you give. Perhaps you know that since I saw you, we have lost my father. I think I should start for Hastings to-day, only that his funeral is fixed for tomorrow.

With kindest regards to Miss Howitt and Miss Parkes, to whom I shall ever feel grateful for her kindness to Miss Siddal at Hastings.

True to his word, Rossetti left for Hastings as soon as the funeral was over, barely staying to comfort his family, convinced he was about to lose Lizzie as well as his father.

By the mid-1850s, Hastings was the fourth largest health resort in the country.[7] The train service from London was regular and efficient,

---

[7] In the 1850s, Hastings was beaten in popularity as a health resort only by Brighton, Great Yarmouth and Dover.

with the direct journey taking just over two hours. Rossetti arrived in the town to find that Lizzie was, as she had declared, not dangerously ill, but simply her usual delicate self. In many ways her health was much improved, not least because she was in good spirits. Her frailty, charm and elegant manners had won her the affection of many of the other residents at her boarding house and a great number of sympathetic ladies had become her willing attendants. She was also being regularly visited by Bessie Parkes, who nursed her selflessly.

Rossetti wrote again to Barbara, thanking her, Bessie and Anna for their attentiveness and recognizing that the fear they had entertained arose from their not knowing how ill Lizzie habitually looked: "I have known her for several years," he wrote, "and always in a state hardly less variable than now; and I can understand that those who have not had so long a knowledge of her will naturally be more liable to alarm on her account than I am. Nevertheless I am quite aware that she is in a most delicate state."

Before his arrival, Barbara had been busy trying to persuade Lizzie that she should be admitted to the Sussex Infirmary, a ghastly thought as hospital hygiene was so appalling that many patients ended their time in hospital in a far worse state than when they had arrived. Lizzie was determined not to go into hospital – apart from the fact that hospitals were such dreaded places, she wanted to be cared for by Rossetti. If she went into hospital, he would be allowed in only at strictly regulated times and they would never be alone together, which also meant she would not know what he was doing in the numerous hours he would be apart from her. There was also the fear that in hospital she would not be able to dose herself with laudanum whenever she craved it. Dr Wilkinson backed up Rossetti in his refusal to admit her, but Barbara continued to suggest hospitalization for Lizzie for the next few years, including the suggestion that Lizzie attend Barbara's cousin's new hospital for women in London – her cousin being

Florence Nightingale, currently on the brink of national fame for her mission to the Crimea.[8]

When Rossetti arrived in Hastings he took a room in an inn on East Parade, but within days he had moved into the same lodgings as Lizzie, at 5 High Street (now in the Old Town), run by a Mrs Elphick. He wrote to his mother, in a letter quite tactlessly happy in tone: "No one thinks it at all odd my going into the Gug's room to sit there; and Barbara Smith said to the landlady how inadvisable it would be for her to sit with me in a room without fire." He raved about the weather, the views, the perfect countryside then, almost as an aside, added that of course he had not been the merriest of companions, mourning his father as he was. Lizzie, he added, had been sketching and her health was vastly improved; she had even been able to take bracing walks with him across the Downs, as well as being able to journey several miles to nearby Robertsbridge to visit Barbara at Scalands Farm. That Dante, at this mournful time, instead of being with his mother, would rather be with a woman they barely knew – and who was brazen enough to allow him to visit her alone in her room – was galling in the extreme.

Rossetti had not intended to stay in Hastings for more than a week, but on May 12 (his birthday) he wrote a somewhat melancholy letter to William Allingham explaining that his plans for returning to town had been thwarted by Lizzie taking a turn for the worse. He was missing his studio and his social life, and finding the daily sight of an increasingly ailing Lizzie an unwelcome addition to

---

[8] At the end of 1854, one of Rossetti's aunts, Ellen Polidori, also went to the Crimea as a nurse. Christina Rossetti begged to go with her, but the authorities turned her down on account of her being too young. A journalist who interviewed the war nurses immortalized Ellen in print as "Miss Polly Dory", causing much hilarity amongst her nieces and nephews. Another notable sibling of Frances Rossetti was her younger brother Dr John Polidori, who travelled for a while with Lord Bryon as his personal physician and was himself a writer. His best-known work was *The Vampire*, published in 1819. Having made the most of his brief life, John Polidori tragically committed suicide at the age of 26, but even his death was to be distinguished. Instead of recording a verdict of suicide, the coroner decided that he had "died by the visitation of God".

the breakfast table. Having come to Hastings without expectations of spending so much money on food and board, he was soon out of cash, finding he did not even have enough to pay for a train ticket home, had he been allowed to leave Lizzie's side. Yet as soon as his uncelebrated birthday was past, and Lizzie started to regain some of her vitality, Rossetti's mood improved. His other correspondence suggests that their time in Hastings and Robertsbridge was one of liberation and fun. On May 23 Rossetti wrote to Madox Brown in high spirits:

> Lizzy ... is looking lovelier than ever, but is very weak, though not so much as one might expect. She has walked a good deal till the last day or two, when we have been working. She has spent two very pleasant days at Barbara Smith's farm, some miles from here, and just while I write a letter reaches me asking us to go down again to-day, but I do not suppose we shall, as it is wet. Everyone adores and reveres Lizzy. Barbara Smith, Miss Howitt, and I, made sketches of her dear head with iris stuck in her dear hair the other day ... There are most wonderful things to paint there, and here and everywhere.

Despite the recent death of Gabriele – or because his father's death had made Rossetti reassess the value of life – this two-month sojourn in Hastings appears to have been one of the happiest times in their life together. They walked contentedly along the cliffs and the beach, noting perfect spots for painting backgrounds. They sat at Lovers' Seat, a resting place for ramblers with views to inspire even the ailing Lizzie. While out walking one day, they met a young girl who was looking after her even younger sister. She had exotic looks, like a gypsy, which Lizzie ached to sketch. The girl came to sit for her a few days later. Rossetti wrote to Allingham that he had been "disgracefully idle" while in Hastings, but his idleness failed to disconcert him. He was rejoicing in this deliciously romantic repose.

It has been claimed that it was during this spring, while walking in the grounds at Scalands Farm, that Rossetti proposed to Lizzie.

Barbara added weight to this theory by revealing that Rossetti carved his and Lizzie's initials into the wood of one of the window-frames (although it seems this was something of a tradition with guests and probably held little extra significance). He may well have proposed – there were several instances in their relationship when he suggested marriage – but any spontaneous proposal was certainly not made official and a wedding remained resolutely unplanned. May 1854 would have been a strategically cunning time for Rossetti to suggest marriage: following the death of his father, a year of mourning would be expected to be observed before a wedding could take place, so he would have been able to make Lizzie happy by proposing but also please himself by knowing he need not marry her yet.

At the end of May, Rossetti postponed his plans to return to London yet again, due to another relapse of Lizzie's health. This time he wrote to his brother, explaining he dared not leave her. These sudden relapses and the constant need to have Rossetti near her may not only have been attributable to Lizzie herself: it is apparent in his letters that Rossetti felt proud about her desperate need for him. It ensured their relationship remained on the footing both of them felt happiest with – Lizzie playing the part of his unchaperoned lover in need of protection and Rossetti assuming the role of her chivalric knight, willing to leave friends and family behind in order to be with her.

It was not only Lizzie's physical health that improved in Sussex. Her mental state also blossomed, not only from the change of air and food but from the knowledge that she did not have to share Dante with anyone. She had no need to feel jealous of the three women at Scalands, all of whom fretted over and petted her as much as Rossetti did.[9] There were no predatory models, no tiresome and

---

[9] It is commonly suggested in biographies that Barbara was quietly in love with Rossetti at this time. Barbara was not a beautiful woman, she was also a passionate believer in women's causes and would not have dreamt of flirting with a friend's partner, so even if she was in love with Rossetti she posed no threat to Lizzie and remained a true friend to the end, and beyond, stalwartly protecting Lizzie's reputation long after her death.

confining family and no high-spirited friends tempting him out to the theatre or to the pleasure gardens. Lizzie was able to keep her lover with her for two glorious months, returning with him triumphantly to London at the start of July.

Back in London, Barbara was still agitating for Lizzie to go into hospital but, as Rossetti confided to Allingham, he thought the atmosphere of so much disease and illness would depress her dangerously. After their two months in Hastings the lovers were used to spending all their time together and Lizzie settled down quite happily to work at her art in the studio in Chatham Place. Her desire to paint provided Rossetti with another excuse for not allowing her to be admitted into hospital, saying, quite truthfully, that she was at her most healthy when occupied in painting and his studio was therefore the most obvious and safe place for her to be. Her time at Hastings had been a wonderfully creative period and this continued after their return. Lizzie had also begun to write poetry though, as none of her poems is dated, it is difficult to tell which date from this period, or indeed if her earliest works even survive.

During their time in Hastings, the two artists had been occupied by sketching or painting. Initially, while she was too ill to work, Rossetti made endless sketches of Lizzie reclining in an invalid chair while she designed in her head all the pictures she would paint when she was better. As her health improved, she started work on *Clerk Saunders*, the first of several intended designs to accompany a book of ballads – Lizzie's favourite poetic form – that Allingham was planning to edit. She also drew illustrations for the old Scottish ballads, "The Lass of Lochroyan" and "The Gay Goss Hawk", both of which tell the story of cruel parents using their powers to prevent – or to attempt to prevent – two young lovers from being together. The countryside around Hastings provided the inspiration for her backgrounds.

Clerk Saunders, now one of Lizzie's best-known paintings, comes from a seventeenth-century ballad about two of Lizzie's most popular themes, those of doomed love between different social classes and untimely death. In the ballad, Clerk Saunders is in love with May Margaret, whom he hopes to marry. When her seven brothers find him innocently asleep beside May Margaret, they are convinced the pair are lovers and murder him as he sleeps. When she wakes it is to the horror that she is lying beside his corpse. On the night after his funeral, his ghost comes back to her; she pleads with it to enter the room and kiss her, but he knows if he kisses her she will die. So he asks her to kiss the branch of a tree amd to lay it on his grave so that the kiss will reach him. Then he tells her she must marry another man, but asks her never to love her husband as much as she loves him. Lizzie painted the scene where Clerk Saunders's ghost has entered May Margaret's room. It is an emaciated figure with a gaunt face and hands outstretched as though pleading with her. She is kneeling on the bed, gazing up at him and kissing the branch she will later lay on his grave. The colours are rich and well chosen, but the most impressive aspect of *Clerk Saunders* is the way Lizzie recreated the differing shades of dawn light. The town outside May Margaret's window is bright in a chilly early morning sun, but the limited amount of light that is able to reach in through her sole window makes the room glow as with the edge of the sunrise. Both faces are illuminated in ghastly white, Clerk Saunders's ghostly, May Margaret's wan with grief, but the other colours in the room reflect the sunlight and give back rich hues of green, blue and red, making the misery of the two figures' faces even more apparent.

Hastings had inspired Lizzie with an artistry she found liberating; when back in Chatham Place, she was determined to feed this flow of creative energy. She began work on an illustration to accompany a macabre poem of Rossetti's, "Sister Helen". The poem tells the story of a woman who wants revenge on her faithless lover, so she makes a wax effigy of him. When he dies, she is executed for murder. In a stark contrast of subject, Lizzie also began an ambitious Nativity scene. The Nativity was a familiar subject for the Pre-Raphaelites

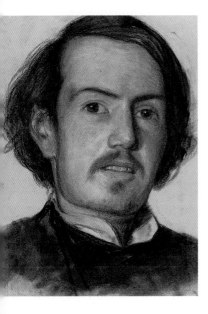

**'Walter Howell Deverell'
by William Holman Hunt (1853)**
Walter Deverell was the first artist to paint
Lizzie. Only one of his paintings, an oil
entitled *A Pet* (1853), was sold during his
lifetime and this portrait was Holman Hunt's
way of celebrating the sale. It was executed
on the night he told Deverell the news. Deverell
was very ill by this time and died about
six months later.

'Twelfth Night' by Walter Howell Deverell (1849–50)
The preliminary sketch for Deverell's painting of *Twelfth Night*, and the first picture for which
Lizzie was the model, she is seated to the left of the central figure, Duke Orsino. A self-portrait
of Deverell was used for the latter and Rossetti modelled for the jester.

'Dante Gabriel Rossetti' by Dante Gabriel Rossetti (1847)
A self-portrait, executed when Rossetti was 19 years old, a couple of years before he met Lizzie. He has chosen to depict himself as a romantic figure with his flowing curls and sultry mouth. It is easy to see why Lizzie found him so attractive.

'Ophelia' by John Everett Millais (1852)
This is the painting that established Millais's reputation and made Lizzie's face famous. The realism exhibited in *Ophelia* was groundbreaking for a painting of its time and held viewers entranced by its exacting execution. It was exhibited for the first time at the Royal Academy in 1852, where it proved a critical success.

'Study for Ophelia' by Millais (1852)
This pencil study of Lizzie's face seems prophetic of the years of illness that lay ahead. Portraying her as the drowning Ophelia, Millais captured an image of a woman plagued by ill health, an image that Rossetti was to recapture time and again in his numerous sketches.

'Self Portrait' by William Holman Hunt (1845)
This oil painting was made several years before Lizzie met the Pre-Raphaelites and shows a very young Holman Hunt, aged just 17. Holman Hunt was one of the first artists to want to paint Lizzie and he employed her as a model on several occasions.

'A Converted British Family Sheltering a Christian Priest from the Persecution of the Druids' by Holman Hunt (1850)
Lizzie modelled for this painting as the girl standing beside the priest, preparing to clean his wounds. Holman Hunt himself wrote that this depiction of Lizzie was not very true to her. The picture, although critically unacclaimed at its debut, is one of Holman Hunt's masterpieces; it is filled with rich symbolism and executed with stunning realism.

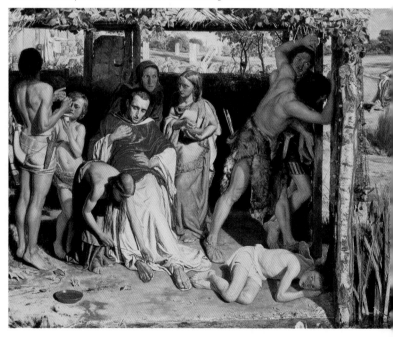

'How They Met Themselves' by Rossetti (1851–60)
Rossetti worked on this for the duration of his and Lizzie's relationship and finally completed it on their honeymoon. The couple – based on himself and Lizzie – encounter their doppelgängers while walking in a forest. The picture echoes Rossetti's assertion to Madox Brown that "when he first saw [Lizzie], he felt his destiny was defined".

Paolo and Francesca da Rimini' by Rossetti (1855)
Lizzie was the model for Francesca da Rimini in this triptych, and Rossetti the model for Paolo. It shows a pair of doomed lovers, whose story was related in Dante's *Inferno*. When their adulterous affair was discovered Paolo and Francesca were executed and their souls damned. The central panel depicts two poets, Rossetti's hero Dante Alighieri (on the left) and Virgil.

'Rossetti Sitting to Elizabeth Siddal' by Rossetti (1853)
In this quickly executed sketch, Rossetti has captured an intimate moment in his and Lizzie's relationship. At this time, Lizzie was a frequent visitor to Rossetti's rooms in Chatham Place, Blackfriars. He had assumed the role of her art teacher and she made regular use of his studio and art materials.

'Writing on the Sand' by Rossetti (1859)
Although not an actual portrait, the facial features bear strong resemblance to those of Rossetti and Lizzie. It was painted during their separation, but seems to be a remembrance of his and Lizzie many walks on the beaches of Hastings and Clevedon.

'Portrait of Mother & Daughter' by Rossetti (1877)
This unsympathetic portrait of Rossetti's mother, Frances, and younger sister, the poet Christina
Rossetti, shows two women made bitter by life. Neither Christina nor her mother believed that
Lizzie was good enough for Dante. Christina, however, was in awe of Lizzie's beauty and talent
and wrote several poems inspired by her sister-in-law.

Photograph of Dante, Christina, Mother and William Rossetti (1863)
This photograph was taken by Charles Lutwidge Dodgson – better known as Lewis Carroll, the
author of *Alice in Wonderland*. It was taken a year after Lizzie's death and shows what a caricature
of his youthful self Rossetti had become. At this date he had grown obsessed with the idea that
Lizzie was speaking to him at séances and that her ghost was haunting him.

'Elizabeth Siddal'
by Rossetti (1855)
Rossetti captures here the
inherent sadness of Lizzie's
disposition. At the bottom left,
the sketch is dated Feb 6, 1855,
a couple of months before Ruskin
became Lizzie's patron and she
met Rossetti's family for the first
time. At this date, her health was
very poor. She spent much of
1855 seeking a cure, both in
England and abroad.

'Elizabeth Siddal'
by Rossetti (1850s)
It is not known when
this sketch was made,
but its subject matter
suggests it was during
one of Lizzie's long
bouts of illness,
perhaps in
Hastings in 1854.

and it is likely Lizzie's choice was influenced by Rossetti, as the Virgin Mary was a favourite subject of his.

The time spent together in Hastings seemed to cement Rossetti's feelings for Lizzie – perhaps he would impetuously have married her if he had not been in mourning. A letter to Allingham written on July 23 seems to suggest so:

> It seems hard to me when I look at her sometimes, working or too ill to work, and think how many without one tithe of her genius or great-ness of spirit have granted them abundant health and opportunity … while perhaps her soul is never to bloom nor her bright hair to fade … How truly she may say, "No man cared for my soul." I do not mean to make myself an exception, for how long I have known her, and not thought of this till so late – perhaps too late. But … I fear, too, my writing at all about it must prevent your easily believing it to be, as it is, by far the nearest thing to my heart.

Unfortunately for Lizzie, long before Rossetti was out of mourning, the depth of his more noble feelings, and his desire to prove to her how much he cared for her soul, were easily suppressed.

At the end of July Lizzie was once again ill and depressed and Rossetti had to write to Ford and Emma Madox Brown to cancel a visit to them as Lizzie was too ill to move. Over the next few months she pined and fretted, fearful that she was losing Rossetti yet again. Meanwhile she painted pictures of tales of chivalry, illustrating stories by Sir Walter Scott and other balladeers about noble knights and their faithful ladies. Rossetti was once again embroiled in his hectic, exciting life, leaving her alone while he spent time with his disapproving family and the friends who thought of her solely as his mistress. He was neglectful, surrounded by the usual London distractions – including Annie Miller, left alone while Holman Hunt travelled in the Middle East.

Fate also decreed that the lovers' cosy existence at Chatham Place had to come to a temporary end. All other concerns were put aside as Lizzie and Rossetti fled Blackfriars in fear of their lives as yet another cholera outbreak swept through London, particularly dangerous to those with homes on the river. Rossetti divided his time between staying with family and friends, while Lizzie stayed in rooms she had rented in a house at 1 Weymouth Street in central London, a short walk from Regent's Park. The house was on the corner where Weymouth Street connects with Great Portland Street; it had a garden and her room looked out onto the branches of a large tree.[10] It was unusual for a woman of her era and uncertain income to choose to rent a place of her own instead of living with her parents, but it is suggestive of the fact that she did not want her family to know the details of her relationship with Rossetti, especially when it concerned the amount of time she spent at his apartment. It is unclear how she supported herself in these new lodgings, but one must assume that Rossetti was paying for her new home, or else paying her a regular wage for modelling (of which no records have been discovered).

In October, when the cholera outbreak was in retreat, Ford Madox Brown called round at Rossetti's studio, where he found Lizzie still very ill but submitting to being drawn again and again. She was too weak to apply herself to her own painting or poetry, but she had enough energy to sit motionless in a chair and be sketched and painted ad infinitum. Some of these pictures are sexual in undertone, others are sympathetic, but all show a huddled, frail figure sapped of energy and vitality. In one, she sleeps in an armchair, a huge pillow supporting her head, her hands crossed gently on her lap but with her spine characteristically erect, even in slumber. In another, she sits in the same chair, supporting her head with her right hand while her left holds a book, which she appears

---

[10] The house that Lizzie lived in on Weymouth Street no longer exists, replaced by a building from the early twentieth century.

absorbed in reading. In a third, she stands by a window, her head tilted so she faces into the room, away from the sunlight. Her right hand is resting on the window-sill and her left hand supports her weight by grasping the arm of a nearby chair. In this drawing, Lizzie looks wan and sapped of energy; the position is forced and seems likely to have been the result of Rossetti visualizing a character in a genre painting. All the pictures seem to breathe a knowledge that the artist and sitter were intimately connected. In their construction is a tenderness and obvious sympathy for the plight of the model. By now Lizzie's laudanum addiction was a constant companion in their relationship and these sketches make her pathetic physical state all too apparent.

Despite being such an invalid herself, Lizzie was surprisingly unsympathetic when Rossetti was ill and was apparently a very poor nurse. In 1853 Rossetti had been plagued by illness, including recurrent and painful boils, thrush and a severe reaction to the medicine prescribed to relieve his symptoms. He chose, however, not to allow Lizzie to nurse him. Instead, he travelled north to stay with his friend William Bell Scott in Newcastle (a place he hated and was very scathing of in letters home), hoping that the change of air would cure him. It did not, so after several sojourns into the countryside on his slow progression down south he returned uncured to London. He did not, however, choose to stay at Chatham Place where Lizzie had been sleeping and painting in his absence; instead he went back to his family so Maria could nurse him. It seems there was only room for one invalid in this love affair.

Lizzie's first artistic triumph had taken place during the time that Rossetti was in Newcastle. This was before she rented her rooms in Weymouth Street, so the chance to live independently in Blackfriars was idyllic. Alone in Chatham Place, she thrived. With no one to disturb her, no sisters to share a bedroom with and no small brothers requiring attention, Lizzie could concentrate on her art. Not only did she have the luxury of time, she had all Rossetti's art materials to hand, with no one else wanting to use them. Prior to this time she had been painting under the close instruction of Rossetti, with him guiding everything she created, but in his absence she chose to do something different from genre painting. Instead of re-creating a scene from someone else's imagination, she decided to take her art in a new direction and attempt to paint a self-portrait – and to paint it in oils. When Rossetti returned to the studio he was genuinely impressed by how good the oil painting was and suggested sending it to the Royal Academy for the Winter Exhibition (a plan that did not reach fruition). Around this time, Lizzie had also come up with designs to illustrate "St Agnes' Eve", a poem by Tennyson.[11] Traditionally, on the eve of St Agnes's Day (January 21) unmarried women performed certain ceremonies – including fasting before sleep – in the hope that they would dream that night of the man they were to marry. In John Keats's famous poem "The Eve of St Agnes", he tells the story of two lovers, fated by belonging to warring families, who sneak away together in the middle of the night. Although Lizzie could have illustrated Keats's poem, by which she could have expressed her own desire for Rossetti to defy his family and marry her, she chose instead to illustrate Tennyson's, in which a novice nun considers her life in the convent and her desire to be "married" to God. She contemplates life and death and her desire to be in heaven with her "Bridegroom"; the musings are similar to Lizzie's own poetic contemplations. There are two reasons for Lizzie choosing to paint Tennyson's version of the poem – in the hope that she might be chosen as an illustrator for future volumes of his work, but also because religious art sold well in the mid-1850s.

Towards the end of 1853, Lizzie was painting another popular poetic subject, one that had been painted by several Pre-Raphaelites, Tennyson's "The Lady of Shalott". Lizzie planned to send it to the

---

[11] In 1848, Holman Hunt had used John Keats's poem about the Eve of St Agnes as the inspiration for one of his paintings and Arthur Hughes exhibited a triptych of the same subject in 1856.

Royal Academy for the Summer Exhibition, although, as with Rossetti's plans for her self-portrait, nothing came of this intention. Like "The Eve of St Agnes", this poem had a special significance for Lizzie. It tells the story of a lady of Arthurian legend who fell in love with one of the Knights of the Round Table, Lancelot. Her love was not returned – Lancelot was too busy falling in love with Arthur's queen, Guinevere – and she died of neglect and a broken heart.[12] In the poem, the Lady is isolated in a tower on the island of Shalott. She is forbidden to look out of her window towards Camelot, and has been told that if she does so she will be cursed. The curse – although she does not know it – is unrequited love. She lives a simple life of weaving and observing the outside world by means of a mirror placed opposite the window. The mirror reflects everything she has, until now, desired to see and she has never previously been tempted to look out of the window. Lizzie depicts the Lady at the pivotal moment of the poem, when she is weaving her "web" at the loom, she has caught sight of Lancelot for the first time in her mirror and impetuously turns to look out of the window to watch him as he rides towards forbidden Camelot:

> *Out flew the web and floated wide;*
> *The mirror crack'd from side to side;*
> *"The curse is come upon me," cried*
> *The Lady of Shalott.*

In Lizzie's picture, the Lady is a demure, unruffled figure in the centre of the room, yet around her all is turning to chaos. Her weaving is unravelling in thousands of broken skeins, billowing out from the loom as though blown by a hurricane; the mirror has not simply cracked from side to side but is a mass of spidery breaks, and

---

[12] The Lady of Shalott is usually identified with the figure of Elaine in Arthurian legend.

a cupboard door has flung open wildly. All that remains calm is a crucifix by the window and the Lady herself, who wears a pained smile – it shows recognition of what she has done but also an expression of stunned happiness in the first flush of love.

By the following spring, Lizzie had moved on from Keats and Tennyson to Wordsworth's poetry, spending months creating and then reworking her design for *We Are Seven*. Although only a handful of her works remain, Lizzie produced many more pictures in her short life than those we know about. Some of her works are documented or photographed if they themselves do not survive, but many of them have been lost, destroyed or forgotten. Her other works include another illustration for "The Lady of Shalott", in which the Lady is floating along the river in her boat on her way to death; a depiction of St Cecilia, the patron saint of music, in a pose not dissimilar to Rossetti's *Beata Beatrix*; and a study of the Jewish martyr, *Jephthah's Daughter*.[13]

Rossetti was always a fervent believer in Lizzie's artistic ability – even when they were separated and barely on speaking terms, he remained convinced of the quality of her work and the depth of her talent. When she was first starting out and her pictures were not selling, he made every effort to reassure her that it was through the ignorance of the buyers, not through any defects of her own, and wrote a limerick to cheer her up:

> *There is a poor creature named Lizzy,*
> *Whose pictures are dear at a tizzy;*
> *And of this the great proof*
> *Is that all stand aloof*
> *From paying that sum unto Lizzy.*

[13] After her death, Rossetti arranged to have Lizzie's works photographed. In some cases, these photographs are now the only visual references remaining.

He knew, however, that no matter how strongly he believed in her and no matter how many poems he wrote her, he could not make the art world take her seriously. He recognized that Lizzie needed a more powerful ally, someone who could champion her cause more effectively and more influentially than he was able to do. Now that she had built up a reputable body of work – with the paintings she had made while he was in Newcastle, together with the works she had created throughout 1854 – she should have been able to make money from them, but he knew that being female meant Lizzie was even less likely to achieve success than the thousands of penniless male artists who filled London's garrets. In order to achieve any measure of independence through art, Lizzie needed a patron.

CHAPTER EIGHT

Rossetti and Ruskin

D ante Rossetti had met John Ruskin for the first time in
April 1854. It was a meeting both men had been keen to
secure and, despite what could have been insurmountable
differences in personality, they became long-term friends. Rossetti's
mind was not wholly on art, however, at this first meeting. He was
worrying about his father and about Lizzie, who was very ill and
about to go to Hastings for her health. He hated it when she went
away from him. Rossetti told Ruskin about his "pupil" and extolled
her abilities as well as her beauty. His enthusiasm was infectious and
Ruskin became fascinated with the idea of meeting Rossetti's muse,
as well as with seeing her paintings.

Rossetti's comments to Ruskin were heartfelt, but he was not
merely chatting disinterestedly. His comments were calculated to
whet the appetite of the susceptible Ruskin – and his wiles were
effective. As Rossetti wrote to Allingham that April, "I have told
Ruskin of my pupil, and he yearneth."

The year 1854 was John Ruskin's *annus horribilis*. It was the
year in which his wife, Effie, began a scandal-inducing court case
to obtain an annulment of their marriage, as a result of which all
sorts of whispers and jokes about him were to circulate in London.
He sought solace in his work and craved reaffirmation of his abilities as a patron and critic of the arts, in lieu of receiving any
commendation for his abilities as a husband or lover. He was also
very much in need of friendship and kindness. Serendipitously,

Rossetti appeared at exactly the right time to benefit himself and Lizzie.

John Ruskin was born in 1819, the only son of wealthy, doting parents who recognized his precocious abilities from a young age and fed them with a rich education and impressive foreign travel. His was a sheltered life and often quite a lonely childhood, with few friends of his own age. He was reluctant to marry until his parents engineered a courtship with a distant cousin, Miss Euphemia Gray, known as "Effie". She was in her teens when they met for the first time and 20 years old when they married in 1848. She was naïve, sheltered and fully prepared to hero-worship her extremely clever and well-respected husband, who was nine years her senior. The reality of marriage, however, was vastly different from the ideal both these innocents had been hoping to achieve. Theirs was a troubled relationship, a mismarriage of minds and a jarring clash of ideals. For whatever reason, their marriage remained unconsummated – a decision of Ruskin's that left Effie miserable and with an overwhelming sense of rejection. Not only was she deprived of love, she was also deprived of the chance to have children, which she desperately wanted.

There is no proof of the reason why Ruskin chose not to sleep with his wife. Biographers have suggested she was afraid on their wedding night and he never tried again, or that they did try and it was too painful for her, that he was only interested in very young girls or simply that he did not like sex.[1] The most commonly held belief – based purely on supposition rather than fact – is that Ruskin, a fervent lover of art from a very young age, had never before seen a

---

[1] The theory that Ruskin was interested only in young girls was borne out by the extraordinary behaviour he exhibited after his marriage. At the age of 39, he became obsessed with a 10-year-old girl, Rose de la Touche, whom he told he intended to marry when she came of age. Effie, alerted to his behaviour, wrote a letter to Rose's parents, which convinced them to stop their daughter spending time with Ruskin, whom they had viewed as a caring family friend. Tragically, Rose later went insane before dying at the age of 26; her death caused Ruskin to undergo a mental breakdown.

woman naked, except on canvas. He was therefore horrified to discover that his wife had pubic hair and thought she was deformed. Whatever the real reason, the Ruskins' marriage remained sexless, as well as being mentally damaging to them both.

In 1852, an eager disciple of Ruskin's requested permission to paint Effie. This keen young artist was John Everett Millais, whose career owed a great deal to Ruskin's championship. He was painting *The Order of Release,* the story of a Highlander's release from prison, where he had been held by the English army. His wife, barefoot, with a young baby slumbering in her arms and the Highlander's dog as her escort, arrives at the gaol to hand over the order of release. The resigned, detached expression on her face and the way in which her husband hides his defeated face against her shoulder illustrates that both are aware of the price she paid to earn his release papers. The picture was exhibited at the Royal Academy in 1853, and it earned a place in history books by being the first ever picture to require a bodyguard to protect it from the eager public.

In the summer of 1853, Millais and his brother William were invited to accompany the Ruskins on holiday to Effie's native Scotland. Holman Hunt had been asked to join the party but had declined, wanting to remain near Annie Miller, who was already proving problematic. In Perthshire, John Millais intended to paint a portrait of the great art critic. Absorbed in his portrait, Millais often remained at the lodging house while the other men went out for the day. Much nearer in age and sympathy to Effie than her husband, Millais was captivated by Ruskin's beautiful wife, who often came to chat to him while he was working, just as they had chatted when she had been modelling for *The Order of Release.* There had been a strong bond between them from the start and Effie had grown to trust him. That summer, unable to bear the suffocating situation any longer, she found herself revealing to Millais the sham that was her marriage. The ardent Pre-Raphaelite youth, weaned on the legends of King Arthur, chivalry and courtly love, was horrified by the misery of Effie's life. Placed in the terrible position of admiring the husband and yet falling in love with the wife, who so desperately needed rescuing, Millais was in agonies. It was the most difficult situation his privileged life had ever beheld and it was one he did not enjoy resolving.

In April 1854, Effie left Ruskin. Under the pretence of visiting her parents for a short holiday, she returned to her family home, from where she announced she was applying for an annulment. The grounds for the annulment were non-consummation of the marriage. Ruskin, aware that it was Millais who had prompted this move, nevertheless continued stoically to pose for his portrait and Millais, equally stoically, continued painting it. *John Ruskin at Glenfinlas* was worth it – it is a masterpiece of portraiture and of Pre-Raphaelitism. It has become fêted as one of Millais's finest portraits and is a sympathetic view of the man whose life he had helped to unravel. In the portrait, Ruskin looks downward, as if avoiding the viewer's gaze. His is a humble visage and also a very sad one. It is easy to believe that any viewer, irrespective of whether they knew the details of its conception, could look at the painting and know that Ruskin was deeply troubled while it was being painted. It is also a great tribute to Millais's professionalism that, despite his emotions towards the man he believed had made his beloved Effie so unhappy, he created a sympathetic and flattering portrait. Ruskin is painted standing beside a flowing Scottish burn, with one foot up on a rock. Millais had painted the background *in situ*, but needed to finish off the portrait after the ill-fated holiday had ended, so Ruskin spent several weeks posing at his London house after their return from Scotland. To achieve the desired position, he stood at the head of the stairs with one leg on the top step and the other on the stair below. He chose to stand at the very top to be as far away as possible from his usurper, whose easel was set up at the foot of the stairs. They did not speak once during the painful process. It was an excruciatingly uncomfortable time for both of them, far worse than Lizzie's *Ophelia* ordeal.

The Ruskin vs. Ruskin court case, which came to an end in July

1854, was one of the most exciting scandals to hit London that year, not least because it involved so moral a figure as John Ruskin. As a wronged husband, Ruskin could easily have contested the case and instead sued Effie for adultery with Millais. Had he done so, the scandal would have been far greater and Effie would, no doubt, have come off worst in the contemporary legal climate. But Ruskin chose to maintain a dignified silence and allowed his "impotence" to be cited.

In 1854, the world was in an unstable state. Britain had entered the Crimean War and the papers were filled daily with fresh miseries from the battlefields. The war was one of the first to inspire dedicated war journalists and war artists, and the reportage was of a calibre – and of such detail – that the British public had not previously experienced. The realities of war were, for the first time, brought directly into every literate home.[2] In such an atmosphere, the Ruskin–Millais scandal provided the public with some light and titillating relief. It was picked over with relish in bawdy pubs and respectable gentlemen's clubs all over the British Isles. Ruskin retreated into his work and attempted to rise above it. When the nightmare was over for all three of the antagonists, Effie and Ruskin were no longer husband and wife and almost exactly a year later she became Effie Millais. It was to be a happy marriage, entirely different from her life with Ruskin. The Millaises had eight children and this time around Effie needed to plead with her husband to leave her alone occasionally.

Ruskin, despite the acute public humiliation, was remarkably magnanimous about the affair. In time he even forgave Millais and contact was resumed, albeit as acquaintances rather than friends. Ruskin could never trust Millais again and Millais could no longer hold Ruskin in awe – he knew far too much about him as a man to

---

[2] The Poet Laureate, Tennyson, was moved to write one of his most famous poems, "The Charge of the Light Brigade" after reading a report of the Crimean War in *The Times*. It was in homage to the "Noble six hundred" who were killed in one of the British army's most ridiculous military blunders or, in the words of the poet, after "Some one had blunder'd".

allow him to remain an idol. For Ruskin, Rossetti was not only a unique and interesting addition to his elite circle, he also filled the gap left by Millais. In 1854 Rossetti had not yet achieved the fame, praise and money which he was later to attain and which was, at this early date, already being granted to Millais. As such, Rossetti was in greater need of Ruskin's guidance and assistance than Millais had been. He was also in awe of the critic and, by this genuine adulation, was able to bolster the fragile ego which had taken such a battering in recent months. Rossetti was keen to learn and eager to impress, and Ruskin no longer had a wife to be tempted away – which was fortunate, as Rossetti had far fewer scruples than Millais.

Throughout 1854, with Lizzie in continually poor health, Rossetti would often need to leave his work and rush to her bedside and, through his correspondence with Rossetti, Ruskin came to know about and to gain yet more interest in this ethereal, sickly creature who had so fascinated his eccentric disciple. He began sending messages to Lizzie, who had not yet met him, and turning to his all-knowing mother for advice to dispense to the invalid.

Realizing that Rossetti was not earning anything like enough money from his painting, and recognizing his extremely rare talent, Ruskin persuaded him to apply for a teaching position at the Working Men's College in Camden. The college opened in October 1854, with Ruskin as one of the teachers. Rossetti was accepted and started his classes in January 1855. He taught a three-hour lesson every Monday night, which proved such a success that he remained attached to the college for several years. Meanwhile, his private "pupil" was becoming more confident in her artistic and poetic abilities. She was now sketching or writing habitually and working on subjects that were likely to prove commercially viable. Rossetti was anxious to improve her awareness of all things artistic. He took her to galleries and private exhibitions, including the second annual exhibition of the Photographic Society in January 1855. Photography was still a new art and something of a phenomenon at this date. There was no exhibition centre dedicated to photography, so the exhibition was held at the rooms usually used by the Society of Watercolour Painters.

In March 1855, Rossetti showed Lizzie's paintings and sketches to Ruskin for the first time. The latter was so impressed that he offered instantly to buy them all. In a single day, through no exertions of her own, Lizzie's paintings earned her more than her entire annual wage at the hat shop. Rossetti – who always retained the altruistic attribute of being genuinely happy about his friends' successes, even if they appeared to overshadow his own – wrote glowingly to William Allingham on March 17:

> About a week ago, Ruskin saw and bought on the spot every scrap of designs hitherto produced by Miss Siddal. He declared that they were far better than mine, or almost anyone's, and seemed quite wild with delight at getting them. He asked me to name a price for them, after asking and learning that they were for sale; and I, of course, considering the immense advantage of their getting them into his hands, named a very low price, £25, which he declared to be too low *even* for a low price, and increased to £30. He is going to have them splendidly mounted and bound together in gold, and no doubt this will be a real opening for her, as it is already a great assistance and encouragement. He has since written her a letter which I enclose, and which as you see promises further usefulness.

Rossetti made all the decisions with Ruskin regarding Lizzie. Although he was reluctant to marry her, he was behaving like her husband. Lizzie's works had nothing of the grandeur of Rossetti's or Millais's work, but they were clever and showed great promise. For a girl who had been brought up with no formal artistic training, and had indeed been using paints for only a couple of years, they seemed portentous of great hidden talent that needed only careful nurturing to blossom. Lizzie's paintings and sketches are naïve in style; some seem awkward and confused, yet in others the lines flow idyllically across the page. Her style is erratic, sometimes drawn with clarity, at other times sketchy and rough – indicative of the amount of laudanum she had taken before starting. If she had not been Rossetti's lover, it is unlikely Lizzie would have had any chance of being noticed by the established art world. As a female artist, even one of brilliance, it was a Herculean task to infiltrate that patriarchal sphere – but the backing of a man such as John Ruskin was the stepping stone she needed to help bring her to the forefront and to be taken seriously as an artist. It is apparent from veiled comments made by other Pre-Raphaelites, including Holman Hunt and Madox Brown, that they considered her work unworthy of such great attention, but Rossetti and Ruskin were convinced; and it was Ruskin's opinion that really mattered.

Her style can be seen as being ahead of its time, looking forward to the days of Bonnard and Matisse. Perhaps Ruskin was an artistic visionary, recognizing that this more naïve style would, in just a very few decades, be perceived as a vitally important step towards artistic modernity. Whatever his subconscious feelings or generous philanthropic reasons may have been when he made the purchase, Ruskin was genuinely interested in the paintings on their own merit and they increased his desire to meet the artist.

The impact of Ruskin's intervention was immediate: within days of the critic first glimpsing her paintings, Lizzie was asked by Moxon, the publisher of Tennyson's latest edition of poetry, for which Rossetti was designing some of the illustrations, if she could provide some illustrations as well. It was a dream come true (although Lizzie's illustrations did not appear in the final published volume). Yet, sadly, Lizzie was to discover that even the fulfilment of dreams could not banish depression or cure a destructive addiction.

CHAPTER NINE

Meeting the Ruskins and the Rossettis

John Ruskin finally met the woman by whom he was so deeply intrigued on April 11, 1855. Ruskin lived with his ageing parents in a grand house in Dulwich, south-east London, and Rossetti and Lizzie were invited to visit. Two days later, Rossetti sent an exuberant letter to Ford Madox Brown in which he related how thrilled the Ruskins had been with Lizzie, that Ruskin himself had described her as "a noble, glorious creature" and Ruskin's father had commented "that by her look and manner she might have been born a countess". He continued in the letter, "His mother, who he tells me has much medical knowledge, was closeted with her awhile, and says she thinks her illness principally weakness, but needing the very greatest care. God send it may be only this; and at any rate the cure will now I hope be possible ... [Mrs Ruskin] has sent her a quantity of ivory-dust to be made into jelly, which it seems is an excellent thing."

For the forbidding Mrs Ruskin to take such an interest in a woman of the lower classes, and one who possibly possessed dubious morals, by Mrs Ruskin's standards, is high testament to Lizzie's ability to charm people. Ivory-dust – the jelly made from which was believed to help build up the body and to build up strength – was very expensive and precious, as it was difficult to obtain. The choice of it as a gift to a girl she had met only once was particularly generous and thoughtful, especially as Lizzie could not possibly have afforded to buy it for herself. Although William Rossetti implies in his memoirs that Lizzie was sullen and untrustworthy, she was perceived by many other people to be captivating. The Ruskins proved no exception. Almost at once John Ruskin took the liberty of bestowing upon her a nickname, a strange thing for a man who was not her lover to do in an age when it took a strong acquaintance for a man to address a woman even by her given name (accepted practice was for men and women to address one another as "Mr" or "Miss" and their surname). Ruskin's chosen nickname for Lizzie was "Ida", after the heroine of Tennyson's poem "The Princess".

In the autumn of 1855, when Lizzie was not only suffering from her usual unexplained maladies but also from agonizing toothache, Ruskin sent her a volume of Wordsworth's poetry to take her mind off the pain. He was able to treat her as an intellectual equal – something Rossetti's family were never able to do.

Lizzie may have been tall and sometimes haughty looking, but there was also something about her that was painfully vulnerable, inspiring feelings of protection in many of those who met her. It was not only men who felt this way, many women, including Georgiana Burne-Jones, Emma Madox Brown, Anna Mary Howitt, Bessie Parkes and Barbara Leigh Smith, went to great lengths to help or protect her. Her lover's family may have shunned her, but other people were fascinated by her.

Mrs Ruskin was not the only one of the family to want to cure Lizzie's frail health. John Ruskin was equally concerned about her. He invited her to stay with him and his parents, offering her the run of the pleasant house and its garden, set in one of London's greenest areas. He told her she could keep to herself and need not be disturbed by them if she so wished. He tried to persuade her that the clean air would make a healthy change from Blackfriars or Weymouth Street. It was when Lizzie declined this offer – she knew she could not behave as she would wish in the Ruskins' well-ordered and eminently respectable home – that Ruskin suggested she go instead to stay in Oxford and be seen by Dr Acland.

Ruskin's patronage began changing Lizzie's life at once. As soon as the annual sum of her allowance had been agreed, Rossetti wrote to Madox Brown asking him if he could take Lizzie shopping to buy her own paints, brushes and other accoutrements of their craft. Until then, Lizzie had used Rossetti's painting tools, but at last she was able to purchase her very own. On April 14, 1855, Madox Brown accompanied an excited Lizzie to the premises of "sundry colourmen", where she chose her palette, brushes and colours. Rossetti was unable to take her because he was in debt to almost every art supplies shop in London and dared not show his face in any of them. In the afternoon, Madox Brown accompanied an increasingly nervous Lizzie to the Rossetti family home in Albany Street, where she was to meet Frances and Maria Rossetti for the very first time.

Almost immediately after experiencing the rapt way in which the Ruskins received Lizzie, Rossetti had decided, at last, to introduce her to his own mother. On April 13, he had sent a letter to Madox Brown, asking "Bruno" and Emma to accompany him and Lizzie to his mother's tea party after the morning's shopping trip. The Madox Browns were intended to be a buffer, to prevent any ugly scenes. Ford was a favourite with Frances Rossetti, although it is doubtful she felt so kindly towards Emma, of whose illegitimate baby she was possibly aware. In the event, Emma was unable to attend, her presence regretted by Lizzie who felt keenly the absence of a friend able to empathize with the difficulty of her situation.

Rossetti felt confident about arranging the party now that Lizzie was not only approved of by the Ruskins but was soon to become a woman of private means. In a couple of weeks she would be the possessor of £150 a year – over six times the amount she had been earning as a milliner's assistant. Since Ruskin had first made the offer, Lizzie had become elevated, in Rossetti's wishful opinion, much nearer to his own social rank; and it was not just because of the money, but because she had been accepted by the Ruskins, a family of higher social standing than his own. Rossetti was hopeful that these things in combination would lead his mother to approve of Lizzie. They did not.

The Ruskins may have embraced Lizzie wholeheartedly, but they did not have to suffer the possibility of her becoming their daughter-in-law. In an ideal world, Mrs Rossetti would have preferred her eldest son to marry a well-born girl of Italian extraction or an English girl of the same class or above. She would also have wished for him to bring home a girl who was not so strangely haughty that she made one feel awkward in one's own drawing room. Lizzie was, of course, acutely aware that Rossetti had not wanted to introduce her to his mother before, and equally painfully aware that the Rossettis knew for how long she had been a part of Dante's life without being deemed suitable for an introduction. Added to this, Lizzie had already met the icy Christina, and neither girl had been particularly friendly to the other. Maria, even more sternly religious, as well as being Dante's only elder sibling, was yet more frightening. None of the Rossetti women approved of the hold this ethereal, redheaded creature had over their dear brother and son. To Frances, Maria and Christina, all devout and prejudiced in their religious beliefs, Lizzie was an affront.

The much-anticipated tea party bore no resemblance at all to the successful, laudatory day Dante and his "dove" had spent in the Ruskins' peaceful Dulwich garden. The atmosphere at Albany Street was frigid with awkwardness as the tea party sat almost in silence. In amongst the china tea cups, the silver and the seed cake, the Rossetti women said barely a word and Lizzie was cowed into silence by their obvious hostility. Dante and Ford attempted to keep the conversation flowing, but it was a thankless task. All participants were greatly relieved when it was time for the party to come to a polite end and for Dante to walk Lizzie home. Ford Madox Brown recorded in his diary that he stayed the night with the Rossettis, and while Dante was out sat up until late talking to the rest of the family. His attempts to intercede on behalf of Lizzie (of whom he was very fond) were listened to politely, but he was unable to persuade the Rossetti women to see the good in Lizzie, as he and Emma did. Dante's "dove" was never to be entirely accepted or loved by his family, but after this disastrous tea party a distinct shift necessarily took place. Although the remaining Rossettis had, until then, made every attempt to pretend she did not exist, Lizzie had just become a real part of Dante's life and her presence could no longer be ignored.

While Dante's family were desperate to prevent him from marrying Miss Sid, Ruskin was equally determined that his new friend should do exactly that. Within two weeks of becoming her patron, he was writing to Rossetti to enquire coyly if he had any "plans or wishes respecting Miss S. which you are prevented from carrying out by want of a certain income, and if so what certain income would enable you to carry them out". Marriage may not have worked out happily for Ruskin, but he was sharp enough to see that for Lizzie it was the only way forward. She had been more or less living at Rossetti's rooms – his neighbours and landlady all assumed she was his mistress, there was no pretence at being his "pupil" in Chatham Place. Ruskin could see with clarity the precarious position in which Lizzie found herself. Rossetti could leave her at any time and, as things stood, she would be left with nothing except a tarnished reputation that would preclude the possibility of marriage to any other man. A week after his first letter, Ruskin wrote to Rossetti again, this time stating far more bluntly that he should marry Lizzie. Rossetti chose to ignore it.

CHAPTER TEN

Seeking a Cure

Ruskin was Lizzie's new saviour and she began their working relationship by placing faith in his instructions for her health, agreeing to meet and be treated by Dr Henry Wentworth Acland.[1] She and Lydia set out from London on the morning of May 21, 1855, taking the train to Oxford. There they stayed at a lodging house chosen by the doctor. The Aclands had offered to have the sisters to stay in their home, but Lizzie preferred to be independent.

Rossetti was dreading her leaving him and a couple of days before she left he wrote to Acland, entreating him to send word to London as soon as he had made his diagnosis. Rossetti wrote again as soon as he had seen Lizzie onto the train, reiterating his request and obviously waiting for an excuse to rush down to Oxford and join her. He did not choose to go with Lizzie to Oxford for the duration of her visit because he knew that the carefully chosen landlady of the lodgings the Aclands had deemed suitable to house Ruskin's prodigy would not be as understanding as Mrs Elphick in Hastings.

In Oxford, Lizzie was treated as a welcome friend of the Acland family and as a minor celebrity, thanks to her association with Ruskin.

---

[1] Ruskin did not arrange the appointment with Acland purely out of interest in Lizzie; he was becoming increasingly concerned with the amount of energy Rossetti wasted in worrying about Lizzie. Ruskin was fearful – as was Madox Brown – that Rossetti's constant fears about Lizzie were affecting his own work. Ruskin asked Acland to examine her as much to put Rossetti's mind at ease as to help Lizzie.

He had led his acquaintances to believe she was nothing short of a genius and the Aclands dutifully escorted Lizzie and Lydia to parties and other events and introduced them to their social circle. Lizzie was honoured to be escorted around the Bodleian Library, by an ancient fellow of the university, where she was shown rare manuscripts. She was also invited to see an original painting by Albrecht Dürer. The painting was of a black beetle and – far less to her liking – the owner went scuttling enthusiastically down to the cellar in order to bring up a black beetle so Lizzie could compare it to the Dürer and discover just how accurate the great master had been.

Toward the end of May, Rossetti visited for a few days, where he spent time closeted with Dr Acland in great hopes of the mystery of Lizzie's health finally being revealed. As far as medical diagnosis went, Acland could find no physical signs of ill health, except for the obvious fact that she was very thin. When pressed he said that if Lizzie's lungs were affected they were only slightly so, and his final diagnosis was that Lizzie's constant illness was due to "Mental power long pent up and lately overtasked". He suggested a few months of travelling abroad, to escape the rigours of a London winter, as well as a few months of abstention from any form of work. Her poor health, he seemed to suggest, was largely in her mind. It seems Lizzie took exception to the diagnosis or that she found the Aclands' interest patronizing because for some reason her behaviour in Oxford was not exemplary and her actions infuriated Mrs Acland. Ruskin had to write her an apologetic letter, in which he attributed Lizzie's behaviour to "artistic temperament" and made excuses for her being an invalid and therefore unwillingly temperamental. If Lizzie was not in the mood to be charming, she was sullen, petulant and uninspiring. Mrs Acland obviously found her so.

In his attempt to soothe her indignation, Ruskin wrote:

> I don't know exactly how that wilful Ida has behaved to you. As far as
> I can make out, she is not ungrateful but sick, and sickly headstrong

– much better, however, for what Henry has done for her … The geniuses are all alike, little and big. I have known five of them – Turner, Watts, Millais, Rossetti, and this girl – and I don't know which was, or which is, wrongheadedest.

It is unlikely that Ruskin genuinely believed Lizzie was in the same league as Turner, Watts *et al*; he was elevating her in order to placate Mrs Acland. He was, however, fervently sure that she had "genius", having already written letters to her and Rossetti about how he felt. When first trying to persuade her to accept his allowance, he had written to Lizzie assuring her he was doing so for her own sake, because he believed in her as a great artist, and not because he was a friend of Rossetti's:

> The plain *hard fact* is that I think you have genius; that I don't think there is much genius in the world; and I want to keep what there is, in it, heaven having, I suppose, enough for all its purposes. Utterly irrespective of Rossetti's feelings or my own, I should simply do what I do, if I could, as I should try to save a beautiful tree from being cut down, or a bit of Gothic cathedral whose strength was failing. If you would be so good as to consider yourself as a piece of wood or Gothic for a few months, I should be grateful to you.

Mrs Acland was obviously sorely affronted and Rossetti also felt the need to apologize for Lizzie's lack of manners. Before leaving Oxford, Lizzie had given Dr Acland one of her watercolour designs for *We Are Seven* to thank him for his treatment of her. By way of an apology for his "pupil", Rossetti also sent one of his own paintings, this time addressed to Mrs Acland, with an effusive letter of thanks for everything she and her husband had done for Lizzie.

Although she had not proved a general success among the spires of Oxford, Lizzie did, however, make one new friend in the city. This was a Miss Pusey, whose family were foremost Tractarian

Christians.[2] Miss Pusey determined that Lizzie needed some time away from Oxford before returning to London and suggested that the two sisters visit a small seaside health resort on the Bristol Channel. Clevedon, which is along the coast from Weston-super-Mare, had recently become famed as the home of Arthur Henry Hallam, the doomed friend of Alfred, Lord Tennyson, and whose death had inspired Tennyson's poem "In Memoriam". Having been largely ignored in Regency times, it became a popular health resort in the later nineteenth century, increasing in popularity toward the end of Victoria's reign. Around the same compact size as Hastings – far more manageable than the bustle of Brighton – and with similar inducements, it was an obvious recommendation for Miss Pusey to make to an ailing friend. The coastline and countryside around Clevedon provided Lizzie with inspiration for her painting. The background for her 1857 painting, *The Ladies' Lament*, from the ballad "Sir Patrick Spens", was based on the town's picturesque coastline. "Sir Patrick Spens" is one of Walter Scott's reclaimed ancient ballads; the story of Sir Patrick, a favourite of the Scottish king, who nobly agreed to set sail and carry out an urgent royal mission – even though he was being haunted by a presentiment of disaster. His premonition proved correct and his ship was wrecked, resulting in the deaths of all on board. Lizzie chose not to illustrate the most obvious choice – the shipwreck – but to imagine what it must have been like for the wives, lovers and children of those who had set sail

---

[2] Miss Pusey's father was the Anglican priest Edward Bouverie Pusey, Professor of Hebrew at Oxford, Canon of Christ Church and a key figure in the Oxford Movement. This group desired to bring about reform in the Anglican Church, including introducing more "High Church" elements into the service. These were controversially perceived as being more closely allied to the Catholic mass than to a Protestant service. Pusey was also instrumental in the creation of the first Anglican sisterhood – interestingly, Maria Rossetti became an Anglican nun in the 1870s, joining the All Saints' Sisters of the Poor. Pusey wrote several prominent tracts, including one on the importance of fasting. This latter was published unusually under his name – most were anonymous – and led to a movement known (often derogatively) as "Puseyism".

with Sir Patrick. Lizzie's command of drawing the female form is not as marked in this painting as it is in drawings such as *Pippa Passes*, suggesting she found the art of painting her sketches quite troublesome. This is unsurprising as she only began using paints around the time she met Rossetti, whereas drawing and sketching were arts she had practised since childhood. Although the women's bodies appear stiff and slightly awkward, their facial expressions are cleverly painted, evoking a stunned, dull acceptance of their men's fate and the internal misery of heartbreak and fear.

Rossetti joined Lizzie in Clevedon and they spent their few days together walking in the nearby countryside, wandering along the banks of the River Yeo, strolling on the beach and visiting Hallam's grave. From a coastal path now known as Poets' Walk, one can see across the Severn Estuary to the Welsh mountains. The path came by its name because it was said to have been a walk taken by the many artists and poets who spent time at Clevedon Court, home of the literary patron Sir Charles Lamb. Among those who walked this route were Samuel Taylor Coleridge and Alfred, Lord Tennyson; Lizzie and Rossetti also meandered along Poets' Walk seeking inspiration from the views that had so impressed their literary heroes. Lydia presumably made herself scarce from many of these outings. In a cosily domestic moment, the lovers spent an afternoon picking wild plants together, which Rossetti took back with him to London to plant on his balcony as a reminder of their short, romantic holiday.

Lizzie's appearance created quite a stir in the small seaside town, her red hair once again proving intriguing. One day she was taking a donkey ride along the beach when a little boy, perched on a nearby donkey, asked her if there were any elephants where she came from. He was so enchanted by her unusual looks that he told her he knew she must come from somewhere very far away and from a place as exotic as the land that was home to the giant animals he had seen the previous year when a visiting circus had come to town.

Lizzie went back to Oxford at the beginning of July, where she was once again examined by Dr Acland, who gave a favourable opinion of her progress. One hopes that his wife had been suitably mollified by the present of Rossetti's painting by the time Lizzie returned. On July 13, the day on which Effie Ruskin married John Everett Millais in a quiet ceremony in Scotland,[3] Lizzie took a train back to London, full of plans to travel to the Continent for the winter and with a renewed fervour to paint and be creative.

A letter from Ruskin to Lizzie suggested that she need not necessarily go abroad, telling her that what she needed was not foreign travel but "to be kept quiet and idle, in good and pure – not over warm – air". He mused over ways in which she could be persuaded not to exert herself but also how to prevent the dangers of becoming bored, and ended with, "You inventive people pay very dearly for your powers."

Lizzie was not interested in the prospect of being quiet and idle at the Ruskins' peaceful home, or in Wales, as he suggested in one letter, or in yet another sleepy seaside town on the English coast. She had been offered a chance that, until recently, she could not have dreamed would be offered to her and she was determined to grasp it. The idea of going abroad provided her with the vitality she had been lacking. It was a purpose she could look forward to and, instead of sitting at home moping and feeling unwell, she began to plan her trip with uncharacteristic enthusiasm. Rossetti was thrilled to have her back in London, and in such a vital frame of mind, and they

---

[3] Effie Millais was not accepted by the upper echelons of society because she had been married before and had had that union ignominiously dissolved. Her second husband was a favourite with Queen Victoria, from whom he accepted a knighthood in 1885, but Victoria would not tolerate the idea of accepting Effie. Even Victoria's own children were unsuccessful in persuading her to relent. In 1896, when Millais was dying, the Queen sent a messenger to his home to ask if there was anything she could do. Millais sent him back with a scrawled message, asking the Queen to receive his wife. Queen Victoria was finally defeated and agreed to admit Effie into her presence. The famed meeting took place in early July; Millais died on August 13, his final wish granted.

began a joint project, planning together architectural designs commissioned by another Oxford friend of Ruskin's, a Mr Woodward from the Oxford University Museum. Woodward had been hoping that Rossetti would not just come up with the designs but would go back to Oxford and carry out the work. Rossetti declined the offer.

Rossetti and Lizzie also collaborated on a picture, *Sir Galahad and the Holy Grail*, which is thought to date from this period. One of the preliminary drawings depicts a fearful-looking Sir Galahad, who is visited by two female angels while kneeling in prayer. They show him the coveted Holy Grail, the chalice used by Christ at the Last Supper. The angel on Sir Galahad's left bears a resemblance to Lizzie. According to legend, the Holy Grail was brought to England, after Christ's Crucifixion, by his patron, Joseph of Arimathaea. Many medieval knights set out on the quest to find it, but they failed because they were flawed in character. It was said that the chalice could only be found by one who was chaste and pure in heart. Sir Galahad was, according to legend, the noblest and purest in heart of all King Arthur's Knights of the Round Table. The story, immortalized by Thomas Malory's *Morte d'Arthur* (1485), was brought to prominence again in the nineteenth century and became a popular subject for the Pre-Raphaelites.

That summer was sociable, with both Lizzie and Rossetti in high spirits. Ford Madox Brown recorded a group of the friends visiting a stately home together in early August and of Lizzie appearing "beautifully dressed for about £3, altogether looking like a queen". In mid-August, the stench of the river drove Rossetti and Lizzie away from Blackfriars to presume upon the hospitality of the Madox Browns. Their home was small and, whenever the couple came to stay, Lizzie had to sleep in Ford's bedroom, while he slept in the sitting room and Rossetti stayed at a local inn. The thoughtless twosome seemed to have had no conception of how irritating their extended presence was to Ford. His diary of the time shows that Rossetti and Lizzie fast outstayed their welcome, an irritation exacerbated by Rossetti throwing a heated tantrum one morning on discovering that Lizzie had gone out shopping with Emma and he would not be able to see her for several hours. His unexpected fury illustrated a growing and unreasonable anger felt by Rossetti about the two women's friendship. He resented Emma, begrudging her any time she spent alone with Lizzie and accusing her of trying to poison Lizzie's mind against him. His anger had no real substance as Emma had always been a good friend to him and Lizzie. He was aware, however, that Emma obligingly cleaned several of the Pre-Raphaelites' studios and was therefore privy to gossip he did not want Lizzie to hear. He was also suffering pangs of guilt because he had not made an "honest woman" of Lizzie, as Madox Brown had done for Emma. He knew that the two friends discussed his reluctance to marry Lizzie – and knew that he could never emerge from such conversations in anything but an unfavourable light. Refusing to accept this problem was of his own making, he turned his anger against Emma, leading to ructions in his own friendship with Emma's husband.

Despite presuming on the Madox Browns' hospitality on many occasions, Rossetti was not at all gracious when it came to returning the favour. In mid-September of the same year, while paying a family visit to Chatham Place, Ford was taken suddenly ill, resulting in him, Emma and their new baby Oliver – "Nolly" – needing to stay in Blackfriars until he was well enough to travel.[4] Being encumbered by the presence of three extra people – including a fractious small baby – was not how Rossetti had anticipated spending his last precious days with Lizzie before she left for several months abroad, and he made his friends feel ostentatiously unwelcome. Madox Brown later recorded in his diary that Rossetti also fought with Fred Stephens, who visited the studio while Madox Brown was recuperating there.

---

[4] Nolly Madox Brown was born in December 1854. He inherited his father's talent and had dreams of being an artist; sadly, he died at the age of 19 from blood poisoning.

Rossetti was bearing a grudge against Stephens, whom he had heard had been "speaking irreverentially" about Lizzie, and refused to talk to him. The relief when Madox Brown was well enough to travel home was tangible. A week later, Ford's diary related that Christina Rossetti had arrived to stay with the Madox Browns for a few days. She had been fighting with Dante because "there is coldness" between her and Lizzie. Dante's family and many of his friends were counting down the days until Lizzie was safely on the boat train and on her way to the Continent.

Around this time, Lizzie's health, which had seemed so much better, began to deteriorate once again. It was unfortunate timing, because Mrs Rossetti had thawed enough to show willing to accept her son's "pupil" by offering to take Lizzie to see their own family physician, Dr Hare. On September 17, Dante wrote to his mother explaining that Lizzie was too ill, and her face too swollen with toothache, to allow her to make the journey into central London and thence to the doctor. The offer was seemingly never made again. Lizzie's ill health (real or imaginary) prevented her from accepting the olive branch and Frances Rossetti was not inclined to proffer it again.

Following the advice of both Acland and Ruskin (who financed the trip), Lizzie had decided to go to France for the winter, perhaps journeying on to other countries if the mood took her. Germany was renowned for its beneficial health spas and Ruskin was particularly desirous that she should visit Switzerland. He approved of her plan to go to the South of France, but told her in no uncertain terms that she should avoid Paris at all costs, as it would make her feel more weak and ill than she was already. In his opinion, Paris could be a dissolute place and one no innocent young Englishwoman should want to visit, let alone feel at home in – particularly not a woman as frail as Lizzie.

The thought of travelling abroad was elating in the extreme to a woman who had never left England before. Until now the furthest extent of her travelling had been to Hastings, and now she was going to France and maybe to Switzerland or Germany as well. Obviously she needed a companion to accompany her on this grand trip and it was decided that Mrs Kincaid, a distant cousin of the Rossetti family, should go with her. Mrs Kincaid, the wife of a solicitor, was chosen because of her "superior knowledge" of France and of "Continental life". She was a comfortable-looking woman in her late forties, prepared to look after the delicate, sickly younger woman in a maternal manner and to be a staunchly respectable chaperone. She came to Blackfriars to meet Lizzie in early September, and the two were pleased with their first impressions of one another – Mrs Kincaid was a welcome change to Lizzie from the rest of Dante's disagreeable relations. The two women arranged to leave for the Continent at the end of the month.

Rossetti expressed several concerns about Lizzie leaving England when her health was so poor, but she recognized this as an excuse to try and keep her with him. Uncharacteristically, she did not rise to the bait and ignored his attempts to stifle her enthusiasm for the trip. She was also quite happy to ignore Ruskin's advice, regardless of the fact that he was paying for her to go abroad. Lizzie was not particularly bothered about visiting the South of France, but she was thrilled to the core at the prospect of seeing Paris. When Lizzie had moved in a world of milliners and dressmakers, Paris had been spoken of with the awe which churchgoers reserved for heaven.

In that same September, five months after the disastrous tea party with Rossetti's mother and sisters, Lizzie attempted to introduce him to her own family – these family meetings are the strongest indication that marriage was now being discussed in a serious manner. The couple arrived unannounced at 8 Kent Place one September evening, only to discover that Lizzie's parents and brothers had gone out and would not be back until late. Rossetti was introduced to one of Lizzie's sisters, with whom they sat and had tea, before heading home to Blackfriars. He was no doubt relieved at having escaped the need to answer any awkward questions from her father.

It seems that the apocryphal stories of Lizzie growing up in a slum stemmed from her own comments. When they visited her home, Rossetti was surprised to see how comfortable it was. For the last five years he had heard stories of a deprived and impoverished childhood – tragic tales that had been repeated to Barbara Leigh Smith – but this brief visit made him realize that Lizzie's stories about her origins were highly embellished. Lizzie's tendency to make her childhood sound more impoverished and emotionally deprived than it was had been designed to make Rossetti feel the need to protect her. She preferred to be known as a romantically tragic figure rather than reveal the truth about her family's shabby working-class respectability. A popular subject with the Pre-Raphaelites was the story of King Cophetua and the beggar maid – the myth's romantic notion of a great man falling in love with a poor but beautiful girl was exactly what Lizzie hoped to inspire in Rossetti. King Cophetua had everything he wanted except a wife. He was thwarted in his quest to marry happily because all the women he met wanted him purely because of his wealth and power. While out riding one day, Cophetua saw a beautiful young beggar woman. She did not know he was the king, so when he started talking to her she answered him as an equal without affectation. This impressed him so deeply that he proposed – and she accepted. Tennyson's poem "The Beggar Maid", published in 1842, brought the fable into popularity.[5] But Lizzie was no longer a beggar maid. She was now a woman with an income, a career and a patron who happened to be one of the most influential men in the London art world.

On September 22, 1855, Mrs Kincaid arrived in London, ready for her journey. Rossetti arranged a small family party at Chatham Place – with Rossetti family members only, not Siddalls – to wish them bon voyage. The next day, the travellers began their journey to France, taking the boat train from London, followed by the steamer to Le Havre, where they took another train to Paris.

---

[5] The poem and its legend inspired several artists, most notably Edward Burne-Jones, who completed his painting *King Cophetua and the Beggar Maid* in 1884.

While in Paris, Lizzie intended to use her time, and money, to bring about an exciting change in her appearance. The floating gowns and flowing hair of the Pre-Raphaelites might be acceptable, and fashionable, in the artistic milieu of London, but in 1850s Paris, a woman needed to be chic – and most definitely corseted – in order to be acceptable. Lizzie and Mrs Kincaid managed to spend an unwisely large portion of her generous allowance in their first few weeks, and they were not yet any nearer to the South of France.

In October, Rossetti received a furious letter from Ruskin, demanding to know why "Ida" had disobeyed him and was spending so much time in Paris. His one plan for her while in Paris – for what he had thought would be a duration of a couple of days while she recovered from the boat trip, before taking the train – was that she should meet the Brownings, who were living there for a while. She had not done so. Ruskin was also jealous of Rossetti's intention to go out and meet Lizzie there and attempted to persuade him not to go. He wanted his remaining "genius" to stay in London and paint as much as possible while his distracting muse was out of the country for a few months. Blustering impotently, Ruskin ordered Rossetti to write and tell Lizzie to "go South directly", insisting that "Paris will kill her, or ruin her". As was his wont, when Ruskin said something Rossetti did not want to hear, Rossetti gently ignored him.

Rossetti arrived in Paris on November 12 and stayed for ten days. He had travelled to France with the sculptor Alexander Munro and both artists were filled with excitement at the prospect of visiting the Paris Exhibition. Rossetti and the newly chic Lizzie visited the exhibition together – taking the opportunity to admire Lizzie in Millais's *Ophelia*, which was one of the prime British exhibits. Munro was left to his own devices, causing him to write his letter to William Bell Scott (in which he commented that he had seen barely anything of Rossetti since they arrived, as he was always with Lizzie).

By now, Rossetti had become socially acquainted with the Brownings and was keen to take Lizzie to meet them. In London, he had already shown Robert Browning one of Lizzie's paintings, an illustration of Browning's poem "Pippa Passes", and hoped that if the great poet could meet and be taken with Lizzie, he might commission her to provide illustrations for his next volume. *Pippa Passes* is an interesting illustration for Lizzie to have chosen, having, as it does, parallels with her own life. In the poem, Pippa is a virtuous but poor girl who works in a silk factory. The episode Lizzie chose to illustrate is of Pippa taking a walk through the town and passing three prostitutes who are sitting on a cluster of steps and gossiping. The contrast between the demurely dressed Pippa and the more provocatively attired seated women is marked. Lizzie could well have silently subtitled the picture, "Lizzie and the loose models". Pippa holds herself awkwardly, her spine and head held proudly erect with her right arm brought in close to her body as though protecting herself; the "loose women" are more fluid in their movements, at ease with their bodies and openly curious about her. They stare and seem to sneer at her, though there is also an obvious fascination on their faces, leading them to appraise the woman passing by. Lizzie's Pippa glances sideways at them. On her face is a look of fear, but there is also a spark of interest. *Pippa Passes* is one of Lizzie's most successful renderings of the human form, capturing a fluidity of movement and nuances of facial expressions.

The portentous meeting Rossetti had hoped to effect between Browning and his adored dove was doomed to be of short duration. Disappointingly, Lizzie was so unwell on the appointed day that she was unable to stay for long and was not at her most impressive or beautiful. The longed-for commission did not emerge: Browning was accustomed to the signs of laudanum addiction, living with a wife who was reliant on the opiate, and he saw every day in his own marriage the obstacles ill health could cause for artistic creativity.

Around the end of November, Lizzie finally forced herself to relinquish the pleasures of Parisian art and fashion and the travellers journeyed on to Nice. By the time they arrived, Lizzie had spent all her money and was prompted to write to Rossetti begging him to send her some more. Her letter put Rossetti into a fever of activity. With a speed that astonished Madox Brown, he began working day and night. Realizing that the paintings he was working on would require too long a period to complete, he started a new, less ambitious work, aimed at pleasing Ruskin, whom he hoped would buy it. It was a triptych of *Paolo and Francesca da Rimini*, which he began and finished in just one week and for which Ruskin was justifiably happy to pay 35 guineas. The story of Paolo and Francesca comes from Dante's *Inferno* and tells the tragic story of Francesca, a thirteenth-century noblewoman, who was unhappily married to Giovanni, Lord of Rimini. Giovanni's younger brother, Paolo, was in love with Francesca and they became lovers. They were both executed for adultery in around 1289.

The left panel of the triptych is a romantic image of Paolo and Francesca seated beside each other, holding hands and kissing. Before being tempted to kiss, they had been looking together at a large illustrated book, reading the story of those other doomed lovers, Lancelot and Guinevere. The book lies open, spanning both their laps and emphasizing their proximity to one another. Behind the lovers, framing the kiss, is an oval window. The figures resemble a young, romanticized Rossetti and Lizzie. Francesca's long hair, highlighted by the light coming through the window, is a burnished red.

The central panel of the triptych is a double portrait of an anxious Dante Alighieri and the ancient Roman poet Virgil. The two men are holding hands in a gesture of poetic solidarity and grief; Virgil has his left hand raised to his mouth in an expression of great sadness. Both men are wearing the laurel wreaths symbolic of poets, but which are also suggestive of victory and immortality. The painting includes a quotation from Canto V of *Inferno*, in which Dante himself speaks of the lovers' plight. It is translated, "Alas, how many sweet thoughts, how great desire, brought them to the woeful pass!" It is a quotation that applied equally to Dante Rossetti and Lizzie, especially towards the end of Lizzie's life.

The right-hand panel is a poignant rendering of the lovers, bound together in death, being blown through the fires of hell. They hold on to one another tightly, locked in an eternal embrace, their eyes closed in death, just as they had been for the kiss. Both look sorrowing, but strangely peaceful. Even the flames of hell, stylized into droplets of Paisley-shaped fire, cannot force the lovers apart.

This painting was not a new idea for Rossetti. He had been working on a design for the subject since 1849, but the speed with which he clarified his thoughts and executed this picture – still managing to produce a masterpiece despite his limited time scale – was the stuff of genius, romantically indicative of the artist's over-whelming passion to see his own Francesca again. Missing Lizzie acutely, he determined to deliver the money in person and booked a passage on the first available steamer to France. He met up with the profligate travellers in Nice and stayed for a week, before coming back to work on the paintings he had laid aside before his frenzy.

After several weeks dependent on one another's company, wit and conversation, the travelling companions decided they had been spending rather too much time together and their affection for one another began to pall. By Christmas, Lizzie was using her poor health as an excuse to remain alone in her room – refusing even to come down for meals, requesting instead that they be sent up to her – to avoid spending time with Mrs Kincaid. The matronly Englishwoman had become all too aware that Lizzie's ill health was partly imaginary and largely due to her consumption of laudanum. Not being in love with Lizzie, she was not prepared to make the allowances Rossetti always did. William Rossetti later recorded that up until the France excursion relations between the Rossettis and the Kincaids had been very friendly, but after the trip, Dante sided with Lizzie in opposition to his cousin. Mrs Kincaid took offence and the two families lost contact with each other. It was a rift that remained permanently unhealed.

From all Lizzie's months abroad, only one letter remains. It was written to Rossetti at the end of December, and displays her eloquence as well as her talent for the sarcasm which so discomfited William Rossetti. Rossetti had sent Lizzie money, which she had needed to fetch from the post office, an experience which she described wittily:

On your leaving the boat, your passport is taken from you to the Police Station, and there taken charge of till you leave Nice. If a letter is sent to you containing money, the letter is detained at the Post-Office, and another written to you by the postmaster ordering you to present yourself and passport for his inspection. You have then to go to the Police Station and beg the loan of your passport for half-an-hour, and are again looked upon as a felon of the first order before [the] passport is returned to you. Looking very much like a transport, you make your way to the Post Office, and there present yourself before a grating, which makes the man behind it look like an overdone mutton-chop sticking to a gridiron. On asking for a letter containing money, Mutton-chop sees at once that you are a murderer, and makes up its mind not to let you off alive; and, treating you as Cain and Alice Gray[6] in one, demands your passport. After glaring at this and your face (which has by this time become scarlet, and is taken at once as a token of guilt), a book is pushed through the bars of gridiron, and you are expected to sign your death-warrant by writing something which does not answer to the writing on the passport. Meanwhile Mutton-chop has been looking as much like doom as overdone mutton can look, and fizzing in French, not one word of which is understood by Alice Gray. But now comes the reward of merit. Mutton sees at once that no two people living and at large could write so badly as the writing on the passport and that in the book; so takes me for Alice, but gives me the money, and wonders whether I shall be let off from hard labour the next time I am taken, on account of my thinness. When you enter Police Station to return the passport, you are glared at through *wooden* bars with marked surprise at not returning in

[6] A famous murderer.

company of two cocked-hats, and your fainting look is put down to your having been found out in something. They are forced, however, to content themselves by expecting to have a job in a day or so. This is really what one has to put up with, and it is not at all comic when one is ill. I will write again when [my] boil is better, or tell you about any lodgings if we are able to get any.

There was an English dinner here on Christmas Day, ending with plum-pudding, which was really very *good* indeed, and an honour to the country. I dined in my room, where I have dined for the last three weeks on account of bores. First class, one can get to the end of the world; but one can never be left alone or left at rest.

Lonely without Lizzie, Rossetti spent New Year's Eve 1855 with the Madox Browns; contrarily, his animosity for Emma had dissipated now that she was no longer able to spend time with Lizzie. Instead of resenting her, he was happy to see her as being a remembrance of Guggum. Ford noted in his diary that Rossetti had by now sent Lizzie £55 in the three months since her departure. He had also bought himself a fantastic set of new clothes – "he looked handsome and a gentleman" – and was talking of buying himself a watch, but was careful not to mention paying back the £15 he owed to Ford. That New Year's Eve was not without its excitement, as Ford also recorded in his diary. Halfway through the evening, Emma realized that the roaring fire in the grate had sparked off a chimney fire. While her husband rushed outside and up a ladder to extinguish the flames, Rossetti decided he could best help by raking all the coals out of the grate to cool off and stop any more sparks going up the chimney. Unfortunately he did so without putting down any protective covering, spilling them out on to the Madox Browns' new Kidderminster carpet and ruining it in the process. As usual, Ford was indulgent in his diary entry, despite his obvious annoyance.

Although he spent his New Year's Eve quietly at home with a married couple, Rossetti did not spend all his time mourning his lover's absence. He had met two new friends, intriguing young men who were interested in the Pre-Raphaelites and in flattering awe of Rossetti. Their names were William Morris (1834–96), known as "Topsy", and Edward Burne-Jones (1833–98), known as "Ned". Morris came from a privileged background. He was financially secure but still threw himself passionately into his work, bursting with creative energy that desired an outlet and with a political soul that led him to become a confirmed and active Socialist.[7] In the mid-1850s, Morris's chief desire was to be a designer – he began his career working with an architect – and a poet, but Rossetti convinced him that any man who had poetry in his soul should also be a painter. In awe of Rossetti, Morris followed his advice and struggled valiantly to paint to his own satisfaction – though his self-judgement was harsh. Like Rossetti, Burne-Jones was a born painter. A motherless child growing up in an impoverished home in Birmingham, he had known from the start that he was destined to be an artist. He and Morris had met in Oxford, realized they shared an ideology and decided to rent a studio together. In London, they rented rooms in Red Lion Square, where Rossetti and Deverell had shared a studio several years earlier.

It was not only Topsy and Ned with whom Rossetti spent his bachelor months. With Lizzie in France and Holman Hunt still safely in the Middle East, Rossetti and Annie Miller found they had ample opportunity to console one another – but a shock was in store. Holman Hunt appeared back in England unexpectedly at the end of January 1856, confident of finding Annie waiting eagerly for him, her

---

[7] Morris held regular Socialism meetings at his home, Kelmscott House, on the river in Hammersmith. (Part of Kelmscott House is now open to the public.) He was a fervent believer in the Socialist movement. On one occasion he was arrested for his beliefs and he was a prominent figure in the 1887 demonstration in Trafalgar Square, the event that became known as "Bloody Sunday" after three demonstrators were killed and 200 maimed or injured by over-zealous police. When Edward Burne-Jones received his title, he was too nervous to tell Morris, his oldest friend, about the honour. Even though Morris had dined with the Burne-Joneses the night before the ceremony, he had left their home in ignorance and found out about Ned's knighthood when he read about it in the newspaper.

manners and morals improved drastically by the education programme he had set in motion for her and her personal habits now suitable for a woman who was to become his wife. One of the first things Holman Hunt was told by Madox Brown after his return was that Lizzie was no longer a model – she was now a serious artist. Strangely, Madox Brown also told him that Lizzie was not Rossetti's fiancée, just his pupil. It is uncertain why he made such a comment, only months after wondering in his diary why Rossetti did not marry her. One must assume that he knew the wandering artist was going to find out about Rossetti's affair with Annie and that he hoped Holman Hunt would be able to forgive Rossetti more readily if he believed he was a single man than if he thought he had been cheating on Lizzie to be with Annie.

With Holman Hunt back and Annie no longer available, Rossetti was once more on his own and missing Lizzie. On February 15, 1856, he wrote a belated Valentine's poem which he posted to Nice. In it he bemoaned his solitary painting labours and described his lonely days spent looking at the clock on St Paul's Cathedral – the hands of which were moving far too slowly for the lovesick artist wishing away the days until Lizzie could come home.

A Valentine

Yesterday was St Valentine.
Thought you at all, dear dove divine,
Upon the beard in sorry trim
And rueful countenance of him,
That Orson who's your Valentine?

He daubed, you know, as usual.
The stick would slip, the brush would fall:
Yet daubed he till the lamplighter
Set those two seedy flames astir;
But growled all day at slow St Paul.

The bore was heard ere noon; the dun
Was at the door by half-past one:
At least 'tis thought so, but the clock –
No Lizzy there to help its stroke –
Struck work before the day begun.

At length he saw St Paul's bright orb
Flash back – the serried tide absorb
That burning West which sucked it up
Like wine poured in a water-cup;
And one more twilight toned his daub.

Some time over the fire he sat,
So lonely that he missed his cat;
Then wildly rushed to dine on tick –
Nine minutes swearing for his stick,
And thirteen minutes for his hat.

And now another day is gone:
Once more that intellectual one
Desists from high-minded pursuits,
And hungry, staring at his boots,
Has not the strength to pull them on.

Come back, dear Liz, and looking wise
In that arm-chair which suits your size,
Through some fresh drawing scrape a hole.
Your Valentine and Orson's soul
Is sad for those two friendly eyes.

During that spring, in her absence, Rossetti and Ruskin were busy promoting Lizzie as an artist and some of her paintings were displayed in an exhibition in Charlotte Street, London. This was a major achievement in an age when female artists were seldom taken seriously – even though two of the founders of the Royal Academy had been female, in the 1850s women were still not allowed to be members of the Academy and women's art seldom made it into the public arena.

Holman Hunt and Rossetti were both invited to the private view of the exhibition and the former unwittingly offended Rossetti with his attempt to be complimentary about Lizzie's works. He told him that, had he not known they were Lizzie's, he would have mistaken them for Walter Deverell's pictures, because the style and colours were so similar. Although he had intended them as a compliment, his words provoked in Rossetti an irrational fury. The fiery Italian turned on his fellow artist in a passion, telling him Lizzie's pictures were better than anything Deverell had ever done. Holman Hunt was understandably taken aback, recording later in his memoirs, "I had thought that to compare the attempts of Miss Siddal, who had only exercised herself in design for two years, and had had no fundamental training, to those of Gabriel's dear, deceased friend, who had satisfactorily gone through the drilling of the Academy school, would be taken as a compliment, but Rossetti received it as an affront." It must be presumed that Rossetti's unpredictable behaviour had more to do with Holman Hunt's untimely return and its interference in his affair with Annie than with his comments about Lizzie's pictures. The incident does, however, demonstrate to what extent Rossetti's obsession with Lizzie was able to affect his judgement.

By the end of April, Lizzie and Mrs Kincaid were preparing for their return to England. Both were relieved at the prospect of their uneasy companionship coming to an end, but Lizzie was not entirely at ease with the thoughts of her homecoming. Ruskin, however, was as excited about it as Rossetti and generously resigned to pay out yet more money to secure her safe homecoming. He wrote to Rossetti, "I am almost certain Ida, or Ida's travelling incubus of a companion, will have more debts than they say. People are always afraid to say all at once. Hence it is best to be prepared for the worst." Although Ruskin had not put any pressure on her to start painting at once, Lizzie knew she would have to start work in earnest soon – and that she would need to work with an attitude she had not needed to summon up since leaving Mrs Tozer. Her health, however, was little improved – laudanum having proved an invaluable ally in her battle to dilute Mrs Kincaid's irksome company – and the idea of working to earn her comfortable living filled her with dread.

Even Rossetti's letters were no longer a tonic. Lizzie was longing to see him, but it seemed he felt less excited about her return than she had hoped. She was grimly aware from the tone of his letters that someone else was currently occupying his mind, and it did not take much detective work to decipher who that someone was. Even with Holman Hunt back in London, Rossetti was continuing to see Annie Miller. He had also become enthralled by a beautiful young actress, currently seducing the London audience nightly, by the name of Ruth Herbert. Lizzie, aware of her slowly advancing age and increasingly delicate body, found these two paragons of lusty vitality and beauty depressingly successful opponents.

CHAPTER ELEVEN

"She hath no loyal Knight and true"[1]

Lizzie's return from the Continent in May was marked by a noticeable slump in her health or, as Rossetti described it, there was "little palpable change in her physical health" from when she had left England. Her health had improved abroad, but she had not managed to loosen the hold laudanum had over her and her return and its resultant depression made her cling to its offer of salvation even more closely. Now her adventure was over, she had no idea when she would next have excitement in her life, and the realization that her special treatment was at an end was enervating. She was examined by a doctor who diagnosed "a continuous decline in vital force". Depression had taken hold and Rossetti's behaviour did nothing to alleviate it. She threw herself back into art, reworking some of her watercolours in oils, a medium she was never fully at ease with, using painting as a means of escape.

Lizzie was not only influenced by Rossetti in her artistic choices. She shared the general Pre-Raphaelite affinity for medievalism in her painting, which was one of the reasons why Ruskin found her art so appealing. In the late 1850s (probably around 1857 or 1858) she finished an oil painting she had been struggling with for a while, entitled *Lady Affixing a Pennant to a Knight's Lance* (also known as *Before the Battle*) a crudely executed image of a young woman in

---

[1] Alfred, Lord Tennyson, "The Lady of Shalott"

medieval dress helping to tie her pennant to the lance her doomed lover will carry to the battlefield. Both the knight and his lover seem aware that he is doomed. The pennant is red, the colour representative of Love, as is demonstrated in many of Rossetti's paintings.

Lizzie also attempted to write similarly themed poetry, such as the chivalric verses "True Love", which could be a continuation of the story in *Lady Affixing a Pennant*. In the poem, a lady has to say goodbye to her murdered lover. She kneels at his grave for a grief-stricken farewell, before leaving to marry his opponent, who has won her in the conflict. She swears that she will be true to Earl Richard, despite being forced to marry another, and looks forward to the day she will join him in death.

True Love

Farewell, Earl Richard,
Tender and brave;
Kneeling I kiss
The dust from thy grave.

Pray for me, Richard,
Lying alone
With hands pleading earnestly,
All in white stone.

Soon must I leave thee
This sweet summer tide;
That other is waiting
To claim his pale bride.

Soon I'll return to thee
Hopeful and brave,
When the dead leaves
Blow over thy grave.

> *Then shall they find me*
> *Close at thy head*
> *Watching or fainting,*
> *Sleeping or dead.*

This poem has more than a faint echo of Dante and Beatrice, although in this instance it is Beatrice who remains alive and Dante's sacred memory that is immortalized by death.

Before travelling to France, Lizzie had begun two new designs: an illustration for Keats's ballad "La Belle Dame Sans Merci"[2] and an original scene entitled *Lovers Listening to Music*. In the latter, two lovers, similar in looks to Lizzie and Rossetti, are seated on a bench listening intently to music being performed by two dark-skinned women, perhaps intended to be Indian. The musicians are seated on the ground at the lovers' feet, playing an unusual stringed instrument. Beside the group is a gate at which stands a young child, dressed in a long robe and representative of Love. The child looks wistfully at the musicians who are themselves caught up in the music and apparently oblivious to anything else. Although Lizzie and Rossetti were of a similar height (approximately five feet seven inches tall), the lovers in this picture are dramatically different in size. She is much smaller and in apparent need of protection, emphasizing Lizzie's desire for Rossetti to become her protector by becoming her husband. The man's arm encircles his lover's waist, drawing her closely beside him. Her head rests on her hand which she has placed lovingly on his shoulder and his head is inclined towards her, resting against the top of her head and cradling it between his cheek and shoulder. The woman's eyes are closed in happiness, though whether this is because she is enjoying the music or luxuriating in her proximity to her lover is open to debate.

---

[2] The late-Victorian artist Frank Dicksee (1853–1928), who was strongly influenced by the Pre-Raphaelites, painted what has become probably the most famous pictorial image of "La Belle Dame Sans Merci" (undated). In his picture, the beautiful woman of the title has flaming red hair, in obvious homage to Lizzie Siddal.

Lizzie's ability to draw the human figure is apparent in this work, as is her command of depicting draperies, evinced in the toga-like apparel of the musicians. The style and subject matter of *Lovers Listening to Music* was strongly influenced by Rossetti. As well as being an obvious reflection on their relationship, it illustrates the ideal they seemed able to attain in Hastings and Paris, but which eluded their relationship so much of the time.

Rossetti's ink drawing entitled *How They Met Themselves* (1851–60), which he worked at for the entire length of their courtship and was still making amendments to on their honeymoon, is another representation of their relationship.[3] It depicts the story of a couple, quite obviously portraits of himself and Lizzie, who are out walking in a wood when they are approached by their doppelgängers. The woman faints and is caught in a swoon by her lover, as the doppelgänger figures look on in concern. The picture is a fascinating depiction of the dual nature of Lizzie's and Rossetti's relationship. On occasion they are Dante and Beatrice, yet at other times they are their own depressing selves, bickering and real, ill, depressed or angry, not at all the poetic figures Rossetti would like them to be.

Other paintings created by Lizzie in early 1855 include *The Haunted Tree* and *The Witch*. The latter was singled out by Ruskin for special praise, though he also suggested she stop working on such ghoulish subjects as he was worried such ghostly thoughts were affecting her health. He was similarly displeased by her working on *Sister Helen*, which he felt an unhealthy preoccupation for a sensitive woman such as his protégée.

After her return from France, Lizzie's new artistic endeavours included reworking her original woodblock engraving of *Clerk Saunders* as a watercolour and attempting an oil version of the watercolour *The Lass of Lochroyan*. Despite the many new influences,

---

[3] Rossetti returned twice to the theme of *How They Met Themselves*, painting two watercolour versions of the picture in 1861 and 1864.

'Regina Cordium' by Dante Gabriel Rossetti (1860)
Rossetti painted his new wife as the Queen of Hearts shortly after their return from honeymoon.
The viewer can appreciate how ill Lizzie was when modelling for this painting, she appears too
listless to be convincing as the intended subject. Like *Beata Beatrix*, *Regina Cordium* emphasises
Rossetti's desire to immortalize Lizzie.

'Emma Hill'
by Ford Madox Brown
(c.1852)
Emma Hill was one of Ford Madox Brown's favourite models. After the death of his first wife, she became his mistress and had a child with him; they married in 1853. Coincidentally, Emma's mother was a friend of Lizzie's mother and the two girls had known one another since childhood. Emma remained one of Lizzie's closest friends until her death.

'Ford Madox Brown' by Rossetti
(1852)
Madox Brown, known affectionately as 'Bruno', was one of Rossetti's earliest teachers and best friends. He was fond of Lizzie and often attempted to persuade Rossetti to stop dallying and marry her. When Lizzie began receiving her allowance from Ruskin, it was Madox Brown who took her shopping to buy her first painting materials.

'John Ruskin' by John Everett Millais (1854)
This is the portrait Millais was working on when he fell in love with Ruskin's wife, Effie. Ruskin proved a valuable friend to Lizzie, becoming her patron and taking a genuine interest in her welfare; he also provided her with the means to be financially independent. Ruskin's book *Modern Painters* played an intrinsic part in the creation of the Pre-Raphaelite Brotherhood.

'Algernon Charles Swinburne' by Rossetti (1861)
In 1861, the poet Swinburne was the Rossettis' most constant companion. On the night Lizzie died, she dined with him and her husband before taking her fatal overdose. Swinburne's colouring was remarkably similar to Lizzie's and their friendship seems to have been like one of devoted siblings; he was one of her most faithful friends.

'William Morris'
by Rossetti (c.1861)
Rossetti sketched this picture of
Morris as a study for the head of
King David. It was made at a time
when Lizzie and Rossetti were
frequent visitors to the Morrises'
home, Red House, in Kent. After
the death of her baby, Lizzie went
to Red House to recuperate, but
found the happy family atmosphere
too upsetting after her
bereavement.

Photo of Jane Morris, 'May
Morning'
by J. Robert Parsons (c.1865)
Jane Burden first met Dante
Rossetti at the same time as
she met her future husband,
William Morris. 'Janey' was
one of the women who caused
Lizzie severe pangs of jealousy,
as she knew how attractive
Rossetti found her. Several
years after Lizzie's death,
Rossetti and Janey began a
long-term affair, which William
stoically turned a blind eye to.

'Helen of Troy'
by Rossetti (1863)
In this striking picture, modelled
by Annie Miller, Lizzie's most
detested love rival, was
painted a year after Lizzie's
death. It is a depiction of the
woman whose beauty brought
about the destruction of Troy
and many thousands of lives;
perhaps it is also indicative of
the destruction Rossetti
allowed Annie to cause in his
and Lizzie's relationship.

'Fanny Cornforth'
by Rossetti (c.1860)
Fanny Cornforth was another
of Lizzie's rivals for Rossetti's
affections, and appears to
have been genuinely in love
with him. This picture was
executed around the time of
Rossetti and Lizzie's wedding,
although Rossetti did not
continue their affair during
his marriage. After Lizzie's
death, Fanny became
Rossetti's housekeeper at his
house in Cheyne Walk.

'The Lady of Shalott' by Elizabeth Siddal (1953)
This little-known sketch is one of Lizzie's most original works. Although this particular poem of Tennyson's was illustrated by many other Pre-Raphaelite artists, Lizzie gave her picture an entirely new interpretation. It shows how much raw talent she was capable of harnessing when not afflicte by illness or under the influence of laudanum.

**'The Ladies' Lament'
(also known as 'Sir
Patrick Spens') (c.1857)
by Elizabeth Siddal**
This subject is taken from
Sir Walter Scott's ballad,
'Sir Patrick Spens' (based
on a 13th-century ballad).
The women and children –
waiting to hear news of a
ship that will never return
– seem stricken in attitudes
of trepidation. The
background was painted
from Lizzie's memory of
the cliffs around Clevedon.

'Pippa Passing the Loose Women' by Elizabeth Siddal (c.1855)
This sketch, made to illustrate one of Robert Browning's poems, shows Lizzie's ability to draw the human form – something she found much more difficult to achieve when using oil paints or watercolours. Pippa's unease is suggested by her awkward, stiff posture, whereas the prostitutes' languid and fluid forms indicate their control over the situation.

'Before the Battle' by Elizabeth Siddal (late 1850s)
This painting is crudely executed and demonstrates the difficulties Lizzie experienced when using oils. The influence of Rossetti's teaching can be seen in the subject matter and the style can be compared to Rossetti's triptych of *Paolo and Francesca da Rimini*.

'Beata Beatrix' by Rossetti (1870)
This is perhaps the most famous painting ever produced of Lizzie. It was painted by her husband after her death and remains an idealised icon to her memory. Rossetti took six years to complete the portrait, in which he identifies Lizzie with the poet Dante Alighieri's great love, Beatrice.

'Study of Hands for Beata Beatrix', by Rossetti (c 1860s)
Before her death, Rossetti drew and painted Lizzie as Beatrice Portinari on many occasions. After her death he had a wealth of studies and sketches to draw upon as inspiration for his masterpiece. Beatrice was the unrequited love of Dante Alighieri. *Beata Beatrix* depicts the precise moment at which Beatrice dies and her soul is taken up to heaven.

experiences, sights and colours she had experienced during her time abroad, she was unable to start anything new, finding it difficult to express herself creatively when depressed. She and Rossetti spent a great deal of their time together that summer, William Allingham recording in his diary that he was often with the two of them during those months, but Rossetti's mind was elsewhere. Annie was back with Holman Hunt and it was infuriating the jealous Rossetti. His obsession was so all-consuming, as once it had been for Lizzie, that he was foolish enough to talk to Lizzie about Annie, making Lizzie not only miserable but terrified of being left alone in case he left her to go to Annie. Her health was failing – her addiction fuelled by the desire to blot out Rossetti's infidelity and cruel ravings about another woman – and as a result she felt unable to work. This led to feelings of guilt that she was taking Ruskin's annuity without being able to offer him any artworks in return.

Throughout July and August, Lizzie confided her miseries to Emma Madox Brown, who had no solution to offer. No other respectable man would be likely to marry Lizzie now, with her reputation of being Rossetti's mistress, as well as her history of modelling (a past she was unable to bury as Millais's *Ophelia* had become one of the decade's most acclaimed paintings). She was, however, in the enviable position of being financially independent, and Ruskin himself was not agitating for Lizzie to work herself to death in return for his patronage. In August 1856, while Lizzie was worrying in London, Ruskin was in Europe with his parents. Despite Lizzie's fears of what he must be thinking about her lack of industry, his most pressing concern was about getting Lizzie's money to her. In the end he entrusted it to a mutual friend, Ellen Heaton, who was fortuitously also travelling in Europe but about to return to England. Lizzie, however, was proud and reluctant to take Ruskin's money if it came as charity rather than genuine artistic patronage. She knew she had to start painting in earnest or be obliged to give up his income. At the moment, marriage to Rossetti seemed further away than it had ever done.

Yet by the end of the summer Rossetti was returning to his senses. His passion for Annie had led to his alienating one of his oldest friends, a situation he was desperate to rectify, and had resulted in his running the serious risk of losing Lizzie forever. Infatuated though he had been with Annie, he could not live without Lizzie and he returned to her, apologetic and adoring. After furious rows she accepted him back and they were a couple once again, outwardly appearing even more in love than previously and talking openly of marriage. As Madox Brown recorded in his diary on September 8, 1856, Rossetti had "foresworn" Annie Miller and "he and Guggum seem on the best of terms now". The following week Emma gave birth to another son, Arthur Gabriel, and Lizzie and Rossetti were asked to be joint godparents.

In October, Rossetti was once again sketching his Guggum as feverishly as he had been wont to do in the early days of Chatham Place, visiting her in her Weymouth Street rooms and sketching her as she slept in a chair, too exhausted to make the journey to Blackfriars. It was in early November of this year that Rossetti confided in Madox Brown his plan to marry Lizzie and take her to Algeria. Barbara Leigh Smith had just been there – her sister Isabella was consumptive and they had gone together to seek a cure – and had come back full of praise for the country.

Yet just a week after Madox Brown recorded Rossetti's intentions in his diary, Rossetti had changed his mind again. Lizzie was incensed and humiliated and, this time, she really did leave him, rushing off to Bath with her sister Clara and refusing to see Rossetti. Just as she had thought marriage was finally within her grasp, he had snatched it away again. She was sick of it and desperately ill yet again.

CHAPTER TWELVE

In Sickness and In Health

I n Bath, Lizzie and Clara stayed at 17 Orange Grove, a lodging house run by a Mrs Green, the wife of a furrier and draper named James Green. Orange Grove was a terrace of elegant houses which had been built in the early eighteenth century and named after William of Orange. It was fronted by gardens and healthy-looking trees, altogether a smarter residence than Lizzie's old invalid lodgings on Hastings High Street and indicative of her more wealthy status. On her arrival in Bath, Lizzie told Clara she would not return to Rossetti, and she refused to reply to his pleading letters. Resolute but miserable, she attempted the traditional Bath remedies for invalids, including drinking the water from the medicinal springs (never a particularly palatable experience). Bath had been England's most fashionable health resort in Regency times, but by the middle of Victoria's reign it was no longer such a popular choice. The railways had led to a renaissance for spa towns in previously inaccessible areas, such as Sussex, added to which was the fashion for travelling to spa towns in Germany.[1] Despite this decline from its Georgian heyday, Bath was nonetheless still famed in the mid-nineteenth century for its Mineral Water Hospital (which remained a popular treatment centre until after the Second World War).

---

[1] Jane Morris, who also became a perpetual invalid, regularly visited the German spa at Ems, in the Rhineland. In 1869 Rossetti sketched a cartoon of Janey looking miserable in a spa bathtub, drinking a glass of spa water, with William sitting beside her reading aloud from *The Earthly Paradise*. It was entitled *The Ms at Ems*.

The town was also renowned for its mild climate and thus recommended as an ideal location to avoid "the worst features of an English winter". It was decreed by local doctors that invalids could gain the most advantage from the hot springs' mineral waters between the months of September and May. The high-calcium and low-sodium content of Bath water made it especially recommended for invalids with stomach complaints, which is one possible reason for Lizzie choosing to visit the town. The baths themselves were divided into first and second class – and priced accordingly – and the swimming baths were open to men and women on alternate days. Invalids were recommended to drink two glasses of Bath water every day, after which they were advised to take "gentle exercise" and to limit their visits to the baths themselves to a maximum of four times a week. When not in the capable hands of the bathing attendants, invalids were expected to relax, to eat in moderation and avoid alcohol.

The Siddal sisters remained in Orange Grove for several weeks with Lizzie trying all the recommended cures but, of course, continuing to rely on her regular fixes of laudanum. Despite the perceived health-giving properties of the Bath spa water, her health continued to deteriorate, and when Rossetti arrived at the lodging house in early December she was too weak – and too relieved to see him – to turn him away. He stayed with her until Christmas and, as usual, her health began to improve as the result of his arrival. Despite the many heartbreaking problems that had prompted her escape to Somerset, they were soon laughing and joking together and their relationship resumed as before. Rossetti was in high spirits now his Guggum was his once again. He made the two girls laugh by pretending to be an invalid, lolling his head mockingly from side to side as they wheeled him around in a Bath chair, pretending to be his nurses. On December 18, a triumphant Rossetti wrote to Allingham that Lizzie had been "terribly ill" but was better.

The couple returned to London together around Christmas-time – it was on this Christmas Eve that Christina Rossetti wrote her poem

"In An Artist's Studio". Lizzie, on Rossetti's recommendation, gave up her tenancy at Weymouth Street and moved into new lodgings in Hampstead, not far from the Madox Browns' home in Kentish Town. It was around this time that Lizzie finished a painting she had been working on since 1854, *Lady Clare*, based on a poem by Tennyson. It is a return to one of Lizzie's recurrent themes: love between two social classes. Ostensibly Lady Clare and her fiancé, and cousin, Lord Ronald are social equals. The day before their wedding, however, Clare discovers that she is in fact the daughter of a servant, the woman she has been brought up to regard as her nurse. She determines to tell Lord Ronald of her low birth and release him from their engagement, and her mother, Nurse Alice, tries to stop her. In response to Alice begging her not to tell, Clare proudly replies:

> *"If I'm a beggar born," she said*
> *"I will speak out, for I dare not lie,*
> *Pull off, pull off the brooch of gold,*
> *And fling the diamond necklace by."*

She then dresses herself in a peasant's dress and goes to tell Lord Ronald of her discovery. He is astonished by her clothes and her story. When she convinces him it is the truth, he replies they will still be married and then she will legally bear the name Lady Clare – as his wife. In the picture, Alice kneels before her daughter, pleading with her not to reveal her secret to her lover. Clare is standing but Alice's hands upon her shoulders attempt to drag her down; Clare's left hand is placed over Alice's face as though she cannot bear to look at what she herself will become and is pushing her away. It is symbolic that, although she is determined to refuse the title she no longer feels she has a right to, Clare resists her mother's physical attempt to draw her down to her own level. In the background is a stained-glass window telling of the biblical story of the wisdom of Solomon, another tale of a child with two claimants to be its mother. The painting is strangely dissimilar to Lizzie's other works – Lady Clare's elongated, quite distorted neck looks as though it could be the work of Rossetti, or at least that Lizzie was guided by him when she painted it. Lizzie believed her story to be the reverse of Lady Clare's; after her father's long evening tales, she believed she had been born into a much lower estate than was rightfully hers. Through marrying Rossetti, she would be making her way back up to where she deserved to be.

In Hampstead, everything seemed cosy and happy, but there was a major element missing: Rossetti did not renew his retracted offer of marriage. This time, instead of running away, Lizzie turned to her other option of manipulation. She stopped eating. A short time after they returned to London she claimed she had not eaten for two weeks. It worked – Rossetti was instantly frantic with worry, though not enough to offer the one solution she wanted. She took to her bed and refused to get up, too listless even to make an arranged visit to the Madox Browns. Rossetti, as usual, revealed his most endearing characteristics by caring for her when she was ill – but another, enormous, row was brewing.

For some time, the idea of an artists' commune had been mooted amongst members of the group. The idea had been to find a large property, or group of homes, where they could live together but keep an element of privacy. The property needed to have a large, picturesque garden which the artists could use for backgrounds in outdoor scenes. It was something Rossetti had discussed with several friends in the past, including Madox Brown, Holman Hunt, William Morris and Edward Burne-Jones; Rossetti had also talked about the scheme in general terms to Lizzie. Assuming that they would have to be married in order to be included, Lizzie was enthusiastic about it. She was not, however, fully aware of the plan; she knew only that the inhabitants would include herself, Rossetti and the Madox Browns. On February 25, 1857, Ford Madox Brown came for dinner with Lizzie and Rossetti and started an innocent conversation about the proposed scheme. The problem was that he mentioned an aspect of the plan Lizzie had not yet heard about: he dropped into conversation that Holman Hunt and Annie Miller were to be a part of the commune. Lizzie descended into fury, not caring that Madox Brown was there to witness it. She began raving violently at the suggestion of her being expected to live in the same house as Annie and Holman Hunt. Madox Brown was embarrassed and utterly bemused as to why Lizzie was making such a scene about a scheme he thought she had already agreed to. He was looking at it purely from an artistic point of view, and to his mind Holman Hunt was an integral member of the group. Quite why Ford and Emma had not discussed the potential disaster of Lizzie and Annie being expected to reside in such close proximity to one another is uncertain, but it seemed genuinely not to have occurred to him that it could be a problem.

The following day, Rossetti wrote an embarrassed letter to Madox Brown, attempting to gloss over what had happened, but Lizzie was already on her way to Kentish Town to find out what else Rossetti had been keeping secret about the proposed living arrangements. Unfortunately Emma was away in Hastings, recuperating after the difficult birth of Arthur, so Ford was forced to cope alone with a hysterical Lizzie. She created another furious, tearful scene, making herself alarmingly distressed before collapsing dramatically. Madox Brown took her home and contacted Rossetti to take care of her, but this made her even more distressed. At last Rossetti told Madox Brown he was ready to marry her and begged him to lend him the money to buy a marriage licence. The money was duly forwarded and Madox Brown heaved a welcome sigh of relief that this tempestuous courtship would at last be resolved. Somehow, however, Rossetti spent the money elsewhere – there were always bills to pay or painting materials to be bought – and his good intentions disintegrated.

Lizzie had been so certain that, at last, she would be married, that this overwhelming disappointment was debilitating in the extreme. To have been so certain of her future after all these years and then, yet again, to have been cheated of it was more than she could bear.

Rossetti's presence could no longer cure her and after a couple of days a scared Ford was moved to write to his beleaguered wife, begging her to come back to London and take care of Lizzie who was refusing, once again, to eat anything – neither would she allow Rossetti anywhere near her. This time Lizzie's refusal to acknowledge him was more prolonged than before and they were not back on speaking terms until the middle of April, around which time Rossetti was called away to a portrait commission in Wales, leaving Lizzie to attend Arthur's christening on her own. Ostensibly they had made up the rift, but the cracks in their relationship were becoming increasingly difficult to heal or ignore.

Rossetti returned to London in time to attend one of the most important events in Lizzie's calendar. On May 25, 1857 the Pre-Raphaelite Exhibition opened in Fitzroy Square, in Marylebone. Several of Lizzie's paintings were being shown, including *Clerk Saunders, We Are Seven* and *The Haunted Tree*, as well as illustrations from Tennyson's and Browning's poems. Among the other painters whose works appeared in the show were Rossetti, Madox Brown, Arthur Hughes, John Brett, Charles Collins, Millais and Holman Hunt – Lizzie was the sole female exhibitor.[2] Rossetti threw himself into Lizzie's cause, writing to his own patrons and acquaintances about her work at the exhibition. In June he wrote to the collector James Leathart, "In case you should visit our little collection with any view to possessing something from it, I cannot forbear directing your attention to Miss Siddal's watercolour from 'Clerk Saunders', which I have marked in the list – a most highly finished & admirable drawing. Mr. Ruskin has hitherto bought most of hers, but has not yet visited Russell Place." *Clerk Saunders* was bought by an American collector, and acquaintance of Ruskin and Rossetti, Charles Eliot Norton from Massachusetts.

[2] In 1984, the Tate Gallery in London held an exhibition of Pre-Raphaelite art. Once again, Lizzie was the only woman whose works were included.

It was around the time of the exhibition that Lizzie suddenly gave up her allowance from Ruskin. Her reasons for doing so are unrecorded, but it seems likely that she did so at least partly because her health was now too poor for her to continue with art, and she could not accept his annuity without giving him anything in return. Her most creatively artistic periods had been when she was at her happiest; giving up her allowance was a sad indication that she did not anticipate being happy again. Ruskin wrote to her, entreating her to change her mind, but she would not capitulate. Ruskin had grown increasingly controlling and Lizzie was frustrated with feeling like his puppet. Ruskin wrote to Rossetti shortly afterwards, pleading to be allowed to be of use to Lizzie again:

> I shall rejoice in Ida's success with her picture,[3] as I shall in every opportunity of being useful to you or her. The only feeling I have about the matter is some shame at having allowed the arrangement between us to end as it did, and the chief pleasure I could have about it now would be by her simply accepting it as she would have accepted a glass of water when she was thirsty, and never thinking of it any more.

Lizzie refused to be swayed. Ruskin's entreaties were ignored and Lizzie left London. Running away to Bath had been only the beginning of her bid for freedom. The reality of her relationship with Rossetti had taken a long time to penetrate through to her, but she was finally having to face up to the sham it had become. By bringing Ruskin's patronage to an end – an arrangement she knew she owed almost entirely to Rossetti's interference on her behalf – and by leaving London, she was making a serious attempt at independence. This time she did not head to Hastings or Bath. She headed north

---

[3] Ruskin is referring to Lizzie's *Clerk Saunders,* which they had great hopes for at the 1857 exhibition.

to take the waters at the hydropathic spa in Matlock, Derbyshire, just a few miles from the disputed family home in Hope.

The visit to Derbyshire was in company with one of her sisters and they stayed at a Temperance hotel in Lime Tree View, Matlock, which was run by a Mrs Cartwright. The sisters spent some of their time sightseeing, visiting the nearby town of Castleton, where they explored the Blue John mines[4] and the area around the Duke and Duchess of Devonshire's grand ancestral home, Chatsworth. They also visited Haddon Hall, whose historic associations had helped to inspire one of Lizzie's favourite authors, Walter Scott. His novel, *Peveril of the Peak*, was about the castle that gave the village of Castleton its name – built by the one-time owner of Haddon Hall. It has been suggested that the grounds of Haddon Hall were the inspiration for the battlefield, glimpsed through the window in Lizzie's painting *Lady Affixing a Pennant to a Knight's Lance*. John Ruskin had described the county of Derbyshire as "a lovely child's alphabet; an alluring first lesson in all that is admirable" and Lizzie was equally impressed by the magnificent scenery.[5]

By giving up London, Ruskin's annuity and Rossetti's "lessons", Lizzie was breaking away from everything to do with Rossetti. He had refused to change her name to his, so she decided to rediscover her own family and mingle with the people she thought she had left behind. She had some money left over from her generous allowance, so did not need to rely on anyone else. This time she did not ignore Rossetti, as she had done in Bath, but wrote to him regularly, occasionally sending him the new poems she had been inspired to write. As usual they were about death, gloom and broken hearts.

---

[4] Blue John is a semi-precious stone, veined in varying hues of blue, from the very palest hint of colour through to a deep, inky-dark indigo. It is found exclusively in the mines in Castleton.

[5] Ruskin first visited Derbyshire at the age of 10, when he travelled there with his parents and was inspired to draw the county's dramatic scenes.

Back in London, Rossetti had little time to fret over Lizzie's absence, faced as he was with more serious concerns. In the middle of July, baby Arthur Madox Brown became suddenly and dangerously ill. Within a week he was dead and buried in St Pancras Cemetery.[6] He had died aged just ten months. Lizzie was not around to comfort her best friend as she mourned the loss of her baby; neither was she there to witness the body of her tiny godson disappearing into its grave. She had attended Arthur's christening on her own and Rossetti had been alone at his funeral. This was the stuff of heart-rending poetry, but no such poem written by Lizzie survives.

After a fortnight of treatments at Matlock, Lizzie decided not to return to London. She had renewed her acquaintance with her second cousins, the Ibbitts, who were obviously enchanted with her and invited her to stay at their home in Sheffield. This was the change that she needed and her health seems to have improved dramatically. In Sheffield she did not need to cultivate her reputation as an invalid because her cousins were quite willing to give her the attention she craved without needing to be emotionally manipulated beforehand. It was also more difficult to consume laudanum in the quantities to which she had become accustomed while living in someone else's home.

This was the one time that Lizzie really dared to strike out on her own. She became a great favourite with her Sheffield family, who were awed by her grand connections in London, but she did not attempt to live on her friends' reputations, as she had done in Oxford. She became particularly friendly with her cousin, William

---

[6] In 1866, the site of St Pancras cemetery was developed to become a grand railway station, complete with hotel. There was a public outcry as many of the graves were just weeks old and passers-by claimed to have seen bones and even a shining head of hair as the site was being made ready for the station's foundations. The architect, A. W. Blomfield, had a young assistant by the name of Thomas Hardy, whose job it was to oversee the relocation and reburials of the desecrated graves. Hardy was not yet known for the books that would make his name famous, but he was so affected by the St Pancras incident that he wrote two poems about it.

Ibbitt (1804–69), who was also an artist, and a town councillor. Ibbitt, who was 25 years her senior, was a prominent local figure and a useful friend to have in a new town. He and Lizzie often discussed art and she agreed to sit for him while he painted her portrait, which he started but did not complete. Lizzie's movements in Sheffield are a little obscure, but it seems that after spending a while with the Ibbitts she moved into lodgings on Ecclesall Road.

She decided to spend her time gainfully, and to learn more about art. She wanted to break out of the role into which she had been cast, no longer content to remain the pupil and property of Dante Gabriel Rossetti (who, by now, was a name to be reckoned with). Lizzie wanted to discover if she had genuine artistic talent and, if so, to improve in whatever direction her art was meant to be taken, not solely by dint of the direction Ruskin and Rossetti thought appropriate for her. Missing the friendship of Emma, she became close to a girl she met through the Ibbitts, Annie Drury, who was a student at the Sheffield School of Art. Through Annie's intervention, Lizzie was permitted to use the school's facilities and attend classes under the tutelage of the school's head teacher, Mr Young Mitchell.

In the 1850s, there were no life classes – the idea of learning drawing from a nude model was not accepted at the school until 1903 – but the students were allowed to study the human figure in the form of casts of antique statues. Lizzie often stayed on after classes to work on her own in the Figure Room. Mr Mitchell was aware of Lizzie's London connections and they had regular conversations about the Pre-Raphaelites and Ruskin. His obvious admiration for this new girl, whom most of the other students thought was stuck up and odd, did not pass unnoticed and she became the object of mild bullying. The Pre-Raphaelite fashion had not made it as far as Sheffield, so her unique style of dressing became a point of ridicule. Annie and Mr Mitchell defended her – the latter discovered a bitchy caricature of Lizzie being handed around the class and punished the girls severely – but it was Lizzie herself who put an end to the snide comments and whisperings. She had brought with her to Sheffield the clothes she had bought in Paris, corsets and all, and turned up on a school excursion to Manchester dressed in a style more grand, and fashionable, than any of her fellow students could possibly emulate.[7]

The excursion, which took place in September 1857, was to see Manchester's Great Exhibition. A special train had been commissioned from Sheffield and held 150 passengers, including William Ibbitt, Lizzie, Lydia (who had travelled up especially) and students and teachers from the Art School. The atmosphere was alive with excitement. At the exhibition, Lizzie was approached by an odd but strangely charismatic figure, who introduced himself as a friend of Rossetti's and Ruskin's and explained that he recognized her from Rossetti's portraits. He was in Manchester, he added, on behalf of John Ruskin, having been appointed his art adviser. The man's name was Charles Augustus Howell.

Howell, known affectionately to his contemporaries as "Owl", was one of the nineteenth century's most fascinating and scurrilous figures. Born in obscurity in Portugal at a date some time between 1839 and 1841, depending on which version is adhered to, he managed to become a pivotal figure of London artistic society in the mid- and late 1800s. He was employed by the highly upright Ruskin as his "art expert" and trusted by all the greatest names of the day – even though they acquired proof of just how untrustworthy he could be. Howell was an inveterate liar, at times perhaps even convincing himself of the lies. At a particularly low financial point in his life, he faked his own death to avoid his creditors. Even his actual death

---

[7] Sheffield Local Studies Library has a file of newspaper cuttings about Lizzie. They consist largely of letters to local papers, written by people who had met her, or had relatives who had met her, when she spent time in Sheffield. One letter was sent in by "A.S. of Ashdell Road", a fellow student at the School of Art. Several decades after Lizzie's death, "A.S." was moved to write: "It was a slight acquaintance I had with her, but it made a lasting impression on my memory."

on April 25, 1890, was complicated. There are two versions of his demise. The first, and most popular because it suggests a man dying as he lived (even if the story is untrue), tells of how he was found at dawn, lying in a gutter outside a Chelsea pub. His throat had been cut and between his rigid teeth had been placed a ten-shilling coin. Still alive, he was taken to hospital, where he later died. The problem with this story, although it makes for a great tale of which Howell would no doubt have approved, is that no police investigation into his death appears to have taken place. The second – and more prosaic – version of his death, and the one that was written in his obituary, was that he died in hospital from pneumonia, developed after a severe bout of influenza.

After his death, Howell's effects were sold off by auction. The celebrated actress Ellen Terry wrote pleadingly to a friend in London, "Howell is *really* dead *this* time – Do go to Christie's and see what turns up." Her correspondent, Graham Robertson, duly made his way to Christie's and made notes of the lots being sold. He later reported on the sale to the artist James Abbott McNeill Whistler (1834–1903), who gleefully punctuated the rendition all the way through with comments such as, "That was Rossetti's ... that's mine ... that's Swinburne's!" Whistler also made the following observation of Howell: "He was really wonderful ... You couldn't keep anything away from him and you always did exactly as he told you."

In 1857, Howell was about 17 years old and had only just begun what was to become an enviably varied career. He was very taken with the society into which he had managed to effect an entrance, although at this date his role in relation to Ruskin was less elevated than he led Lizzie to believe.[8] His recognition of Lizzie flattered her, and impressed any remaining sceptics in her student entourage. The doting Mr Mitchell was in awe.

---

[8] Howell worked as Ruskin's secretary for over a decade, until his dismissal in 1870. In 1872 he began working for Rossetti.

While Lizzie was proving a triumph in Sheffield, Rossetti was in the thick of an exciting new art project of his own. In company with the younger Pre-Raphaelites, including William Morris and Edward Burne-Jones, Rossetti was in Oxford, working on the murals for the Oxford Union. The project had been his idea and he threw himself into it with a passion. The architect Benjamin Woodward was excited about Rossetti's offer to cover the white walls of his new buildings with murals, aware of the importance his friend Ruskin afforded to the young eccentric. The university agreed to let the painters lodge free, feed them and supply the paint. Rossetti brought together a party of men, including Morris, Burne-Jones, Val Prinsep, John Roddam Spencer-Stanhope (1829–1908) and Arthur Hughes. The gathering had about it an atmosphere reminiscent of the early days of the Pre-Raphaelite Brotherhood – a group of young artists, excited and enthusiastic about the future, determined to change the face of the artistic world by their own endeavours. "Topsy", "Ned" and co. were as young as Rossetti, Deverell, Millais, Holman Hunt and the others had been when they began the PRB, and Rossetti was infected by their vitality and their passionate ideals. In Oxford, surrounded by adoring disciples, he was no longer the slightly jaded lover of a woman he knew he had wronged. He could be the young Dante again, going out to the theatre and concerts with his single friends, looking for stunners and wondering feverishly if the beautiful girl a few seats away would agree to sit for her portrait. The naked adulation in the faces of Ned and Topsy was intoxicating; it was the kind of unmitigated admiration Lizzie had once shown him every time they met.

One evening in October, a group of the enthusiastic mural painters were at a play when Morris spotted a stunner in one of the seats below their balcony. The impressionable young men excitedly concurred that Topsy had found the genuine article, a woman they all longed to paint. The tall, dark-haired young woman who had magnetically drawn the artists' attention away from the stage was a 17-year-old from a downtrodden area of Oxford. Her father was a stable groom and she had grown up, as Lizzie had done, believing nothing exceptional was ever likely to occur to her, in a life mapped out by financial necessity. She was certainly striking in appearance, with unusually exotic colouring and clearly defined features – and, unlike Rossetti, Morris needed to have no concerns about marrying for money. He had plenty of his own. The stunner's name was Jane Burden, later known affectionately to their circle as "Janey". The group, in true PRB fashion, were all smitten with her, but it was understood from the start that she was the "property" of Topsy. Rossetti was irritated that Morris had staked his claim first, but his friends all knew about Lizzie; he was not expected to be seeking to meet other women. As far as his friends were aware, Rossetti complied wholeheartedly with Morris's romance, but in reality he was as equally in thrall to Jane Burden as Morris was. His male friends remained unsuspecting at this early date, but Lizzie, although a great distance away, was made suspicious by the manner in which he wrote about Topsy's new stunner (Jane had, by now, agreed to be painted by Morris as Queen Guinevere).

On November 14, Rossetti was called away urgently to Matlock, where Lizzie had suddenly been taken terribly ill. Her success in Sheffield had not been able to negate her feelings for Rossetti and, in lieu of absence making the heart grow fonder, she had recognized the signs that he was, instead, enjoying living without her. Jane Burden was not the only problem. There was another new model in London, a voluptuous blonde replacement for the discarded Annie Miller. This new model was, in contrast to Lizzie, so large that she was often referred to as "The Elephant". Her name, or at least the name she assumed for modelling, was Fanny Cornforth (her real name was Sarah Cox).[9]

---

[9] Fanny Cornforth is usually dismissed as a prostitute Rossetti picked up on the street, but recent research is strongly suggestive that she was never a prostitute.

Fanny was a tender-hearted, working-class girl with a dissolute past and a genuine love for Rossetti. His friends derided him for dallying with a woman many of them perceived as unattractive, but he adored her face, her rippling blonde hair and her energizing vitality, so different from a Lizzie grown whiningly discontent through the years. In 1857 Rossetti had conceived an idea for the first painting he was to make of Fanny Cornforth, *Bocca Baciata* which, translated from the Italian, means "the mouth that has been kissed". The subject was taken from the fourteenth-century *Decameron* by Giovanni Boccaccio. It is the story of a woman who has had eight lovers before marrying her ninth. Unlike the moral message in most literary works of its era, the woman is not condemned for her sexually liberated behaviour. Instead, she is hailed as the most beautiful woman in the world, a woman in full command of her sensuality and generous in its bestowal. She is perceived as a heroine who gives and receives exquisite pleasure without any repercussions of bitterness or regret and who luxuriates in a fulfilled, happy and faithful married life. The full quotation, in translation, reads: "The mouth that has been kissed does not lose its fortune, rather it renews itself as does the moon". By 1858 there was little doubt whom the mouth had been kissing during the painting of *Bocca Baciata*.

From Sheffield and Matlock, Lizzie was in correspondence with Emma. In recent letters she had been receiving worrying communications about Rossetti's new model in London. In addition, Rossetti's own letters were making her equally nervous about this new girl in Oxford, discovered just as Lizzie had been, and full of the potential excitement Rossetti's inattentions had smothered in her own once-eager personality. Rossetti's letters may have pretended that Jane was Topsy's "property", but Lizzie had learned the painful way that, when it came to sex versus friendship, Rossetti was not a loyal friend. Even worse was the fact that Jane was just 17 years old. Lizzie was acutely aware that in the years she had been waiting for Rossetti to marry her she had metamorphosed from a

fresh young girl of 20 to a listless woman of 28, who was still
unmarried. Knowing she could not supersede the physical tempta-
tions of a 17-year-old beauty, Lizzie reverted to the proven method
of getting Rossetti's attention. She languished and sent word that
she needed him – that she was frightened she might die. It worked,
as always, and Rossetti rushed away from the painting party, of
which he was supposed to be in charge, and made his way as fast as
possible to Derbyshire.

In 1858, Matlock was a small but lively town surrounded closely
by limestone quarries and other disfiguring signs of the Industrial
Revolution and, a little further out, by idyllic, unspoilt countryside.
The Romans had settled in Matlock to glean lead from its rich mines
and the nineteenth-century manufacturers were determined to
finish off what their ancestors had started. Nearby Matlock Bath had
been renowned as a spa since the seventeenth century and Lord
Byron had described it as "a romantic fragment of Switzerland set in
the heart of England". The first spa-fed pool was built in Matlock
Bath in 1698 and, to the hoteliers' delight, a second spring was soon
discovered. An industry in invalids grew up rapidly as the town
emulated the success of fashionable Harrogate.[10]

Throughout the eighteenth and nineteenth centuries, expensive
hotels were built, including therapy pools fed by the spa water, but
these facilities were aimed exclusively at the wealthy, not at the local
population of miners and factory workers, a large proportion of whom
were in desperate need of treatment for work- and poverty-related
ailments. By the late 1830s, the price of a simple plunge-bath or a cold
shower was a shilling per person; to take a dip in a thermal pool, or to
have a hot shower, cost half-a-crown, prices that the hard-working

[10] In 1883, the Matlock Bath Hydro was opened to the general public. Every day
600,000 gallons of natural thermal spring water rushed through the purpose-
built pools, requiring no heating and minimal maintenance. Today the hydro's
pools are still in use as part of the town's aquarium. The gout-ridden old colonels
and delicate young ladies of yesteryear have been replaced by ornamental fish,
terrapins and piranhas.

locals were unable to afford. In the 1850s a local manufacturer and mill owner, John Smedley, decided to change all that.

Smedley was a philanthropic eccentric who owned a hosiery-making business and preached Methodist principles to any of his employees who would listen. In his spare time he read books about medicine, teaching himself about illness and its cures and deciding that he now knew as much as a doctor (most of whom he dismissed as no better than quacks). Having himself been treated successfully at a spa for a breakdown, he was brought to a firm belief that the best form of medicine was hydropathy, or water treatments, and he deter-mined to built a hydropathic centre. The centre would not only be opened to paying invalids, it would also be a place which his mill workers could visit for absolutely free treatments.

Smedley's first water therapy experiments were conducted in 1853 at a small house he had bought for the purpose. His grand plan, however, was far more exalted – he wanted to build a hydro-pathic centre on a sparsely inhabited hill on the outskirts of Matlock, an area known as Matlock Bank.[11] It is a long, imposing, dark stone building, crenellated all along the top like a fortress. The treatment rooms were decorated with wood panels, marble columns and stained glass.[12] It was to Smedley's hydropathic spa that Lizzie went for treatment.

Lizzie really was ill this time. The years of laudanum addiction had taken hold and her symptoms were advanced and pathetic. She was unable to ingest anything without vomiting, she was weak, terribly thin and could summon up little creative energy. She could not paint, she could only write poetry about death and unhappy love affairs. Her daily routine had become dependent on when she was

---

[11] John Smedley also built the typically Victorian folly Riber Castle, which stands on a hill outside the town and overlooks Matlock; the castle is also easily visible from the hydropathic centre.

[12] Today Smedley's hydropathic centre houses the offices of Derbyshire County Council, near the appropriately named Smedley Street.

able to take her next dose of the drug. She was at this stage physically incapable of leaving Matlock, being far too ill to undertake the long journey back to London, so she remained there for several months.

For those tiresome months Rossetti travelled back and forth between London and Derbyshire, unable to find time to go back to Oxford and help finish off the project, which was a pity as the murals were doomed to failure. The artists – Rossetti included – had not known enough about fresco painting to realize that they should have primed the walls before laying the paint onto them. It was not apparent straight away, but eventually the images began to fade away.[13] As his band of happy artists continued their carefree painting party, Rossetti juggled his time between the corpulent vitality of Fanny in London and the wan misery of Lizzie in Matlock, dividing his energies feverishly between perfecting *Bocca Baciata* and attempting to prevent Lizzie from dying.

In the meantime, Lizzie's reputation as an artist was suffering as miserably as her health. The Pre-Raphaelite exhibition, which had proved such a success in London's Fitzroy Square, had crossed the Atlantic where it had been eagerly awaited as part of the American Exhibition of British Art. Unfortunately, not all the works were as well received as had been hoped – amongst them Lizzie's, which was derided. By the time the travelling exhibition had reached Boston, *Clerk Saunders,* which had shown so much promise and had already been bought by the American collector Norton, was withdrawn from view. Heated correspondence had begun between the exhibition's backers in America and William Rossetti, complaining about the quality of art on display. One of the organizers, William Stillman, included in a letter to William Rossetti: "You should have thought that the eccentricities of the school were new to us, and left out

---

[13] The murals have since been renovated but it is impossible to recreate the brilliant colours the artists used.

things such as Hughes's *Fair Rosamond* and *April Love, The Invasion of the Saxons,* with Miss Siddal's *Clerk Saunders,* and *The London Magdalene*; all of which may have their value to the initiated, but to us generally are childish and trifling..." When *Clerk Saunders* was withdrawn, Dante Rossetti was drawn into the fray, corresponding cajolingly with Norton who was uncertain whether he should also withdraw his offer to purchase Lizzie's painting now it had been so criticized by his compatriots.

Norton was not Rossetti's only preoccupation that spring. While Lizzie fretted in Derbyshire about her advancing age, Rossetti was fast approaching the age of 30. At the start of May 1858 he was in Matlock with Lizzie, but he left her before his birthday, on May 12, to return to London. The birthday was an important landmark for him and he wrote enthusiastically to Bell Scott, "I am 30 this year, and want to try if I am ever to begin anything." This proclamation did not, however, relate to marriage or parenthood. He was at an exciting stage in his career, not only were his paintings being appreciated but he was gaining a staunch reputation as a literary translator of Italian texts.

After his birthday, Lizzie was relieved to welcome Rossetti back to Matlock, but he did not stay with her for her own 29th birthday at the end of July. As the ultimate in treachery, he left her side to travel to Oxford, where he drew a portrait of Jane Burden. Lizzie must have been aware that Morris was currently travelling in France, and the knowledge of Rossetti and Jane spending time together was gnawing at her.

For whatever reason, Rossetti was being deliberately hurtful to both Lizzie and Morris, who was by now one of Rossetti's closest friends and a man who admired him more than any other of his disciples. Morris, pitifully in love with Janey, was to spend their married life stepping back and allowing Rossetti to be her lover, all the time pretending to turn a blind eye to the affair. At this early stage Rossetti and Janey were not lovers, but he was nonetheless cuckolding Morris through his art. Morris was painfully aware of what he believed to be his inferior abilities as an artist. While Rossetti and Ned Burne-Jones had the confidence to know that their work was good, Morris always felt his paintings came a poor second best. When painting Janey for the first time, as Guinevere, desperate for her to know how he felt about her and becoming increasingly despondent about the way the image of her in his mind was translating to the canvas, Morris wrote in chalk on the back of the canvas – the side the model would see – "I cannot paint you but I love you." He was forever to feel belittled by Rossetti's ability to make Janey appear on canvas far more beautiful than she was and by his own perceived inability to live up to his friend's great genius. If Rossetti had been the possessor of Morris's inherited riches – an income of £900 a year – the story could have ended very differently. Janey was never content with Morris, telling him after Rossetti's death that she had never been in love with him. During their marriage she had two long-term affairs, the first of which was with Rossetti. She married, however, as any intelligent Victorian woman born into poverty would have been expected to do if offered the chance. Her matrimonial decision was a financial one, not one dictated by love.

The summer of 1858 was a time of illness for much of the group. While Lizzie was languishing in Derbyshire, Emma, at home in Kentish Town, was also extremely ill, causing Ford to fret tirelessly over her; she had not been strong since Arthur's birth and had not recovered from his death. Ned Burne-Jones, who was engaged to an adoring girl named Georgiana Macdonald, known as "Georgie", became so very ill that summer that he was swept off to Little Holland House, the beautiful Holland Park home of Valentine Prinsep's parents, where Val's mother nursed him back to health. Georgie and Ned had met when she was a child and he a pupil at school with her older brother. He had proposed in 1856, when she was 15 years old, but both knew their engagement would – out of financial necessity – be a long one.

When Ned was ill, Georgie worried impotently. Her vivacious older sister had died of consumption just a few years previously, and she was unsure how to cope with the sudden onslaught of calamities as so many of her new circle of friends seemed blighted by ill health. She wrote in her memoirs that she had been thrilled when a distracted Madox Brown, unable to cope with his children, the incapacity of his wife and his worry about her, coupled with the pressing need to work and earn money to pay for the medical bills, gratefully allowed Georgie to take three-year-old Nolly Madox Brown back to her parents' home and to care for him there until his mother was better.

While all these concerns were occupying the group in London, Lizzie's movements in Derbyshire and Yorkshire are uncertain. After July 1858, any mention of Lizzie disappears from Rossetti's letters, Madox Brown's diary and all other Pre-Raphaelite memorabilia. No letters to her, or from her to Emma or her family, survive and her whereabouts and what funds she was living on remain an unsolved mystery to this day. She may have remained in the north of England, visited her sister Annie in Scotland or returned to the family home in Southwark. The death of her father occurred in July 1859, and it seems likely that Lizzie was at home with her family around this time.

Of Rossetti, during this period, there is a wealth of information. He is known to have spent months vying with his friend George Boyce for the affections of Fanny Cornforth and then, at the end of 1859, after Holman Hunt finally ended his engagement to her, vying with Boyce for the affections of Annie Miller as well. He and Morris were rowing over Janey, with Morris's uncontrollable temper alienating himself from most of his friends – even the faithful Burne-Jones. Rossetti seems to have been the only one in the group who did not shrink from Morris's fury, despite being the object of it. He was painting and translating as usual, but of Lizzie or their relationship there is no mention at all. It is possible that she was mentioned in correspondence or diaries that did not survive, but to all intents and purposes Lizzie seemed to disappear from Rossetti's life altogether until April 1860, when she was once more terribly ill.

CHAPTER THIRTEEN

"So we two wore our strange estate: Familiar, unaffected, free" [1]

When Lizzie's family became convinced that this time she really was going to die, they contacted Ruskin, who instantly relayed the news to Rossetti. He rushed to Hastings to be at her side and realized how fervently he wanted her to live. Lizzie's emaciated frame was being tortured by her addiction, her limbs were now so weak she could barely move at all. She was a heart-rendingly pathetic sight, lying inert on her rented bed. Every day Rossetti willed her to keep going and prayed she would not die. Day and night she vomited, seemingly unable to keep enough sustenance in her body to sustain life. Her body was by now in such a terrible state that she longed to die just to be rid of the pain. This was no longer a ruse with which to manipulate her errant lover; Lizzie's laudanum addiction was destroying her body and she believed this was truly the end. Suddenly Rossetti could not stop talking about marriage. Every day he told her if she could just make it to the church at the bottom of the High Street, they would be married – he had even purchased the licence. For the first time in nine years, Lizzie did not want to talk about weddings. All she wanted to do was be free from this agonizing pain.

---

[1] Coventry Patmore, "The Angel in the House".

On April 13, 1860, Rossetti wrote to his mother, "Lizzy and I are going to be married at last, in as few days as possible ... Like all the important things I ever meant to do ... this one has been deferred almost beyond possibility. I have hardly deserved that Lizzy should still consent to it, but she has done so, and I trust I may still have time to prove my thankfulness to her." But the wedding was not to take place so soon. Although the church was no real distance from the house – just a short walk down to the bottom of the hill or a negligible amount of time in a carriage – Lizzie was far too ill to leave her bed. Rossetti's letters back to London grew increasingly desperate as he fought to keep his Guggum alive long enough to marry him. His guilt at having deferred the marriage for so many years was almost overwhelming as he gazed at the emaciated creature lying listlessly still on her lodging house sheets, moving only to vomit, screaming from the gut-wrenching pains. He was aware that most of her miseries had been prompted by his negligent behaviour.

A few days after writing to his mother, Rossetti wrote to William:

I assure you I never felt more in need of such affection as yours has always been, than I do now. You will be grieved to hear that poor dear Lizzy's health has been in such a broken and failing state for the last few days as to render me more miserable than I can possibly say. The spectacle of the fits of her illness when they come on would be heart-rending to a stranger even.

There seems to-day to be a slight rally, but till yesterday she had not been able to keep anything – even a glass of soda-water on her stomach for five minutes, and this has been the case more or less for a long while. She gets no nourishment, and what can be reasonably hoped when this is added to her dreadful state of health in other respects? If I were to lose her now I do not know what effect it might have on my mind, added to the responsibility of much work commissioned and already paid for, which still has to be done – and how to do it in such a case? I am sorry to write you such a miserable letter, but really it does me some good to have one person to whom I can write it, as I could not bear doing to any other than you.

His letters continued in a similar vein, with Rossetti becoming increasingly fretful about his paintings being left unfinished and his overwhelming fear that Lizzie's failing health would cheat him of his bride. The letters are a jumble of emotions, of pity and love for Lizzie followed by self-pity or self-reproach. Emma suggested she should travel to Hastings and nurse Lizzie, but Rossetti refused her permission, writing to Ford: "Emma made a kind offer of coming here … but I find Lizzy prefers being alone with me, and indeed it would be too painful for anyone to witness. I assure you it has been almost too much for me." Despite the last eighteen months – the cosy tea parties at Fanny's rooms and the flirtatious boat trips with Annie Miller – Rossetti still wanted Lizzie all to himself. If she were going to die, she would do so in his arms, not while being held by Emma.

When April ended and the licence was still languishing in his drawer, Rossetti determined they should make it a double celebration and be married on his birthday, but May 12 also went past without Lizzie being well enough to travel to the church. She was, however, beginning to regain something of her old adoring personality, her health was showing marked improvement and he was no longer so fearful that she would die unwed. His presence had seldom failed to revive her in the past, so he stayed with her, talking about where they would go on honeymoon and how they would live now he was more financially stable than he had ever been before. He told her of the artworks they would create together and proudly designed a monogram of her married initials, which she could use on her poems and paintings as soon as they were husband and wife. It had taken nine long years, but she was finally going to be E.E.R. instead of E.E.S.

The wedding took place on Wednesday, May 23, 1860, at St Clement's Church. They had no family or friends present, just a couple of witnesses whom they had asked in Hastings. The church of

St Clement's is famed in history for taking a direct hit from a cannon-ball when the town was under fire from Dutch ships. The missile remained lodged in the outer wall of the tower, looking down on Rossetti and Lizzie as a decade of courtship finally culminated in wedding vows, of which none must have been more poignant to Rossetti than the line "In sickness, and in health". No doubt Lizzie was eagerly listening out for "Forsaking all others".

The period 1859–60 was a popular time for romance and marriage among Rossetti's group of friends: William and Janey Morris had been married in April 1859; in 1860 Lydia Siddall walked down the aisle, four months pregnant, to marry Joseph Wheeler; Ned Burne-Jones married Georgiana in June, just a couple of weeks after Rossetti and Lizzie finally made it to the altar; and Charles Collins married Katey Dickens in July. Meanwhile, a heart-broken Fanny Cornforth was in London, mourning Rossetti and too miserable to eat or even get out of bed. Within a few months she was also married, to a mechanic called Timothy Hughes, distinguished only by his capacity for alcohol consumption.[2]

After the wedding, as soon as Lizzie was well enough, the Rossettis left for their honeymoon in France. They travelled to Folkestone where they took a boat to Boulogne; here they stayed with the Maenzas, friends of the Rossetti family with whom a young Dante had spent an enjoyable few months in the autumn and winter of 1843. The Maenzas, according to Dante, "quite fascinated" his new wife, whose health continued to fluctuate wildly. After Boulogne they returned to Paris, where they had been so happy with one another five years previously. On arriving, they checked into the Hotel Meurice, one of the city's most popular and expensive hotels, but after a week

[2] Timothy Hughes was also a model and was painted by Rossetti as the young "David as Shepherd" in the left side panel of the Llandaff Cathedral triptych. William Morris modelled for the more noble "David as King" (the right side panel) and, after rejecting his preliminary drawings of Ruth Herbert as the Virgin, Rossetti asked Janey to be the model for Mary in the middle panel, which depicted the Nativity (a linking scene emphasizing King David being Jesus's ancestor).

decided they could not afford to keep paying such high prices and moved into lodgings run by an English landlady, Mrs Houston, at 128 rue de Rivoli (the less desirable end of the street).

On their honeymoon, Dante reworked the slightly macabre *How They Met Themselves*, which may seem a strange choice of picture for one's honeymoon, but was absolutely in keeping with the feeling of predestination he had experienced the first time he had met Lizzie. They spent their time wandering slowly around Paris. Lizzie was still too weak to enjoy the rigours of being a tourist, but they were content with each other. They read books, one listening as the other read aloud, and sketched and painted together. As Rossetti observed, Paris agreed with Lizzie as well as it had done before, and her health was gradually improving. They befriended a couple of stray dogs, "a big one and a little one" as Rossetti wrote home with glee, adding that when they returned home, he planned to bring the dogs too.[3]

It had been hoped that Ned and Georgie Burne-Jones would join them for a joint honeymoon, but Ned was ill again so a disappointed Georgie had to write to Rossetti and tell him they were unable to make the journey to Paris. After receiving her letter, the newlywed Rossettis heaved a collective sigh of relief that their honeymooning was over and they could return home. In Dante's own words, they were tired of "dragging about" and looking forward to seeing all their friends and settling down again to the "refuge" of London life. "We are quite sick of it here," he wrote to Georgie, "as she is not well enough to enjoy sightseeing much."

On their return, they rented a cottage not far from Hampstead

---

[3] Rossetti had a passion for animals, although his love for them was not matched by an understanding of how best to look after them. After Lizzie's death he moved into a house in Cheyne Walk, Chelsea, where he proceeded to introduce all manner of animals, some meant to be domestic and others intended to live in the wild – and often not reared to live in the UK. He had a lifelong passion for wombats, of which he bought a couple; he also possessed an armadillo, a couple of kangaroos, a raccoon, a dormouse and a peacock. These unfortunate animals – and others – appeared randomly, and often expired with equal rapidity.

Heath, near Lizzie's former lodgings and an easy distance from the Madox Browns. Spring Cottage was very small and their rooms did not contain a studio, so Dante left every day to work in Blackfriars, leaving Lizzie alone with her thoughts. The depression and illness soon began to return. She had no idea who Rossetti was with all day and the possibility of him taking up again with Annie Miller, or Fanny, or some other new model was slowly eating away at her. She was, however, feeling creative once more and started her own work again. In the first few months after marriage, she worked on the aptly titled *The Woeful Victory*, another medieval battle scene. This painting has not survived, but a series of Lizzie's preliminary drawings are still in existence. They tell the story of a princess whose beauty has inspired two knights to fight a tournament to win her hand. The princess is in love with one of the knights – but it is his opponent who is victorious and her lover is killed. The story is identical to that of her poem "True Love".

For a few weeks after they returned from their honeymoon Lizzie was too ill to go out – even though in Paris her health had seemed so much improved – but by July she was back in good spirits and ready to enjoy her new status as a married woman. They were a perfect little group now she and Rossetti were legally a couple. They saw the Madox Browns as often as possible and also met regularly with the Burne-Joneses. On July 26, they had a joint day out at Regent's Park Zoo, after Rossetti sent Ford and Ned notes requesting them all to meet at "The Wombat's Lair" at 2 p.m. They appeared as three happy-go-lucky couples without a care or whisper of ill health between them. It was the first occasion that Georgie and Lizzie had met and Georgie wrote a letter the following day describing Lizzie as being "as beautiful as the imagination". Ned's new young wife remembered the whole day with great fondness, especially recalling a feud at the zoo that occurred between Dante and an owl: "The moment their eyes met they seemed to rush at each other, Gabriel rattling his stick between the cage bars furiously and the owl almost barking with rage."

At the end of a perfect afternoon, the Burne-Joneses went back for tea at Spring Cottage. Georgie, several years younger than Lizzie, was obviously in awe of this worldly, beautiful and quite tragic woman, who had been brought back from the brink of death and whom men took seriously as an artist. Lizzie was kind to her and a firm friendship was established. When they reached the cottage, Lizzie took Georgie upstairs to her room so they could take off their bonnets and rearrange their appearance. The moment made a deep impression on Georgie who recalled it exactly, 44 years later:

> I see her in the little upstairs bedroom with its lattice window, to which she carried me when we arrived, and the mass of her beautiful deep-red hair as she took off her bonnet; she wore her hair very loosely fastened up, so that it fell in soft, heavy wings. Her complexion looked as if a rose tint lay beneath the white skin, producing a most soft and delicate pink for the darkest flesh-tone. Her eyes were of a kind of golden brown – agate-colour is the only word I can think to describe them – and wonderfully luminous: in all Gabriel's drawings of her and in the type she created in his mind this is to be seen. The eyelids were deep, but without any languor or drowsiness, and had the peculiarity of seeming scarcely to veil the light in her eyes when she was looking down.[4]

Lizzie also showed Georgie her design for *The Woeful Victory*, before taking her back downstairs to join their husbands. The trip to the zoo was not the only occasion the three couples spent together – during that summer they were almost inseparable. They visited Henry VIII's old palace, Hampton Court, in Surrey, where they braved the famous triangular maze and got lost among the hedges. They spent

---

[4] William Rossetti, who later wrote a description of Lizzie's physical appearance, described her eyes as greenish-blue. His full description of her reads: "a most beautiful creature, with an air between dignity and sweetness, mixed with something which exceeded modest self-respect, and partook of disdainful reserve; tall, finely-formed, with a lofty neck, and regular somewhat uncommon features, greenish-blue sparkling eyes, large perfect eyelids, brilliant complexion, and a lavish heavy wealth of coppery-golden hair."

time at one another's homes, painting or sketching and talking about grand plans for the future. Lizzie, with the air of a practised artist, encouraged a tentative Georgie in her newly discovered art of wood engraving and they even talked of doing joint illustrations. Lizzie was finally in the role she had longed to play, that of a respectable wife in the fashionable areas of London; but she was also still addicted to laudanum and by the end of July she was once again too ill to leave the house.

Since returning from honeymoon, Lizzie had not made any effort to see her new in-laws, neither had they called on her (although convention dictated that she should have made the first visit). Her new mother- and sisters-in-law had not seen her for several years, but Lizzie claimed she felt too ill to make the journey to Albany Street – in spite of having been energetic enough to jaunt out to Surrey with the Madox Browns and Burne-Joneses. In answer to a letter that had asked Christina about her brother's new wife, the poet replied:

> Some years ago I knew her slightly; she was then extremely admired for beauty and talent ... His marriage would be more of a satisfaction to us if we had seen his bride; but owing I dare say in great measure to the very delicate state of her health, we have not yet met. She suffers much from illness ... I hope we shall be good friends some day.

They had made no effort to make her feel welcome when she would have welcomed it; now Lizzie felt no need to make an effort in return. At the beginning of August she was too unwell to attend a small dinner party for family and close friends hosted by Dante's mother. It was the first such family party since they had been married and the bride did not put in an appearance. Lizzie did, however, have a genuine reason for not attending the party – she was suffering from morning sickness.

CHAPTER FOURTEEN

The Queen of Hearts

or the first few months of her pregnancy Lizzie was a contented artist's model, just as she had been when they met, happy to pose for her husband and thrilled at the prospect of having a baby. Everything she had once feared denied to her was now tantalizingly within reach. Rossetti painted her as the Queen of Hearts in *Regina Cordium*. It is a little-known but beautiful picture in which Lizzie appears wistful and even sorrowful.[1] In the preliminary sketch, Rossetti's usual monogram and the date appears inside a stylized heart. In the finished oil painting, the same motif is used, worked into a golden background of hearts. The sketch is a much more flattering portrayal of Lizzie than the oil painting. In the latter, her drooping eyelids and the pallor of her skin – unfortunately appearing an unhealthy greenish hue against the rich gold of the background – are more suggestive of a woman in an advanced state of ill health than the captivating queen of the title. There is, however, an exquisite chalk drawing of *Regina Cordium*, in which Lizzie appears beautiful and alluring – though strangely untouchable. Rossetti was to use the title *Regina Cordium* again for pictures of other models, but the depictions of Lizzie as the Queen of Hearts demonstrate his feelings at the time of their marriage and are a fitting tribute to a marriage so many have derided as an unmitigated sham.

---

[1] The version of *Regina Cordium* for which Lizzie Rossetti was the model is now on display in the Johannesburg Art Gallery.

In early September 1860 Ruskin turned up at Chatham Place, unannounced, to offer his congratulations on their marriage – he had been abroad when the couple returned from honeymoon. There was no one in the studio but, in common with all Rossetti's friends, Ruskin knew where the key was kept, so he let himself in. He wandered around the studio looking at the paintings and discovering a wealth of new pictures of Lizzie. He was so touched by these that when he returned home he wrote Rossetti a letter about how wonderfully he drew when Lizzie was the subject:

> I looked over all the book of sketches at Chatham Place yesterday. I think Ida should be very happy to see how much more beautifully, perfectly, and tenderly you draw when you are drawing *her* than when you draw anybody else. She cures you of all your worst faults when you only look at her.

Ruskin was genuinely happy for the couple and relieved to see his Ida respectably married at last.

Lizzie was once more convalescing. This time she and Lydia had gone to Brighton, on the south coast, a popular health resort, more expensive and more lively than Hastings. Lizzie's decision to choose Brighton instead of returning to Mrs Elphick is illustrative of the new phase in her life. Hastings was where she had been as an unmarried woman, not all her memories associated with the town were happy and Hastings was a small place where people had long memories. In Brighton no one knew her. They had not known the unwed, miserable Lizzie. Here she was a married woman, expecting her first child with a hopeful and excited outlook on life – an outlook of the kind that she had not experienced for five years, since the first weeks of her trip to France.

While Lizzie was in Brighton, Dante was worrying about their home. Spring Cottage was much too small, especially with a baby so imminent, but finding a suitable place to rent near the Heath was proving a Herculean task. He was particularly disappointed after losing out on renting a place which had a "glorious old-world garden", which he knew would have been the ideal location for painting most of the backgrounds to his pictures, thereby saving him at least £200 a year in travelling expenses and rental fees. He knew that Hampstead had the best air for an invalid such as his wife, but properties in this invalid-ridden age were nigh on impossible to discover before someone else snapped them up. Meanwhile, paying rent on Chatham Place as well as Spring Cottage was fast clearing out his bank account. Lizzie was also agitating to come home and he was worried that she would make herself more ill by doing so. A letter, in which she apologizes for threatening to return home early, survives:

My Dear Gug,

I am most sorry to have worried you about coming back when you have so many things to upset you. I shall therefore say no more about it.

I seem to have gained flesh within the last ten days, and seem also much better in some respects, although I am in constant pain and cannot sleep at nights for fear of another illness like the last. But do not feel anxious about it as I would not fail to let you know in time, and perhaps after all I am better here with Lyddy than quite alone at Hampstead...

I should like to have my water-colours sent down if possible, as I am quite destitute of all means of keeping myself alive. I have kept myself alive hitherto by going out to sea in the smallest boat I can find. What do you say to my not being sick in the very roughest weather? I should like to see your picture when finished, but I suppose it will go away *somewhere* this week. Let me know its fate as soon as it is sealed...

I can do without money till next Thursday, after which time £3 a week would be quite enough for all our wants – including rent of course.

Your affectionate

Lizzie

She also came up with a solution he had not dared offer and by which he was vastly relieved. She suggested they move back to Chatham Place permanently. She wanted them to be together in the same house all day. There would be no more mornings of her husband leaving for the studio and his models and Lizzie having no idea of what he was up to or what time he would be home. Rossetti spoke to his Blackfriars landlord, who also owned the next-door building. He obligingly agreed to knock through the wall between the two houses, giving them rooms in number 13 as well as number 14 and transforming them into one large apartment.

They moved in in October 1860 and spent several months turning the bachelor flat into a marital home, having curtains made, buying carpets and decorating, all of which Lizzie found exhausting. Rossetti, however, threw himself into the decorating with enthusiasm, writing to his mother to send them any reliable curtain maker she might know of (something Lizzie was supposed to have arranged, but had not). He had by now developed a passion for buying yards of sumptuous materials, which he wound around and pinned on to his models when he painted, transforming them on canvas into rich gowns or ethnic clothing. These fabrics appeared from his studio and were draped over unglamorous furniture, making the rooms rich with colour.[2] In

---

[2] By the end of his life, Rossetti's obsession with buying rich materials to use as costumes had become a joke with his friends, as he had so many lengths of fabric he was unable to store it all. In the 1920s Max Beerbohm (1872–1956) published a cartoon in which he had sketched Rossetti surrounded by mountains of cloth attempting to persuade a dour, unimaginatively clad Christina into having a dress made up from a length of it. Although Beerbohm was not born until a decade after Lizzie's death, he was well acquainted with the popular stories of the Pre-Raphaelites, in particular with the story of Dante and Lizzie Rossetti.

addition, Rossetti proudly covered the walls of the new drawing room with Lizzie's paintings, made new wallpaper by hand and installed a birdcage to house Lizzie's pet bullfinch.[3] The couple shared a passion – in common with the rest of the group – for collecting blue-and-white china. Examples of this were displayed around their home – even the tired-looking ancient fireplace was given a new lease of life by the addition of blue-and-white tiles. This china passion was mentioned in the only note Georgie ever received from Lizzie. It was written when Lizzie was happy and vivacious and the younger woman kept it as a memento of her friend. "My dear little Georgie, I hope you intend coming over with Ned tomorrow evening like a sweetmeat, it seems so long since I saw you dear. Janey will be here I hope to meet you. With a willow-pattern dish full of love to you and Ned, Lizzie."[4]

Lizzie, however, was far too exhausted and listless to become involved in the decorating of Chatham Place with anything approx-imating enthusiasm. Pregnancy was absorbing all her energy and she had no more at her disposal to allow her to become excited about soft furnishings. She was also perfectly content to let her husband take command and create a home for her, something she had been longing for him to do for ten years. In early November she was, once again, too ill to visit her mother-in-law. The Rossetti family's feelings toward Lizzie had, however, mellowed since discovering she was having a baby. Christina in particular was overjoyed at the prospect of becoming an aunt. In February 1861 she wrote happily to her friend Mary Haydon, "Some day I suppose I shall rival you in

---

[3] After her death, the bird was moved to Albany Street to be cared for by her sisters-in-law.

[4] Rossetti's home in Cheyne Walk was well known for his vast collection of the china and caricatures of him often include this motif; Whistler was also an enthusiastic collector, as was William Morris. At the Morrises' Red House, one of the few aspects of the décor that was not brand new were the blue-and-white Delft tiles used to decorate some of the fireplaces.

Auntship ... My sister-in-law proves an acquisition now that we know her better ... you cannot think how quaintly and prettily they have furnished their ... drawing room." For some years now Frances had resigned herself to the fact that there might be no grandchildren: her daughters were getting beyond the age when they could be expected to marry and have children and neither of her sons had seemed to show much propensity toward matrimony. Yet her prayers were being answered. Even if Lizzie was not the ideal daughter-in-law, Frances could forgive a great deal in return for the gift of a grandchild.

Dante's and Lizzie's plan was not to stay in Blackfriars indefinitely. After the baby was born, they planned to move somewhere "more suburban", as Rossetti wrote to Bell Scott, hopefully into a shared home with the Burne-Joneses, who were also expecting their first baby. The idea of an artists' commune had not been forgotten and, now Annie Miller was well and truly out of the frame, Lizzie embraced the idea wholeheartedly. As Rossetti also included in his letter to Bell Scott, Lizzie had been "rather better on the whole of late" and the future looked considerably more reliable than he had previously dared to hope.

After the first three months of pregnancy, Lizzie began to feel much less nauseous. Unfortunately, for those first months her discomfort had been relieved by the accepted remedy for morning sickness: laudanum. During her pregnancy, both Rossettis had to accept the possibility that the baby might not survive. Lizzie's addiction and general poor health stacked the odds against them; added to which was the fact that many babies born in England in the 1860s did not live, as had been brought home to them by the death of Arthur Madox Brown. Pregnancy was also a highly dangerous time for the mother-to-be, the possibility of death following miscarriage or during the birth was an ever-present spectre and women who experienced healthy pregnancies and safe births often died needlessly through haemorrhaging after childbirth or developing an infection due to the deplorable lack of hygiene practised by so many medical workers. With every month that passed, however, Lizzie and Rossetti could relax a little more and believe that – just maybe – this pregnancy would be uncomplicated.

Lizzie wrote the melodramatic poem "At Last" during her pregnancy. It is the story of a young woman who dies in childbirth, bequeathing the care of her baby son to her mother. The poem voices the trepidation all prospective mothers of the period must have felt. It is a fitting tribute to Lizzie's sense of the melodramatic and her desire to write great ballads in the style of Lord Tennyson or Sir Walter Scott.

At Last

O mother, open the window wide
And let the daylight in;
The hills grow darker to my sight
And thoughts begin to swim.

And mother dear, take my young son,
(Since I was born of thee)
And care for all his little ways
And nurse him on thy knee.

And mother, wash my pale pale hands
And then bind up my feet;
My body may no longer rest
Out of its winding sheet.

And mother dear, take a sapling twig
And green grass newly mown,
And lay them on my empty bed
That my sorrow be not known.

And mother, find three berries red
And pluck them from the stalk,
And burn them at the first cockcrow
That my spirit may not walk.

And mother dear, break a willow wand,
And if the sap be even,
Then save it for sweet Robert's sake
And he'll know my soul's in heaven.

And mother, when the big tears fall,
(And fall, God knows, they may)
Tell him I died of my great love
And my dying heart was gay.

And mother dear, when the sun has set
And the pale kirk grass waves,
Then carry me through the dim twilight
And hide me among the graves.

With her medical history it is not surprising that Lizzie was assailed with trepidation about the birth and whether she would survive it. At the age of 31 she was old to be having her first baby, especially as she was living in an era when every birth – no matter how ideal the circumstances – held the possibility of causing the mother's death.

But Lizzie's pregnancy was not just a period of worry and sickness, it was also a time when she felt emotionally energized and alive. She was artistically creative, poetically inspired and happy to be sociable – with their friends, if not with her in-laws. The poet Algernon Swinburne (1837–1909) moved to London in October 1860 and became an inseparable friend to both the Rossettis. He was included in most of their social engagements and was constantly at their home. Swinburne did not try to hide the fact that he adored Lizzie, he looked upon her as a favoured sister, whom he would do anything to protect. When Rossetti spent long hours working in his studio, Swinburne would come and keep Lizzie company, reading aloud to her on days she felt too weak to venture outdoors. She took great pleasure in his visits and felt comfortable enough in his company to lie back on her invalid's couch and listen to him reading or participate in brilliant conversation. Even while Rossetti was painting a delectable model behind closed doors, Swinburne could make Lizzie cry with laughter.

Although Swinburne was notorious for his attempts to seduce almost every woman he met, he was always respectful and brotherly to Lizzie. He had had an awkward childhood and recognized in her someone who had also dealt with life's difficulties. He had often been derided for his nervous twitch, slight stature and flame-coloured hair, but Lizzie found him wonderfully appealing. Their affinity for one another was increased by the coincidence of their hair being almost exactly the same shade of red. Swinburne had been teased for his colouring all his life, but Lizzie had made red hair acceptable. She had even succeeded – in certain quarters of society – in making it fashionable.[5]

Rossetti, normally jealous of anyone close to Lizzie, was uncharacteristically happy about her friendship with Swinburne. The poet was no threat and he kept Lizzie amused and happy so Rossetti could get on with his work without feeling guilty. Lizzie had been growing increasingly difficult about his models, paranoid from early experiences, but when Swinburne was around, Rossetti knew he needed to worry less about suffering a sudden jealous outburst while he was working. At this time Rossetti was not only painting increasingly sensual pictures, his career as a writer and translator was also

---

[5] Helen Rossetti Angeli wrote of their friendship: "Swinburne's devotion to Lizzie would appear to be the only deeply felt platonic attachment of his life ... Of all her husband's friends he was the one she liked best and with whom she felt most at home ... Swinburne elicited more of her real thoughts and personality than Gabriel's other friends or his family."

in the ascendant. In 1860 Rossetti had realized a dream – he had been commissioned to produce a volume of translations from the early Italian poets, including Dante Alighieri's *Vita Nuova*. This was to be published in December 1861 and the volume dedicated to Lizzie. Rossetti's increased and more cerebral workload meant he needed to work longer hours and did not have the time to be with Lizzie as often as she desired; the comical redheaded poet was therefore a welcome addition to Chatham Place. Swinburne's biographer, Edmund Gosse, described them in the following way: "Rossetti was much entertained by their innocent intimacy, occasionally having to call them both to order, as he might a pair of charming angora cats romping too boisterously together."

That autumn of 1860 was a time of friendship and sociability. Chatham Place once again became the scene of parties and small gatherings of friends. They would sit around in the studio for hours by candlelight, watching the river and making sketches of one another or planning future projects. Lizzie improved her intimacy with Georgie Burne-Jones, in whom she confided and to whom she talked about art, but Lizzie was never fully happy just to be on her own with Georgie, or anyone else, panicking when Rossetti was out of her sight. Georgie later recalled how nervous Lizzie would be whenever Rossetti was out of the room, her whole body on edge as she waited anxiously for him to come back in, whereupon she would uncoil and sit reassured with him beside her, finally able to take an interest in the conversation.

Georgie also remembered an evening at the theatre, when a group of them went to see the play *Colleen Bawn*. There was such a large number in their party that they filled an entire row, with Swinburne sitting at one end and Lizzie at the other. According to Georgie's memoirs, the two shocks of red hair were a terrifying sight to a superstitious boy who was selling programmes: "[He] looked at Swinburne and took fright, and then, when he came round to where she was, started again with terror, muttering to himself, 'There's another of 'em!'" The play was one that must have had a certain resonance for

Lizzie, being about a marriage of two social unequals. *Colleen Bawn,* written in 1860, was a popular melodrama set in Killarney. In it a matchmaking mother attempts to arrange a marriage between her son, Hardress, who is in danger of losing his estates through lack of finances, and his wealthy cousin, Anne, whose money could save the family's home and reputation. Unknown to his mother, Hardress is already married, having wed in secret a poor but beautiful peasant girl, Eily O'Connor, known as the Colleen Bawn. Having grown bored with his young wife and eager to taste wealth again, Eily's husband arranges to have her murdered. Despite his behaviour, she still loves him and – having been rescued from her fate – makes a dramatic appearance as he is about to marry Anne. When the shock is past, Eily is accepted into Hardress's family and no longer shunned for her poverty. Anne, who has also been reconciled to her ex-lover – whom she was attempting to spite by marrying Hardress – agrees to pay off the mortgage, allowing Hardress and Eily to live together in comfort. Sitting in the stalls, Lizzie must have been embarrassingly aware of how similar her own situation was to Eily's, with a mother-in-law who had viewed her, before her pregnancy, as the canker in her son's life because of her social status.

In October 1860, while Rossetti was busy working, Lizzie went to stay with William and Janey Morris. They had recently moved into the brand-new Red House, which had been built beside the hamlet of Upton, near Bexleyheath in Kent. It was created for Morris by his designer friend and colleague Philip Webb (1831–1915).[6] The house is L-shaped, with a tower in the middle,

---

[6] Philip Webb was an architect and designer who became an integral part of the Arts and Crafts movement. He first met William Morris in 1856, when they were working together at the architectural practice, G. E. Street. In 1858 Webb set up his own practice specializing in country residences; Morris was one of his first clients, with his commission for the Red House. A few years later Webb joined Morris's new company, Morris & Co., where he worked as a designer, overseeing amongst other things the famous Morris & Co. stained glass. The two men also collaborated in the creation of the Society for the Protection of Ancient Buildings.

and was inspired by Gothic and medieval architecture. Its name derived from the red brick used for its construction as well as the red roof tiles.[7] After visiting Upton, Rossetti wrote to Charles Norton saying, "I wish you could see the house which Morris, who has money, has built for himself ... It is a most noble work in every way, and more a poem than a house ... but an admirable place to live in too ... It is a real wonder of the age that baffles all description."

The Pre-Raphaelites helped Morris design some of the furniture and to decorate the interiors. During her stay in the autumn, Lizzie helped with the painting of murals. In company with many visitors to the house, she also modelled for the wall paintings.[8] Rossetti went to join them when he was able to take time away from his studio and he and Lizzie appeared happy and optimistic together. He painted three panels about love – a Garden of Eden, an allegory about Love, and Dante's last meeting with Beatrice. For a time Renaissance Florence was forgotten. Dante and Beatrice were now married and expecting a baby. For a short time at least, in the autumn of 1860, life and love seemed to be allowing them to be happy. Lizzie's health was improved also by the visit – Upton was then in the middle of countryside and, as Georgie described, visitors to Red House "were met with this fresh air full of sweet smells" and an exquisitely laid out garden with "roses growing thickly".

---

[7] Today Red House is owned by the National Trust and is open to the public.

[8] Unfortunately most of Lizzie's work on the Red House murals has been lost due to the artists' lack of awareness about painting murals – the group had learnt some lessons from the Oxford Union mistakes, but not enough to prevent similar problems at Red House. There is, however, a Philip Webb cabinet, now in the entrance hall, on which Morris painted a scene from Malory's *Morte d'Arthur* for which Lizzie was one of the models. The features of Morris, Janey, Ned and Georgie are also discernible in the figures. Lizzie can also be seen in Burne-Jones's *Sir Degrevaunt* murals in the drawing room and her features can be perceived in the female figure in Burne-Jones's drawing *The Backgammon Players* (1861), the background of which was taken from the garden of Red House.

Red House in the early 1860s was a place of house parties and friendship. Almost every weekend visitors would arrive to stay and help decorate the house, play bowls or croquet on the lawn and go for rides in the eccentric carriage Philip Webb had designed for William and Janey to gad about in. Their daughter May later described this vehicle as being like "an old-fashioned market cart" which was hung with brightly patterned fabric in various patterns. It caused the local villagers much hilarity as the eccentric young arty couple from the new red-brick house drove their equally eccentric friends around the surrounding countryside, although the pious locals were less than impressed by some of the "exotic" clothing worn by guests and shocked by the Morrises holding tea parties on Sunday afternoons. To reach Red House from London, visitors took the train to Abbey Wood where they were fetched by the carriage. Georgie later recalled wistfully, "Oh the joy of those Saturdays to Mondays at Red House ... the getting out at Abbey Wood station ... and then the scrambling swinging drive of three miles or so to the house, and the beautiful roomy place where we seemed to be coming home."[9] The house had four bedrooms and no bathrooms (which was usual for a house of that period). The water source was a well in the garden, from which water was hand-pumped into the house, and vegetables were grown in the kitchen garden. The Morrises and their guests lived mainly on the first floor, while the ground floor was the domain of the servants. Georgie wrote about a particularly splendid medieval banquet, for which Morris and Rossetti had improvised a minstrels' gallery and after which the extra guests were accommodated on "beds strewn about the drawing room" while Swinburne slumbered on the sofa.

[9] In the end, it was this four-hour journey from London – almost impossible when attempted as a commute – which brought the parties at Red House to an end. In November 1865 the Morrises were very reluctantly forced to sell their idyllically secluded home and return to London, where William could concentrate on his newly founded business, Morris, Marshall, Faulkner & Company (later known as Morris & Co.).

Around Christmas-time the Rossettis went once again to stay at the Morrises' new home, in company with the Burne-Joneses. It was a happy party with all three couples expecting their first babies. In Georgie's words there was "certainty of contentment in each other's society. We laughed because we were happy." For Morris it was a dream come true – the incarnation of his desire to found an artistic working community. He was already making designs for an extra wing to the house in which he hoped Ned and Georgie would live, the Morris and Burne-Jones children growing up as one happy family. That Christmas their lives seemed blessed and content. They sang together, played cards, painted and drew, dined on delicious food and drank Morris's carefully chosen wines. The atmosphere could not have been perfected – until Rossetti, eaten up by jealousy about Janey and over William's idyllic new home for his prospective family, started to mock his host's ability to paint. The two men had a furious row and a cloud formed over the celebrations, Morris's irascible temper was legendary and the party was ruined for everybody. The Rossettis and Burne-Joneses soon returned to London, with the pregnant Lizzie excruciatingly aware of her husband's feelings for the wife of his friend.

Though relations with the Morrises were temporarily soured, those with Rossetti's family continued to improve. Lizzie was aware she had been accepted not for herself but as the mother of the next Rossetti generation, but for the moment she was reasonably happy and the future was exciting.

CHAPTER FIFTEEN

"The hour which might have been . . ."

In January 1861, Lizzie was ill again. She was so ill that, even though Frances Rossetti was also unwell, Dante could not leave his wife to visit his ailing mother. Meanwhile, he was making sure everything was ready for the birth of their child. He found a suitable doctor, an obstetrician and a live-in nurse. The latter was described by Georgie as, "a delightful old country woman, whose words and ways we quoted for years afterwards; her native wit and simple wisdom endeared her to both Gabriel and Lizzie, and were the best possible medicine for their over-strained feelings".

As was quite usual, the Rossettis' baby would be born at home – most Victorian babies were born at home as "lying-in" hospitals were best avoided at all costs. In these hospitals, there was an incredibly high risk of developing puerperal fever (also known as childbed fever or lying-in fever), which usually resulted in death. No one had yet worked out the causes of this mysterious killer and Rossetti was not willing to risk the lives of his wife and child.[1]

---

[1] It was Barbara Leigh Smith's cousin, Florence Nightingale, who helped to discover the causes of puerperal fever. She was shocked to discover that, despite centuries of a horrific percentage of new mothers contracting it, no research had ever been carried out. She insisted the research be undertaken and commissioned a study into the illness. The fever was largely caused by frighteningly unsanitary hospital conditions.

Rossetti voiced his fears in a letter to William Allingham, in January 1861:

> Lizzie is pretty well for her, and we are in expectation (but this is quite in confidence as such things are better waited for quietly) of a little accident which has just befallen Topsy and Mrs. T who have become parients [sic]. Ours, however, will not be (if at all) for two or three months yet.[2]

Even at this early stage, Rossetti's parenthetical "if at all" revealed his fears that Lizzie would never be able to carry a foetus to full term.

In the middle of April, Lizzie sensed that something had gone badly wrong. Thus far the pregnancy had progressed as expected, the feared miscarriage had not happened and her confinement was due in just a couple of weeks, but suddenly the baby seemed to have stopped moving inside her. Although a doctor and an obstetrician were called in by Rossetti, there was nothing they could do. There were no medical scans or emergency procedures available. At that date Caesareans, despite having been performed for millennia, were still little understood by British medics and usually proved fatal to the mother. In the first half of the nineteenth century, Caesareans brought about death in 75 per cent of cases. A doctor would choose to perform the procedure only if he was convinced the mother was going to die anyway and he was battling to save the baby. There was no way to find out what was wrong. When her baby stopped moving, Lizzie Rossetti had no choice but to pray and to wait.

Able to observe at first hand the abuse Lizzie dealt her body, Rossetti must have been aware from an early stage that his baby was fighting against difficult odds to survive. It was this knowledge that

---

[2] Janey Morris had just given birth to her and William's first daughter, Jenny.

allowed him to write to his mother quite stoically on May 2, 1861, "Lizzie has just been delivered of a dead child. She is doing pretty well, I trust. Do not encourage any one to come just now – I mean, of course, except yourselves." Rossetti's main fear now was that Lizzie herself would not recover from the birth and her bereavement. His letters to friends over the ensuing hours and days are all tinged with a sense of relief – relief that he did not lose his wife as well as his daughter.

He wrote to Madox Brown, "Lizzie has just had a dead baby. I know how glad Emma and you will be to hear that she seems as yet to be doing decidedly well … I dare say she would be very glad if Emma could look in for a little tomorrow."

And to a family friend, Mrs Dalrymple:[3] "My dear wife has just given birth to a still-born child. However she herself is so far the most important, and seems as yet to have got through so much better than we ventured to hope, that I can feel nothing but thankfulness. God send she may continue to do well!"

Although Rossetti's letters written at the time of the birth may appear to modern readers to be quite heartless, this was an act as he struggled to be strong for his grieving wife. Rossetti loved children and longed for his daughter to be alive. The loss of their baby may not have seemed to affect him at this stage, but it was something he never stopped thinking about.[4] Years after Lizzie's death, he wrote a poem entitled "Stillborn Love", about a dead baby waiting in the afterlife for the arrival of its parents:

---

[3] Mrs John Dalrymple was the aunt of Valentine Prinsep and sister to Mrs Prinsep, who so attentively nursed Edward Burne-Jones through his worrying illness. The Prinseps lived in Little Holland House, Holland Park, very close to Frederic, Lord Leighton, G.F. Watts and other members of the artistic milieu known as The Holland Park Circle. They were important connections for the Pre-Raphaelites.

[4] Recent research has shown that the partners of postnatally depressed women develop an increased tendency to depression themselves. Rossetti suffered from severe depression in the final years of his life.

Stillborn Love

The hour which might have been yet might not be,
Which man's and woman's heart conceived and bore
Yet whereof life was barren, – on what shore
Bides it the breaking of Time's weary sea?
Bondchild of all consummate joys set free,
It somewhere signs and serves, and mute before
The house of Love, hears through the echoing door
His hours elect in choral consonancy.

But lo! what wedded souls now hand in hand
Together tread at last the immortal strand
With eyes where burning memory lights love home?
Lo! how the little outcast hour has turned
And leaped to them and in their faces yearned:–
"I am your child: O parents, ye have come!"

But while Lizzie was prostrated by the death of their baby, Rossetti could not afford to dwell on the daughter he had lost. He knew there was still a danger Lizzie could die from the rigours of the birth and fussed over her just as he had for the long weeks before their wedding. Even after the doctor pronounced Lizzie out of danger their problems were by no means at an end. After giving birth to a dead baby, Lizzie would never be the same again. The baby girl had died inside her two or three weeks before the birth and Lizzie's body was suffering the ill effects. Poisons from the dead foetus were leaching into her own system, causing distressing physical problems, while her mind was suffering equal torments from the knowledge her baby had died and she had not been able to save her. This was combined with an acute nagging guilt that her dependence on laudanum might have been the cause of death. Although both Lizzie and Rossetti had been aware for a while that the baby was probably dead and it was something they had been warned was a possibility from the outset, Lizzie had blocked such an eventuality out of her mind. By the time the birth took place, Rossetti had forced himself to accept the probable outcome, but Lizzie was never able to do so. Her usual tendency to depression, combined with a new pressure of postnatal depression and bereavement, led her to a dangerously increased dependence on laudanum. Her addiction worsened dramatically as she attempted to numb the physical and mental torment – Rossetti later admitted that he had known her take up to a hundred drops of laudanum in one dose. Shortly after the birth, Lizzie wrote the following poignant poem:

Lord May I Come?

Life and night are falling from me,
Death and day are opening on me,
Wherever my footsteps come and go,
Life is a stony way of woe.
Lord, have I long to go?

Hallow hearts are ever near me,
Soulless eyes have ceased to cheer me:
Lord may I come to thee?

Life and youth and summer weather
To my heart no joy can gather.
Lord, lift me from life's stony way!
Loved eyes long closed in death watch for me:
Holy death is waiting for me –
Lord, may I come to-day?

My outward life feels sad and still
Like lilies in a frozen rill;
I am gazing upwards to the sun,
Lord, Lord, remembering my lost one.
O Lord, remember me!

How is it in the unknown land?
Do the dead wander hand in hand?
God, give me trust in thee.

Do we clasp dead hands and quiver
With an endless joy for ever?
Do tall white angels gaze and wend
Along the banks where lilies bend?
Lord, we know not how this may be:
Good Lord we put our faith in thee –
O God, remember me.

CHAPTER SIXTEEN

"How is it in the unknown land?"

Following the loss of her child, Lizzie was permanently altered. She would sit in the drawing room for hours without moving her position, just staring silently into the fire. If there was no fire, she would simply stare into space, apparently not seeing anything in front of her. Once more she refused to eat and became increasingly emaciated. The nurse hired as a maternity carer was living with them and taking care of her, but Lizzie was too wrapped up in grief to be aware of anything except her loss. When Ned and a heavily pregnant Georgie came to visit her, Lizzie was in her room alone, staring at the empty baby's cradle, which she would rock tenderly from side to side as though soothing her daughter to sleep. As the door creaked open she looked up and told them to be quiet so as not to wake the baby. The pregnant Georgie found this heart-rendingly sad; Ned thought Lizzie was being ridiculously over-dramatic.

In June, she was invited to stay with the Madox Browns for a while. Rossetti could not cope with Lizzie's misery and needed a break from caring for her and absorbing all her grief while suppressing his own. He also needed to be able to work. Their finances, although improved, were not yet stable and the birth and its attendant medical costs had been expensive. It was hoped that being with Emma would help Lizzie to grieve and be comforted, but Emma had a child and staying in the Madox Browns' house with the constant reminder of the child she did not have was excruciating for Lizzie. The young Lucy Madox Brown, who was staying with her father and stepmother at the time of Lizzie's visit, found the bereaved mother highly disturbing, with her vacant expression and silent staring.

After just a few days, Rossetti was astonished to find Lizzie back in Chatham Place – she had left the Madox Browns' without a word and made her own way back to Blackfriars. Lizzie could no longer bear to be in the home of such a happy family when she herself could not be a part of one. Lizzie was also paranoid that Rossetti would be with another woman in her absence – this became an obsession throughout the last months of her life and, given her husband's past history of infidelity, her fears were not without basis. It seems, however, that they were groundless: Val Prinsep, who had become a good friend of Rossetti's, wrote an article after the deaths of both Lizzie and Rossetti, in which he declared Rossetti was wholly faithful to Lizzie once they were married.

Rossetti wrote an embarrassed letter to the Madox Browns, explaining that Lizzie had felt ill and, not wanting to trouble Ford and Emma with needing to look after her, had thought it best if she returned to her husband. He ended the letter with, "I hope if she comes again she may be better and give you less trouble. I write this word, since her departure must have surprised you as her return did me." Today it seems unthinkable that a woman would be expected to suffer no ill effects from a stillbirth and that her friends – who had themselves endured the death of a young baby – would not have understood what she was going through. Rossetti's letter is indicative of the nineteenth-century misconception about postnatal depression. Any form of depression or any other mental illness was considered something shameful, to be covered up and lied about in order to preserve a façade of "normality".

When the time approached for Georgie to have her baby, Lizzie decided she was going to give the Burne-Joneses all her carefully prepared baby clothes. Rossetti wrote to Georgie begging her not to accept them because he was frightened that her doing so would prove a bad omen for him and Lizzie. Lizzie already felt certain she would die childless, but Rossetti was blindly optimistic. He thought another baby would cure Lizzie of her depression; he believed they would get through the nightmare together and go on to have more children.

In July, Lizzie was persuaded to go away from home again, this time to Red House to stay with the Morrises. Rossetti was desperate to work and could not while he needed to take care of her. He was also fearful because Lizzie's physical health was once again precarious and he knew she needed a change of air from the summer-heated stench of the Thames and the smoke from the belching steamers. Upton was a country haven, a place where Lizzie could sit in tranquillity surrounded by greenery and flowers and, hopefully, start recovering from the birth and bereavement. The house was surrounded by an apple and cherry orchard through which Lizzie could wander. As well as the fruit trees, the gardens were dotted with oaks, limes, hawthorns and horse chest-nuts and the air was scented by the carefully chosen flowers – white jasmine, rosemary, lavender, passion flowers, honeysuckle, sunflowers and the thickly stocked rose beds. Beyond the house and gardens were fields and woodland, the ideal location for an artist seeking inspiration. It was hoped she would also feel entirely at home in the house which was a monument to the Pre-Raphaelite movement. The stained glass in the windows had been created by her husband, Morris and Burne-Jones, who had also painted the majority of the tiles and furniture (much of which had been specially designed for Red House by Philip Webb). Perhaps, however, Lizzie felt the strongest affinity with the motto Morris had carved over his drawing room fireplace: ARS LONGA VITA BREVIS – art endures, life is brief.

Lizzie was not Rossetti's only worry that July – one of his patrons, Thomas Plint, a wealthy stockbroker from Leeds, died very suddenly. Plint's death dealt a financial blow not only to Rossetti but to Madox Brown and Burne-Jones, whose patron he had also been.[1] In addition to losing the chance of future commissions, they all found themselves having to pay back money they had been given. The dependably wealthy Plint had, it seemed, experienced financial worries of his own and had died insolvent. As a result, Plint's executors requested the return of all advances paid on unfinished pictures. Rossetti, who had stopped teaching at the Working Men's College a couple of years previously, now returned to teaching.

In spite of his fears after her ignominious return from Kentish Town, Lizzie stayed without incident at Red House, prompting Rossetti to believe she was at last on her way to recovery. She wrote him a letter from Kent, signed "your affectionate Lizzie", after hearing of the death of one of their friends and fellow artist, Joanna Boyce Wells, who had died in childbirth. That summer, the Morrises and various artistic friends were employed in decorating their home by painting murals and patterns not only onto the walls but onto the furniture as well. Lizzie was having difficulty with her artwork, feeling inadequate in her ability to paint figures. "If you can come down here on Saturday evening, I shall be very glad indeed…" she wrote to her husband. "I want you to do something to the figure I have been trying to paint on the wall. But I fear it must all come out for I am too blind and sick to see what I am about."

A couple of months later, choosing to ignore the depressive undertones in her last letter from Upton, and feeling relieved by

---

[1] When Arthur Madox Brown died, Ford was in such dire financial straits – having footed the bill for the 1857 salon and not yet been paid back by Lizzie, Rossetti, Millais or any of the other exhibitors – that he could not afford to pay for his baby's funeral. He had turned to Plint who had given him the money.

the apparent stability in Lizzie's health, Rossetti accepted a commission in Yorkshire. He had been asked by one of his most dependable patrons, Ellen Heaton (1816–94), to paint a portrait at her Georgian home in Leeds.[2] Eager to make up the money he had lost after the death of Plint, he arranged for Lizzie to stay with the Morrises again. This time it was all too much for her. The beautiful Janey Morris – with whom Lizzie was aware her husband continued to be sexually enthralled – not only had her eight-month-old daughter, Jenny, but she was pregnant again. It seemed that everywhere Lizzie turned for solace she found new babies, young children or the optimism of pregnancy – even her once closest ally, her sister Lydia, was a new mother. Janey's contented fecundity was more than the postnatally depressed Lizzie could cope with and she ran away yet again. A frantic Rossetti, unable to leave Yorkshire, wrote an urgent letter to his mother requesting her to go to Chatham Place and take Lizzie some money as he knew there was none in the house and he had no idea what she could be doing for food.

By the end of the year, Lizzie was once more accepted as an immovable invalid, lying listlessly in her chair to be sketched or staying in bed for most of the day. Neither she nor Dante had ever been early risers, regularly choosing to stay in bed until midday, to their visiting friends' annoyance, but now she wanted to stay in bed continually.[3] On Christmas Eve 1861, Rossetti wrote to his mother that, as Lizzie was so ill, there was "very little prospect of our coming tomorrow, but if we can we will".

Throughout December, Rossetti tried to re-create the happier days of being together, sketching Lizzie as Princess Sabra and as a

---

[2] Ellen Heaton was a friend of the Brownings, Millais, Ruskin and Christina Rossetti, as well as being Dante Rossetti's patron. She and Christina corresponded for almost three decades. Ellen, who did not marry, became a woman of independent wealth after the deaths of her parents. She was acquainted with Rossetti's ill-fated patron Thomas Plint.

[3] One of the most apparent signs of postnatal depression is a feeling of intense tiredness that worsens throughout the day.

sanctified Beatrice. Princess Sabra was the daughter of an Egyptian king, in a land that was terrorized by a dragon. Every year a virgin girl had to be sacrificed to the dragon to prevent his ravages to their kingdom. Eventually, it was the turn of the king's daughter herself, a beautiful girl who was awaiting her fate with terror and increasing desperation. Her prayers for salvation were answered by the arrival of a passionate suitor, an Englishman we now know as St George. He slayed the dragon and rescued the princess, whom he married. Her Muslim father was overjoyed – until he discovered that George intended to take his new bride back to England where she would become a Christian, whereupon the king arranged to have his new son-in-law killed.

In *The Wedding of St George and Princess Sabra*, Lizzie – as the princess – has her face raised heavenward (as in *Beata Beatrix*). She is clasped in the arms of St George, who has just rescued her from the dragon, lying dead on the ground beside them, but both figures wear an expression of misery, portentous of the danger that awaits them. The attitude of the lovers, his protective arms drawing her to him and her compliance, are similar to the attitudes adopted by the lovers in Lizzie's *Lovers Listening to Music*.

By January, however, Rossetti had to face the fact that he could not slay Lizzie's personal dragons. His brave Princess Sabra and saintly Beatrice was once again dangerously ill and relying ever more increasingly on laudanum. Even the knowledge that she was pregnant again was unable to encourage moderation in the amount she consumed.

CHAPTER SEVENTEEN

"Lord May I Come?"

The evening of Monday, February 10, 1862 started out like almost any other evening in the Rossettis' diary. The lack of cooking facilities at Chatham Place meant they were accustomed to eating dinner at a restaurant and on this particular evening, Dante and Lizzie were joined by Swinburne, their most regular dinner companion. The couple set out at about six o'clock to meet the poet at one of their favourite restaurants, La Sablonière, in Lizzie's old haunt, Leicester Square.[1]

Rossetti later explained that he had been concerned at the start of the evening because his wife seemed to be fluctuating between being drowsy and over-excited when they set out from home (although he was used to it, her laudanum addiction having been his constant companion for the last twenty months). He realized she must have taken quite a large dose of the opiate before leaving and asked if she would rather they turn the cab round so she could stay at home instead of coming out to dinner – the implication being that he was worried she would embarrass him in the restaurant. Lizzie being embarrassing in public was something Rossetti was painfully used to by now. Lizzie, however, wanted to go out and dine, so they continued on their way to meet the faithful Swinburne, in whose eyes Lizzie could never be an embarrassment.

The three enjoyed a spirited meal. Swinburne later wrote that

---

[1] The restaurant and the hotel it was attached to no longer exist.

nothing untoward or unpleasant had happened during dinner and that Lizzie had seemed in very good spirits, although at the inquest he commented that he had been worried because she had seemed to be even weaker than usual that evening. They finished eating at around eight o'clock and, after agreeing he would call round the following morning so Rossetti could continue painting his portrait, Swinburne left them to make their way back to Blackfriars. Lizzie and Rossetti returned home by cab. By this time Lizzie was feeling the soporific effects of the laudanum and was ready to go to sleep. They may have had an argument, as has often been suggested. If so, the incident is unrecorded. At about nine o'clock Rossetti left her, already in bed, and went out to the Working Men's' College. It has been suggested by several sources that Rossetti was, in fact, going out to meet another woman, leading Lizzie to turn in desperation to her laudanum bottle that evening. Val Prinsep's assertions belie this suggestion, however, and no evidence has ever been discovered that he did not go to work that evening. It is likely, though, that Lizzie, by this time a serious and paranoid addict, had convinced herself he was going to meet a lover, even if his errand was genuinely innocent. Rossetti's past infidelities and her own very disordered mind, increasingly unstable after the stillbirth, had led her to become highly erratic in her behaviour.

When he returned home at half past eleven, Rossetti found Lizzie snoring very loudly and disconcertingly. The bottle of laudanum beside the bed, which had been half-full earlier in the day, was now empty and ominously a note addressed to him was pinned to her nightgown. It was a suicide note asking him to take care of Henry, her disabled young brother.[2] A distraught Rossetti made a tremendous

---

[2] Dante Rossetti and, after his death, William Rossetti, continued making payments to the Siddall brothers for many years. It has been suggested this was "guilt" money, because her family realized it was suicide and Rossetti had covered it up. It is more likely, however, to have been a genuine desire on the part of Rossetti to carry out Lizzie's last request.

effort to wake her, but it proved impossible. Removing the note, he yelled for a neighbour and friend of Lizzie's, Ellen Macintire, and his landlady, Sarah Birrill. Dr Francis Hutchison, who lived in nearby Bridge Street, was called to treat Lizzie. He was the doctor who had attended at the stillbirth and knew Lizzie's medical history. By the time Hutchison arrived she was already in a coma. The doctor tried both pumping her stomach to remove the laudanum and then washing her stomach out, but had no success at reviving her. At the inquest Hutchison stated that her stomach contents smelt overpoweringly of laudanum. When Hutchison's attempts failed to bring her round, Rossetti called out a second doctor; later he called out a third and a fourth, but they could do no more than Hutchison had already done.

A desperate Rossetti set out for the Madox Browns' house in Kentish Town, with Lizzie's note concealed in his pocket. He also sent urgent messages to Lizzie's family in Kent Place. The unconscious Lizzie was left in the care of the four medics, Ellen Macintire, Mrs Birrill and her daughter, Catherine, who had sometimes acted as a maid when Lizzie had needed one. They were all painfully aware of how little any of them could do.

Rossetti reached the Kentish Town house in the early hours of the morning. When he and Ford were alone together, Rossetti showed him the note. After reading it, Ford threw it on the fire and they agreed not to mention it to anyone else. Suicide was not only highly scandalous, it was also illegal. The Rossetti and Siddall families' names would be tarnished permanently but – which was far worse – Lizzie would be unable to receive a Christian burial and would be buried in unconsecrated ground. This was a stigma that it would be intolerably difficult for her relations to recover from, as well as being an unbearable end for a woman whose religion had been an important part of her life.

Lizzie's sister and brother, Clara and James, had rushed from Southwark as soon as they had received Rossetti's message, reaching

Blackfriars at about 3 a.m. They held her hands and spoke to her, but she did not regain consciousness and they had no idea if she even knew they were there. Despite the best attempts of the medical men and the ministrations of her doting siblings, Lizzie was on the brink of death and nothing could pull her back. Ford returned to Blackfriars with Rossetti, leaving a miserable Emma at home with the children to wait for any news. They arrived at Chatham Place at five o'clock in the morning.

At around twenty past seven on the morning of February 11, 1862, Lizzie Rossetti was pronounced dead by all four doctors present. She was just 32 years old and pregnant – yet another baby destined not to survive. Perhaps Lizzie had again felt her baby stop moving inside her and knew it was dead, or maybe she felt she could not risk the possibility of another stillbirth and its miserable repercussions.[3] Perhaps her postnatal depression had tragically led her to believe she would be a bad mother and brought about a decision not to bring her child into the world, or maybe the thought of motherhood inside such a tormented marriage was overwhelming. We will never know.

Dante Gabriel Rossetti was devastated. He had lost his wife and another baby and the memory of the suicide note was eating away at his conscience. Of all his friends, only a handful genuinely grieved at his wife's death. Algernon Swinburne, Ford and Emma Madox Brown, William Allingham and Georgiana Burne-Jones were amongst the few genuinely saddened that such a young woman, and their friend, had died. Allingham noted in his diary, "Short, sad and strange her life; it must have seemed like a troubled dream." Swinburne later wrote, "To one at least who knew her better than most of her husband's friends, the memory of all her marvellous charms of mind and person – her matchless grace, loveliness, courage, endurance, wit, humour, heroism and sweetness – it is too dear and sacred to be profaned by any attempt at expression."

---

[3] How advanced Lizzie's pregnancy was is unrecorded.

Rossetti's family, however, and many of his friends were secretly relieved that such a tragic and troublesome woman had finally gone out of Rossetti's life for good.[4]

Lizzie's poem "Early Death", although undated, is believed to have been written just a few months before her suicide:

Early Death

Oh grieve not with thy bitter tears
The life that passes fast;
The gates of heaven will open wide
And take me in at last.

Then sit down meekly at my side
And watch my young life flee;
Then solemn peace of holy death
Come quickly unto thee.

But true love, seek me in the throng
Of spirits floating past,
And I will take thee by the hands
And know thee mine at last.

---

[4] Lucy Madox Brown was a frequent visitor to Albany Street in 1862, as at this time she was being educated by Maria and Christina and had come to be viewed as one of the family. She later recalled the "sense of relief" felt by Dante's family when the news of Lizzie's death was broken to them.

CHAPTER EIGHTEEN

The Coroner's Verdict

He and She and Angels Three

Ruthless hands have torn her
From one that loved her well;
Angels have upborn her,
Christ her grief to tell.

She shall stand to listen,
She shall stand and sing,
Till three winged angels
Her lover's soul shall bring.

He and she and the angels three
Before God's face shall stand;
There they shall pray among themselves
And sing at His right hand.

Elizabeth Siddal
date unknown

An inquest on the death of Lizzie Rossetti was held at Bridewell Hospital, London, on Thursday February 13, 1862. Many of Rossetti's friends and relations were fearful that despite the non-appearance of a note, there would still be grounds to claim Lizzie took her own life. They were unaware of the note that had been burned in the Madox Browns' hearth,

199

but Lizzie's mental state had left most people who had known her in little doubt as to what had really happened that evening. Rossetti, Swinburne, Clara Siddall, Mrs Birrill, Catherine Birrill and Ellen Macintire were called upon to give evidence. For some reason, Swinburne's name does not appear in any of the newspaper reports of the inquest.

Ellen Macintire told the coroner that she had been with Lizzie on the evening she died, at about half past eight, just after she and Rossetti had come home from the restaurant. They had talked in her bedroom and, she reported, Lizzie "seemed cheerful then". She added that Lizzie, "told me once that she had taken quarts of laudanum in her time".

Ellen's words backed up Rossetti's own evidence: "She was in the habit of taking large doses of laudanum. I know that she has taken a hundred drops." In case the coroner was still veering towards suicide, Rossetti added:

> She had not spoken of wishing to die. She had contemplated going out of town in a day or two and had bought a new mantle the day before. She was very nervous and had I believe a diseased heart.[1] My impression is that she did not do it to injure herself but to quiet her nerves. She could not have lived without laudanum. She could not sleep at times nor take food.

Clara Siddall was slightly more circumspect in her account, telling the coroner she had seen her sister the previous Saturday, when she "seemed in tolerably good spirits". She added that Lizzie was in the habit of taking laudanum and that she did not suspect anyone else of causing Lizzie "any harm". It is noteworthy that Clara did not state that she did not suspect Lizzie of causing harm to herself.

---

[1] It is uncertain when Rossetti had formed the impression that Lizzie had a weak heart or who had made the diagnosis.

Strangely, Clara got her sister's age wrong, claiming Lizzie was only 29 at her death when she was, in fact, 32.

Sarah Birrill, the loyal housekeeper, admitted to having known Lizzie for nine years – although she only admitted to Lizzie living in the house since her marriage. She told the court that she knew Lizzie kept a phial of laudanum under her pillow. Fearing for the safety of her dear Mr Rossetti, she felt moved to add, "I knew of no hurt to her nor don't suspect any. Her husband and herself lived very comfortable together." The latter statement had obviously not been true for much of their relationship, especially following the death of their child after which Lizzie had often been abusive and manipulative.

Catherine Birrill backed up her mother's assertions and told the court:

I had not bought any laudanum for the deceased for 6 months... I bought a shilling's worth... The Phial was about half full.... The Phial found was the one she generally used.... I never saw her take any... I know of no hurt to her... I waited upon her and they lived very happily together.

Swinburne's evidence was brief, as he had not been there on the night she died. He arrived on the scene the following morning for his arranged portrait sitting, and found the household in devastation. He told the court that at dinner, "I saw nothing particular in the deceased except that she appeared a little weaker than usual."

The worst was past. The coroner returned a verdict of accidental death and Rossetti was free to arrange his wife's funeral.[2] At first he

---

[2] That the coroner chose to believe it was an accident is due partly to the relatively common occurrence of accidental deaths from laudanum at the time. The year after Lizzie committed suicide, there were 80 recorded deaths from laudanum or syrup of poppies and in 1864 there were 95 such deaths in Britain. These figures do not include deaths from all other forms of opiate.

refused to believe she was gone, reportedly standing by her open coffin and pleading with her to come back to him. He even asked a surgeon friend of Madox Brown to come round and attend to her as he could not accept her death and was certain something could be done to revive her. In the end she was buried near Gabriele Rossetti, the father-in-law she had never been deemed good enough to meet, in the family plot at the western side of Highgate Cemetery. Over the years, Frances and Christina would also be buried there. It is an odd location for Lizzie's grave, among all those disapproving Rossettis and none of her own family. Lizzie was destined never to be reunited with her husband – on his death, in 1882, his will included strict instructions that he should "on no account" be buried at Highgate.[3]

Lizzie's funeral took place on February 17. Despite the ravages of the doctors' and coroner's medical attentions, she was laid in an open coffin at their home. Rossetti, in the early stages of the insanity that was to dog his later years, was inconsolable. He believed that love had died with Lizzie and that nothing was any use without her. He forgot all the irritations and misery of their later years together and mourned her as his flawless, innocent Beatrice. For several years he had been composing a volume of poetry, of which he had only one copy. Fired by the sudden, and erroneous, thought that the poems had all been inspired by Lizzie, he decided to bury them with her. Just before the coffin was taken to the hearse, he slipped into the room where she lay and, lifting her hair, tenderly laid the slim volume of poetry between it and her cheek. He also placed her Bible against her hair. As he watched his wife, his unborn child and his manuscript disappear into the north London soil, Rossetti believed he would never write poetry again.

---

[3] It is not possible to see Lizzie's grave; unfortunately, visitors to the Western Cemetery are allowed in only on a guided tour, which does not include seeing the Rossetti family plot.

A month after the inquest, Swinburne wrote to his mother giving a more elucidating account of the death than he had admitted in court:

> I am sure you will understand how that which has happened since I last wrote to you has upset my plans and how my time has been taken up.... I would rather not write yet about what has happened – I suppose none of the papers gave a full report, so that you do not know that I was almost the last person who saw her (except her husband and a servant) and had to give evidence at the inquest. Happily there was no difficulty in proving that illness had quite deranged her mind, so that the worst of all was escaped ... I am only glad to have been able to keep his company and be of a little use during these weeks.

For years after her death, Rossetti was haunted by images of Lizzie. He told his doctor and his family that she was not at peace, that her ghost visited him every night. He was unable to remain at their shared home – staying with his family or friends until he could relocate – but, wherever he slept, Lizzie's ghost apparently found him. He was determined to move house and within weeks had moved his possessions out of Chatham Place, with its unhealthy air and unhealthy memories, and was setting up home with Swinburne in Cheyne Walk, a fashionable and extremely desirable riverside area of Chelsea. It was a location which would have been much more suitable for one of Lizzie's delicate health than the riverside at Blackfriars. Rossetti's poem "The Portrait", one of the collection that he buried in Lizzie's coffin and which was presumably written during a melancholy moment in which he believed her to be dying, encapsulates the loneliness he felt after Lizzie's death:

The Portrait

This is her picture as she was:
It seems a thing to wonder on,
As though mine image in the glass
Should tarry when myself am gone.
I gaze until she seems to stir, –
Until mine eyes almost aver
That now, even now, the sweet lips part
To breathe the words of her sweet heart: –
And yet the earth is over her...

In painting her I shrined her face
Mid mystic trees, where light falls in
Hardly at all; a covert place
Where you might think to find a din
Of doubtful talk, and a live flame
Wandering, and many a shape whose name
Not itself knoweth, and old dew,
And your own footsteps meeting you,
And all things going as they came...

Here with her face doth memory sit
Meanwhile, and wait the day's decline.
Till other eyes shall look from it,
Eyes of the spirit's Palestine,
Even than the old gaze tenderer:
While hopes and aims long lost with her
Stand round the rimage side by side,
Like tombs of pilgrims that have died
About the Holy Sepulchre.

Now Lizzie really was dead, but she was not to be allowed to rest in peace. Instead, she was destined to become more famous in death than she had ever been in life. Her demise began a series of ugly rumours, suggestions that it had not been accidental. The whispered suggestions were not, however, of suicide, but of murder perpetrated by her husband. The stories were fuelled by those who were jealous of Rossetti, who disliked him or simply by those who enjoyed a scandalous gossip. The stories remained in existence for decades. One of the most famous of those to spread the vindictive rumours was the playwright and celebrated wit Oscar Wilde (1854–1900), who was still a child at the time of Lizzie's death. Never one to be perturbed by suspicions about the veracity of a good story, Wilde created his own version of a scene that had succeeded the dinner at La Sablonière with Swinburne. Years after the event, he was telling his own depiction of that evening, a story that began with Rossetti being incensed by Lizzie's unseemly behaviour at dinner. This was elaborated grossly, building up to the crescendo of the story, which included a spectacular row and culminated in a murderous Rossetti thrusting a full bottle of laudanum at Lizzie and ordering her to "take the lot" before striding out of their home to meet another woman.

Lizzie's death did not only begin a campaign of rumours against herself and her husband, it also began the first rumours of a legend that would be created around her life – the legend of a woman who had been the first supermodel, in a world where the term had not yet been coined.

CHAPTER NINETEEN

Without Her

It was not only Dante Rossetti who became haunted by the vision of Lizzie. William Rossetti, Swinburne and even William Bell Scott began to believe in ghosts and the spirit world. Dante became obsessed with the idea of séances, regularly inviting a medium to his Cheyne Walk home, where he and his brother or friends attempted to reach the "other side". William Rossetti, usually so rational and conventional, became entirely convinced, telling Bell Scott that Lizzie rapped out answers to the medium about things that only she could possibly have known. Several years after her death, by which time the once-abstemious Dante Rossetti had become addicted to chloral and was a regular drinker, he became convinced that her soul had migrated into a bird's song, certain that via the voice of a specific chaffinch he was being communicated with by Lizzie from beyond that Highgate grave.

Rossetti took solace in the only way he knew how. Burying himself once again in the works of Dante Alighieri, Rossetti spent much of the 1860s attempting to paint the perfect memorial to his own Beatrice. Drawing from memory and from all those drawers full of Guggums, Rossetti created an oil painting that has come to be known as one of his masterpieces, *Beata Beatrix* (1864–70).[1] The picture is a beatification of his dead bride, the image in which he wished Lizzie had remained: not a drug addict, not a depressive,

---

[1] Now in the Tate Britain, in London.

but a deeply religious, saintly young woman, her eyes closed, her face raised to heaven and her hands held in prayer. A woman with attributes more keenly akin to his sisters than to his lover, but it was an image he pretended to himself he had sought and found in Lizzie. Flying towards her, with a flower in its beak which it intends to place in her hands, is a dove, not only indicative of his loving nickname for her and the symbol he used to depict her in letters but also the bird of peace, a symbol of love and a symbol of the Holy Spirit, guiding the soul to heaven. It is a red dove, the colour of Lizzie's hair as well as the colour traditionally associated with Beatrice, love, heaven and the saints. In the background are two dimly discerned figures, Dante Alighieri and an angelic figure, dressed in a red robe and indicative of Love. A sundial marks the passing of time and the passing of life and there is a bridge which could represent the Ponte Vecchio, symbol of Florence, though it could also suggest Blackfriars Bridge, the span, at the start of their romance, between Rossetti's and Lizzie's homes and the site of their marital home. There is, however, a more disturbing way in which to analyse *Beata Beatrix*. The flower the dove is carrying is a white poppy, the provider of opium. Usually a white poppy is an innocent depiction of sleep or death, but in a work of art in homage to Lizzie Rossetti it is a sad indicator of the manner in which she died. Beatrice's religious ecstasy can also, more prosaically, be read as Lizzie's own expression after drinking laudanum; the ecstasy of an addict who has taken her fix. Rossetti described the work as "not a representative image of death ... [but] ... an ideal of the subject". The overdose of his wife and its vividly undignified results could not allow him to look on death as a peaceful process.[2]

---

[2] Rossetti made several replicas of *Beata Beatrix* in watercolour and chalk and, towards the end of his life, began a second oil painting, in which the bird flying to Beatrice became a white dove carrying a red poppy. The original was sold to the collector and patron William Graham, who paid Rossetti the princely sum of 900 guineas.

Seven years after Lizzie's death, Rossetti published a collection of sonnets entitled *The House of Life*; contained within it was the poem, "Without Her". It is a reflection on life once love has departed:

Without Her

*What of her glass without her? The blank grey
There where the pool is blind of the moon's face.
Her dress without her? The tossed empty space
Of cloud-rack whence the moon has passed away.
Her paths without her? Day's appointed sway
Usurped by desolate night. Her pillowed place
Without her? Tears, ah me! For love's good grace,
And cold forgetfulness of night or day.*

*What of the heart without her? Nay, poor heart,
Of thee what word remains ere speech be still?
A wayfarer by barren ways and chill,
Steep ways and weary, without her thou art,
Where the long cloud, the long wood's counterpart,
Sheds doubled darkness up the labouring hill.*

Peaceful though *Beata Beatrix* may appear, Rossetti was not at peace, and neither would he allow Lizzie to remain so. In 1869, by which time he had started his tortuous affair with Janey Morris, as well as writing equally tortured poetry, Rossetti was keenly regretting the grand gesture of burying his poems with his dead love. Or, at least, of not having made a copy of them before doing so.

It was his agent, the utterly unscrupulous Charles Augustus Howell, who suggested to Rossetti the idea of retrieving the poems.

Helen Rossetti Angeli, Dante Rossetti's niece,[3] believed that Howell did so partly out of fear for Rossetti's mental health; she claims Howell was convinced that the loss of his poems was worsening Rossetti's mental illness and depression. Howell was, however, a shrewd businessman. By 1869, the name of Dante Gabriel Rossetti was famous; by association with him and the poems, which were bound to create good publicity, Howell would also gain glory. Howell's magnetism, which had worked so well in convincing less mentally tortured souls to place their trust in him, persuaded Rossetti to take up his suggestion. On August 16, 1869, Rossetti wrote to Howell: "I feel disposed, if practicable, by your friendly aid, to go in for the recovery of my poems if possible, as you proposed some time ago. Only I should beg *absolute* secrecy of *everyone*, as the matter ought really not to be talked about…"

Howell needed no further prompting and instantly communicated Rossetti's wishes to the Home Secretary, Mr Bruce. Howell requested from Bruce an exhumation order to retrieve the poems, impressing on him the need for secrecy. Howell and Rossetti were wise to insist on secrecy – after all, Lizzie had been buried in a communal family grave. Gabriele Rossetti was buried in the same plot and the owner of the grave was Mrs Frances Rossetti. The rigidly Christian Mrs Rossetti senior would never have agreed to desecrate any grave, let alone her husband's, neither would Maria or Christina have approved of their father's grave being opened and plundered. Yet, somewhat astonishingly, the order for the exhumation was granted without the Home Secretary questioning Howell's suggestion that the grave be opened without permission from the plot's owner. Mr Bruce apparently stood in awe of Rossetti and illegally

---

[3] Helen Rossetti Angeli was the daughter of William Rossetti and his wife, Lucy Madox Brown (Ford Madox Brown's daughter by his first wife, Lizzy). She was the person who finally laid to rest rumours about Lizzie's death; in her 1949 biography of Rossetti she revealed the existence of a suicide note, finally exonerating Rossetti from his unwilling role as potential murderer.

agreed to waive the need for Frances Rossetti to add her signature to the written permission for the grave to be reopened. Dante Rossetti, eager to dissociate himself from the action he was about to sanction, signed over Power of Attorney to Howell, authorising the latter to act for him "in all matters as he thinks best".

Rossetti's feelings of guilt did not allow him to attend the exhumation. He remained at Howell's home in Fulham, nervously awaiting news and being attended to by Howell's wife, Kitty. There were very few people present at the cemetery. In addition to the diggers, there were only Howell and the official lawyer, who had the ironic name, for an observer of such a deed, of Mr Virtue Tebbs. So as not to upset visitors to the cemetery or mourners, the deed had to be carried out at night. There was no light in that part of the graveyard so a large fire was built to help the diggers see what they were doing, as well as to keep the observers warm. Howell declared that, when the coffin was opened, Lizzie remained fully preserved. She was not a skeleton, he claimed, she was as beautiful as she had ever been in life and her hair, which had kept growing after death, now filled the coffin and was as brilliantly copper-coloured as it had been in life, glinting mesmerizingly in the firelight.

The character of Howell, as well as the obvious impossibility of the facts, prevent his words from being taken seriously, but they have been repeated time and again in stories about Lizzie, obviously sometimes believed, as though poor dead Lizzie had become some kind of saintly miracle. Howell's words, however, were not only prompted by his fantastically over-active imagination but also by a desire to comfort a guilt-consumed Rossetti.

Indebted to Howell's gloriously conceived fiction is the myth of the prevailing beauty of the original supermodel, even in death. It is a story that continued to be played out long after Lizzie's demise. Even today the mythical beauty of her untainted corpse can still be found repeated on numerous adulatory websites. Alive, she had often not been appreciated, but in death Lizzie apparently remained a thing of extraordinary beauty.

Gone

To touch the glove upon her tender hand,
To watch the jewel sparkle in her ring,
Lifted my heart into a sudden song
As when the wild birds sing.

To touch her shadow on the sunny grass,
To break her pathway through the darkened wood,
Filled all my life with trembling and tears
And silence where I stood.

I watch the shadows gather round my heart,
I live to know that she is gone –
Gone gone for ever, like the tender dove
That left the Ark alone.

Elizabeth Siddal
date unkown

Notes

CHAPTER ONE

The Red-Haired Model

Information about the area around Cranbourne Street courtesy of the local studies library in St James's. Information about Mrs Tozer and her shop obtained from Robson's and Pigot's commercial directories of London.

The exact date on which Allingham met Lizzie and the date she began modelling for Deverell are unknown. It is generally accepted that it was the winter of 1849–50; as Deverell's painting was displayed in the spring of 1850, she must have begun modelling for him around the end of 1849 or very early in 1850.

CHAPTER TWO

A Pre-Raphaelite Muse

Information about the Siddall family and their family business obtained from the Family Records Office in Islington, the censuses for 1841, 1851 and 1861, the local studies library in Holborn and Robson's and Pigot's commercial directories of London. Information about Hope and the Crossdaggers courtesy of the Hope Historical Society and the Old Hall pub in Hope.

The rates of pay for an artist's model are quoted by Diana Holman Hunt.

CHAPTER THREE

Dante and Beatrice

That Charles Siddall was influenced by Rossetti's changing of their surname to "Siddal" is shown in the census: in the 1841 census it was spelt as Siddall, but in the 1851 census the family is listed as Siddal. In the census of 1861, by which time Charles was dead and Elizabeth listed as the head of the household, the spelling is returned again to Siddall. For the rapidity with which Charles Siddall changed it back again, see Watkin's commercial directory of London businesses for 1852, in which it is once again Siddall.

Valentine Prinsep quoted by Georgiana Burne-Jones.

For Christina's comment that her brother was too ensnared by Lizzie to go abroad and about Lizzie's dislike of Holman Hunt, see Diana Holman Hunt.

CHAPTER FIVE

Falling In Love with Ophelia

The description of Emma Hill is taken from Helen Rossetti Angeli's biography of Dante Rossetti.

CHAPTER SIX

"Why does he not marry her?"

Victorian contraception information obtained from the Wellcome Institute library.

CHAPTER SEVEN

Lizzie's Mysterious Illness

Lizzie has previously been assumed to have taken possession of the rooms in Weymouth Street in 1856, but Fredeman claims a letter sent by Rossetti asking William Allingham to join him and Lizzie at Weymouth Street and "take a chop" with them before going on to a theatre was sent in April 1854. As Lizzie was not yet receiving Ruskin's pension, Rossetti must have been paying her rent at this date.

CHAPTER TEN

Seeking a Cure

The date for Rossetti arriving in Paris is from Fredeman's edition of DGR's letters and corrects an earlier assertion made by Oswald Doughty.

CHAPTER TWELVE

In Sickness and In Health

Dr Jan Marsh has looked into the genealogy of the Ibbitts and the Siddalls and found no evidence that they were actually related. However, correspondence and newspaper cuttings at the Sheffield Local Studies Library, dating from the early twentieth century, demonstrates that the Ibbitts and Siddalls believed themselves to be related. Even if there was no actual connection, both Lizzie Siddal and William Ibbitt believed themselves to be cousins by marriage, both descended from the Greaves family and, prior to that, from the Eyres.

CHAPTER THIRTEEN

"So we two wore our strange estate: Familiar, unaffected, free"

The fact of Lydia Siddall being pregnant when she married is reported by Jan Marsh in her biography of Rossetti.

CHAPTER SEVENTEEN

"Lord May I Come?"

For notes on their final evening and the death, see DGR's letters; Swinburne's letters and biographies by Humphrey Hare and Edmund Gosse; coroner's notes (quoted in Violet Hunt); and Jan Marsh's books.

The suicide note was originally mentioned in William Bell Scott's memoirs, but was edited out by William Rossetti before publication. Violet Hunt asserted in her 1932 book that Lizzie had committed suicide and left a note – a claim that was roundly refuted by Dante Rossetti's niece and Ford Madox Brown's granddaughter, Helen Angeli Rossetti. It was therefore surprising that, in her own biography of Rossetti, published in 1949, Helen Angeli Rossetti admitted the existence of a suicide note, revealed its contents and related that her grandfather and uncle had made the decision to burn it.

Lucy Madox Brown's feelings about the death of Lizzie recorded by Jan Marsh.

Valentine Prinsep's article was printed in the *Magazine of Art* and quoted by Brian and Judy Dobbs.

Helen Rossetti Angeli remembered her father receiving occasional visits from a man she was told was Lizzie's brother. They always went into her father's study and she assumed he was receiving some kind of payment.

CHAPTER EIGHTEEN

The Coroner's Verdict

Rossetti's housekeeper's name is spelled variously as Birrill, Birrell and Burrill.

CHAPTER NINETEEN

Without Her

For a description of the exhumation and Lizzie's body being perfect in death, see Hall Caine's recollections.

Bibliography

Alighieri, Dante, trans. John D. Sinclair, *The Divine Comedy: Inferno*, OUP, Oxford, 1961

Alighieri, Dante, trans. Mark Musa, *Vita Nuova*, OUP, Oxford, 1992

Allingham, H., & Baumer Williams, E., eds., *Letters to William Allingham*, Longmans & Co, London, 1911

Banks, J.A., *Victorian Values*, Routledge & Kegan Paul, London, 1981

Banks, J.A. & Olive, *Feminism and Family Planning in Victorian England*, Liverpool University Press, Liverpool, 1964

Barrett, Gladys, *Blackfriars Settlement: a Short History*, Blackfriars Settlement, London, 1985

Barron, Caroline M., with Penelope Hunting & Jane Rowse, *The Parish of St Andrew Holborn*, Corporation of London, London, 1979

Baum, Paull Franklin, ed., *Dante Gabriel Rossetti's Letters to Fanny Cornforth*, John Hopkins Press, Baltimore, 1940

Beerbohm, Max, *Rossetti and His Circle*, William Heinemann, London, 1922

Berridge, Virginia, *Opium and the People: Opiate Use and Drug Control Policy in Nineteenth and Early Twentieth Century England*, Free Association Books, London & New York, 1999

Birch, C.A., *The Medical History of Hastings*, private publication, Hastings, 1980

Browning, Robert, *Selected Poetry*, Penguin, London, 1989

Burne-Jones, Georgiana, *Memorials of Edward Burne-Jones*, in 2 vols., Macmillan & Co, London, 1904

Burton, Hester, *Barbara Bodichon 1827–1891*, John Murray, London, 1949

Champneys, Basil, ed., *Memoirs and Correspondence of Coventry Patmore*, G. Bell & Sons, London, 1900

Coombs, Scott, Landow & Sanders, eds., *A Pre-Raphaelite Friendship: The Correspondence of William Holman Hunt and John Lucas Tupper*, UMI Research Press, Michigan, 1986

Daly, Gay, *Pre-Raphaelites in Love*, Collins, London, 1989

De Villiers, P., *Hastings as a Health Resort*, Hastings, 1879

Dobbs, Brian & Judy, *Dante Gabriel Rossetti: An Alien Victorian*, Macdonald & Jane's, London, 1977

Doughty, Oswald, & Wahl, John Robert, eds., *Letters of Dante Gabriel Rossetti*; Clarendon Press, Oxford, 1965

Douglas Kerr, J.G., *Popular Guide to the use of The Bath Waters*, Bath, 1884

Dunn, Henry T., *Recollections of Dante Gabriel Rossetti and his circle*, Elkin Mathews, London, 1904

Erskine Clement, Clara, & Hutton, Laurence, *Artists of the 19th Century and Their Works*, Osgood & Co., London, 1879

Finalyson, Iain, *Browning: A Private Life*, HarperCollins, London, 2004

Firth, J.B., *Highways and Byways in Derbyshire*, Macmillan & Co., London, 1905

Fredeman, William E., ed., *The Correspondence of Dante Gabriel Rossetti: The Formative Years, 1835–1862*, D.S. Brewer, Cambridge, 2002

Gaunt, William, *The Pre-Raphaelite Tragedy*, Jonathan Cape, London, 1975

Gosse, Edmund, *The Life of Algernon Charles Swinburne*, Macmillan & Co., London, 1917

Hall Caine, Thomas, *Recollections of Dante Gabriel Rossetti*, Elliot Stock, London, 1882

Harding, Geoffrey, *Opiate Addiction, Morality and Medicine: From Moral Illness to Pathological Disease*, Macmillan, Basingstoke, 1988

Hare, Humphrey, *Swinburne: A Biographical Approach*, H.F.&G. Witherby, London, 1949

Harvey, Peter, *Street Names of Sheffield*, Sheaf, Sheffield, 2001

Hawksley, Lucinda, *Essential Pre-Raphaelites*, Parragon, London, 1999

Hayter, Alethea, *Opium and the Romantic Imagination*, Faber & Faber, London, 1968

Hilton, Timothy, *The Pre-Raphaelites*, Thames & Hudson, London, 1993

Hodgson, Barbara, *Opium: A Portrait of the Heavenly Demon*, Souvenir Press, London, 1999

——, *In the Arms of Morpheus*, Greystone Books, Vancouver, 2001

Hollamby, Edward & Wood, Charlotte, *Architecture in Detail: Red House*, Architecture, Design & Technology Press, London, 1991

Holman Hunt, Diana, *My Grandfather, His Wives and Loves*, Hamilton, London, 1969

Holman Hunt, William, *Pre-Raphaelitism and the Pre-Raphaelite Brotherhood*, Macmillan & Co., London, 1905

Hunt, Violet, *The Wife of Rossetti: Her Life and Death*, John Lane, London, 1932

Jenkins, Clare, 'Portrait of the Artist', *Westside* magazine, April 1991

Landow, George P., *William Holman Hunt's Letters to Thomas Seddon*, John Rylands University, Manchester, (no date given)

Lang, Cecil Y., ed., *The Yale Edition of the Swinburne Letters*, Vol I, Yale, New Haven & London, 1959

Lethbridge Kingsford, Charles, *The Early History of Piccadilly, Leicester Square and Soho*, Cambridge University Press, Cambridge, 1925

Lewis, Roger C., & Lasner, Mark Samuels, eds, *Poems and Drawings of Elizabeth Siddal*, Wombat Press, Canada, 1978

London Topographical Society, *The A-Z of Regency London*, London Topographical Society, London, 1985

——, *Tallis's London Street Views 1838-40*, London Topographical Society, London, 1969

McLaren, Angus, *Birth Control in Nineteenth-Century England*, Croom Helm, London, 1978

Mainwaring Baines, J., *Historic Hastings: A Tapestry of Life*, St Leonards-on-Sea, 1986

Marchant, Rex, *Hastings Past*, Phillimor, Chichester, 1997

Marryat, H. and Broadbent, Una, *The Romance of Hatton Garden*, J. Cornish & Sons, London, 1930.

Marsh, Jan, "Knights and Angels: The Treatment of 'Sir Galahad' in the work of Gabriel Rossetti, Elizabeth Siddal and William Morris", *The Journal of the William Morris Society*, Vol VIII, No. 1, Autumn 1988, pp.10–15

——, *Elizabeth Siddall, Pre-Raphaelite Artist (1829–1862)*, Ruskin Gallery, Sheffield, 1991

——, *The Legend of Elizabeth Siddal*, Quartet Books, London, 1992

——, *Christina Rossetti, A Literary Biography*, Jonathan Cape, London, 1994

——, *Dante Gabriel Rossetti*, Weidenfeld & Nicolson, London, 1999

Mee, Arthur, ed., *Derbyshire, The Peak Country*, Hodder, London, 1949

Millais, John Guille, *The Life and Letters of Sir John Everett Millais*, Methuen and Co., London, 1899 (repr. and abridged in 1905)

Morrissey, Kim, *Clever as Paint*, Playwrights Canada Press, Toronto, 1998

National Trust, The, *Red House*, The National Trust, London, 2003

Pearsall, Ronald, *The Worm in the Bud: The World of Victorian Sexuality*, Weidenfeld & Nicolson, London, 1969

Pigot & Co.'s Directory, 1828

Reilly, Leonard, *Southwark: An Illustrated History*, London Borough of Southwark, London, 1988

Robson's London Directory, 1826

Robson's London Directory, 1828

Robson's London Directory, 1829

Robson's London Directory, 1830

Robson's London Directory, 1831

Robson's London Directory, 1832

Robson's London Directory, 1833

Robson's Classification of Trades, 1836

Robson's London Directory, 1839

Robson's Commercial Directory of London 1840

Robson's London Directory, 1843

Rossetti, Christina, *Selected Poems*, Carcanet, Manchester, 1984

Rossetti, Dante Gabriel, *Poems*, Roberts Brothers, Boston, 1882

——, *Rossetti's Poems and Translations*, J.M. Dent & Sons, London, 1954

——, *Poems*, J.M. Dent & Sons, London, 1961

Rossetti, William Michael, ed., *New Poems by Christina Rossetti*, Macmillan & Co., London, 1896

——, ed., *Dante Gabriel Rossetti: Classified Lists of His Writings with the Dates*, 100 copies privately printed, 1906

——, ed., *Ruskin: Rossetti: Pre-Raphaelitism, Papers 1854 to 1862*, London, George Allen, 1899

Rossetti Angeli, Helen, *Pre-Raphaelite Twilight: The Story of Charles Augustus Howell*, Richards Press, London, 1954
——, *Dante Gabriel Rossetti: His Friends and Enemies*, Hamish Hamilton, London, 1949
Royal Academy of Arts, *Pre-Raphaelites and Other Masters*, Royal Academy of Arts, London, 2003
Scottish Intercollegiate Guidelines Network, *Postnatal Depression and Puerperal Psychosis*, June 2002
Silvester-Carr, Denise, 'Red House', *History Today*, July 2003
Surtees, Virginia, *Rossetti's Portraits of Elizabeth Siddal*, Scolar Press, Oxford, 1991
Tate Gallery, *The Age of Rossetti, Burne-Jones & Watts*, Tate Gallery, London, 1997
Tennyson, Alfred, *In Memoriam, Maud and Other Poems*, Dent, London, 1974
The Review of the Pre-Raphaelite Society, Vol VIII, No. 2, Autumn 2000
The Review of the Pre-Raphaelite Society, Vol X, No. 2, Summer 2002
The Review of the Pre-Raphaelite Society, Vol X, No. 3, Autumn 2002
Treuherz, Julian; Prettejohn, Elizabeth; & Becker, Edwin, *Dante Gabriel Rossetti*, Walker Art Gallery, Liverpool, 2003
Vallance, Aymer, *The Life and Work of William Morris*, Studio Editions, London, 1995 (repr.)
Vickers, J. Edward, *A Popular History of Sheffield*, E.P. Publishing, Wakefield, 1978
Walford, Edward, *Old and New London*, London, (no date given)
Watkin's London Directory, 1852
Watkinson, Ray, "Red House Decorated", *The Journal of the William Morris Society*, Vol VII, No. 4, Spring 1988, pp.10–15
Waugh, Evelyn, *Rossetti*, Duckworth, London, 1928
Wildman, Stephen, *Visions of Love and Life: Pre-Raphaelite Art from the Birmingham Museums and Art Gallery*, Art Services International, Virginia, 1995
Wilson, A.N., *The Victorians*, Arrow, London, 2003
Wojtczak, Helena, *Notable Women of Victorian Hastings*, Hastings Press, Hastings, 2002

Index